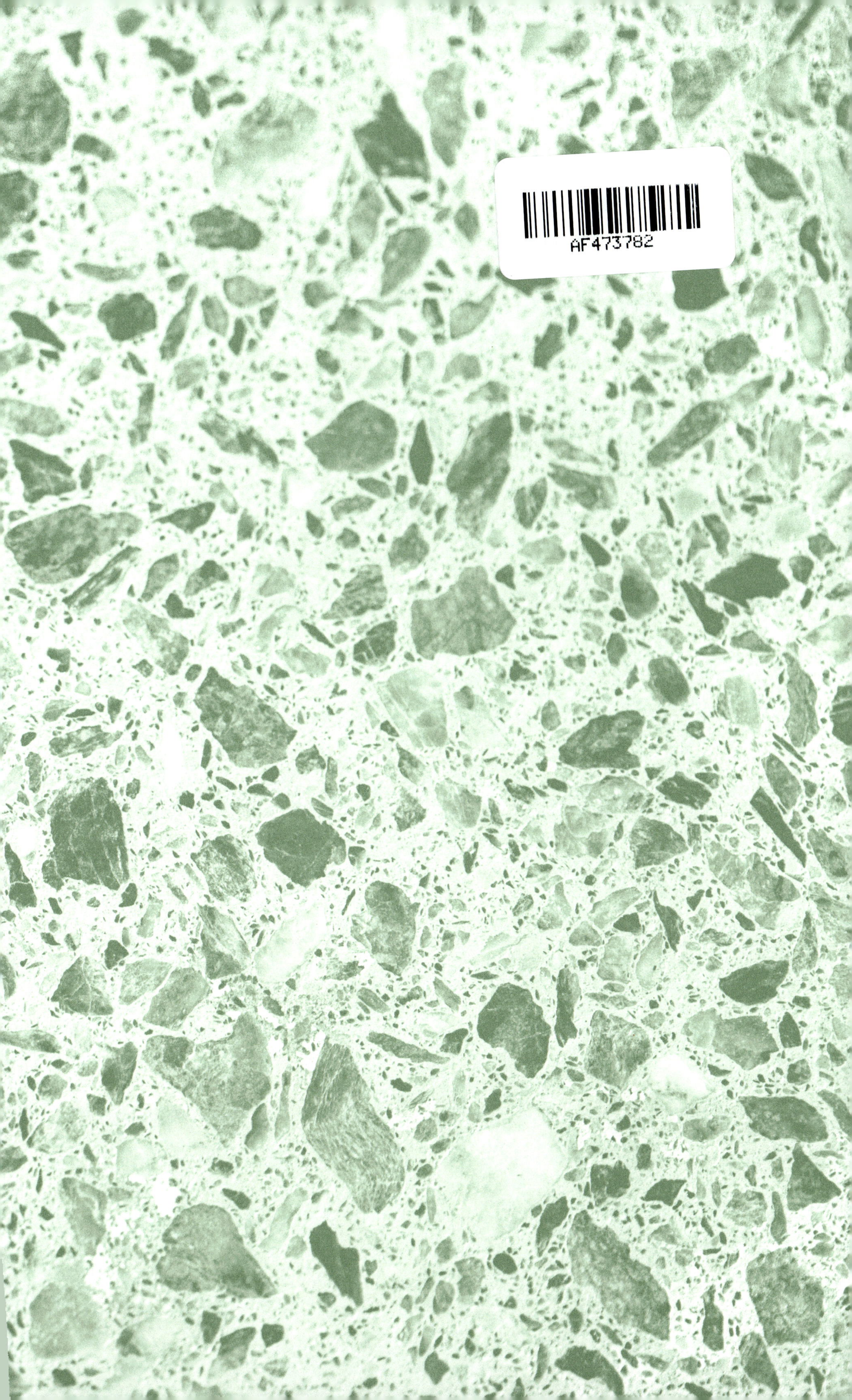

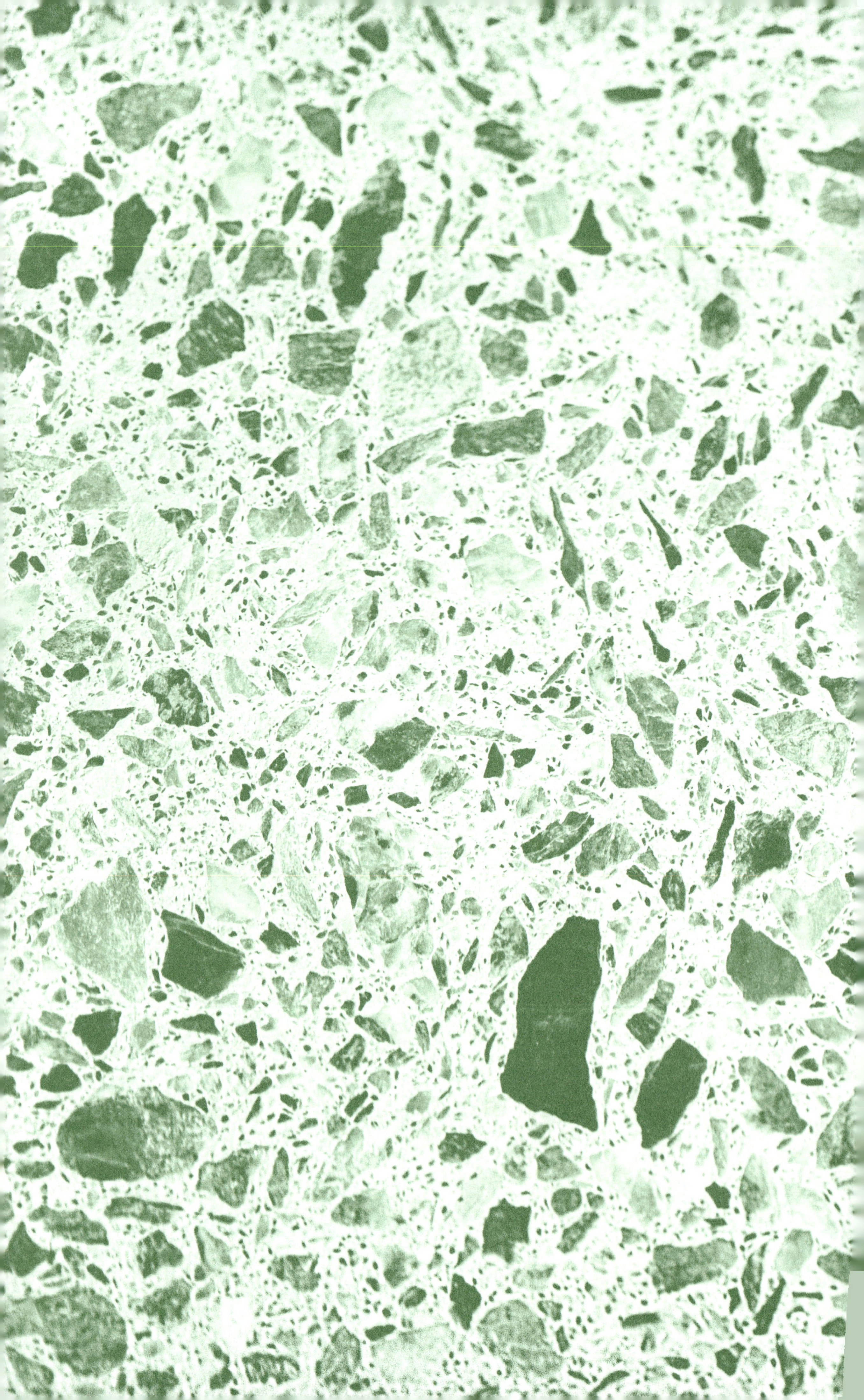

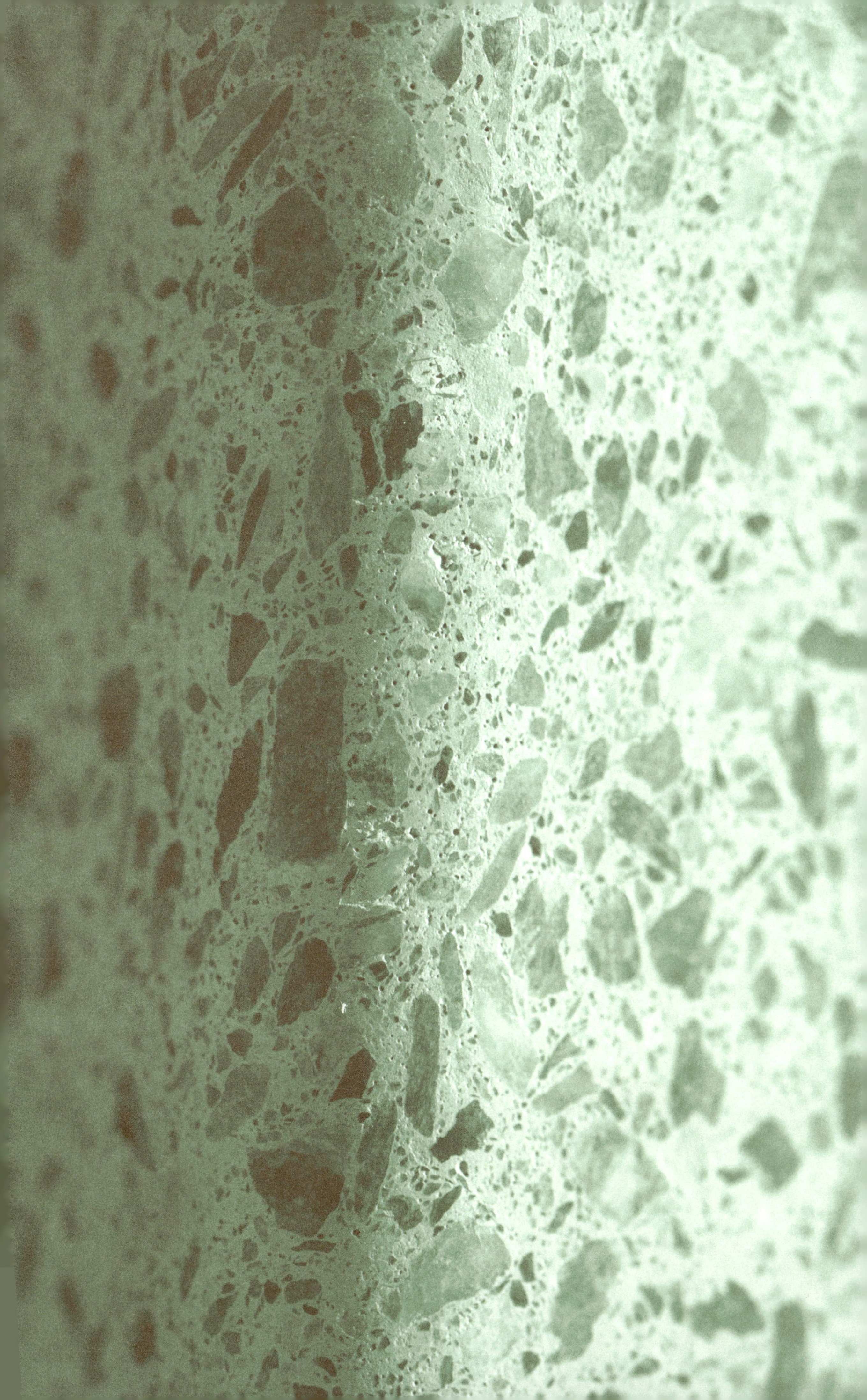

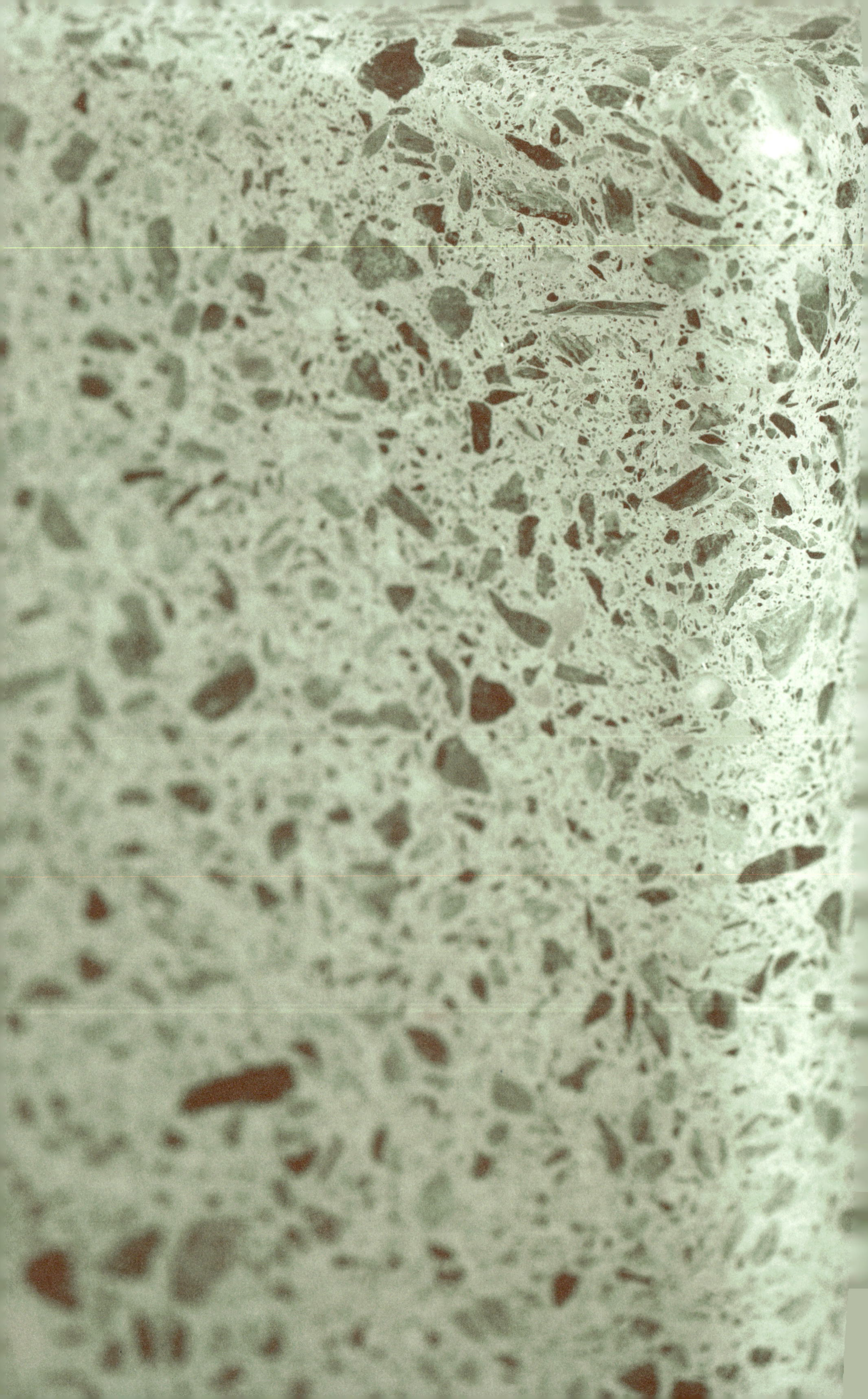

FLORIAN GRAF

SCHOOL MODELS

Archetypische Spiele

Teresa
Fankhänel

Teresa Fankhänel ist Architekturkuratorin, Autorin und Chefredakteurin der *Architectural Exhibition Review*. Zu ihren jüngsten Ausstellungen zählen *African Mobilities* (2018), *The Architecture Machine* (2020/21), *Built Together* (2021), *Shouldn't You Be Working?* (2023) und *Andrea Canepa: As We Dwell in the Fold* (2023/24). Seit 2024 ist sie Vertretungsprofessorin für Architekturtheorie am KIT in Karlsruhe.

Als Schuljunge war Florian Graf anfänglich eingeschüchtert von seinem Schulhaus. Er hatte das Gefühl, von dem übermächtigen Gebäude verschluckt zu werden. Seine Muschelkalksteinskulpturen *School Models* (2023) überwinden dieses architektonische Schreckgespenst mit einem einfachen und doch gewichtigen Kunststück: Massstabsgetreu verkleinert, erlauben es die drei steinernen Schulskulpturen jedem und jeder, die den Hof umgebenden realen Gebäude für sich zu «besetzen». Im verkleinerten Massstab «begreifen» die Schüler*innen auf dem Pausenhof spielend ihre Schule.

Die Miniaturen der denkmalgeschützten Schulhäuser versinnbildlichen auf räumliche Weise Archetypen der sich stetig ändernden Lehrmodelle aus drei Jahrhunderten. Sie balancieren auf übergrossen roten und grünen Terrazzobauklötzen – Orangerot steht für die Ziegeldächer aus dem 19. Jahrhundert und Grün für die historischen Korridore, durch die sich Generationen von Schüler*innen bewegt haben.

Wer selbst mit Spielklötzen aufgewachsen ist, weiss, dass in jedem Baukasten ein eigenes System, eine eigene Welt steckt. Ob Anker- oder Stabilbaukasten, Lego oder digitale Blockbauspiele wie Minecraft – der Bausatz bestimmt die Grenzen der Fantasie. Und jeder Kasten bringt seine ganz eigenen Spielregeln mit. Die Architekturgeschichte kennt eine Reihe von bereits im Kindesalter tätigen Blockbaumeister*innen, deren späteres Werk auf eine frühe Modellaffinität und das Spielen mit baulichen Archetypen zurückschliessen lässt: Architekt Walter Gropius zum Beispiel oder der Pionier der Computerarchitektur, Ivan Sutherland, sollen beide bereits im Kindergartenalter «gefröbelt» haben. Ähnlich wie Le Corbusier, der die geometrischen Grundformen der Architektur in den Bauten des antiken Roms sah, brachen sie die komplexe gebaute Umwelt auf einfache Baublöcke herunter.

Die meisten Architekt*innen lieben Modelle. Ihre Faszination bewegt sich zwischen einem Materialfetisch, einer gottgleichen Beherrschbarkeit der verkleinerten Wirklichkeit, einem händischen Umgang mit den Details des Entwurfs und einer greifbaren Ideensammlung. Massstab und Detailgrad sind im Modell immer untrennbar miteinander verbunden. Bei den Skulpturen von Florian Graf wurden die feinen Grate der sitzbankhohen Schulhäuser teilweise per Laserstrahl in den Stein gefräst und dann geschliffen. Dort, wo die Maschine nicht weiterkam, wurde von Hand weitergearbeitet. Dass nun die überdimensionierten Spielsteine teils die Modelle der Schulhäuser überragen, ist Teil des Charmes, den dieses Wechselspiel mit den Grössenverhältnissen birgt. Die schematische Architektur der Klötzchen und die euklidischen Grundformen ihrer dreidimensionalen Geometrie – Pyramide, Zylinder und Quader – scheinen beinahe eine Karikatur der zugrunde liegenden Architekturtheorien der Schulgebäude und der ihnen innewohnenden, immer auch auf Vereinheitlichung zielenden Erziehungsmodelle zu sein. Vor allem der fünften Fassade, der Dachlandschaft der Gebäude, kommt in den Modellen eine neue Bedeutung zu: vom historischen Walmdach über das so lange kontrovers diskutierte Flachdach der Moderne bis hin zu der (heute immer noch beliebten) skulptural gefalteten Sheddach-Landschaft, die eine Beleuchtung durch Oberlichter ermöglicht. Sonst selten für die Bewohner*innen sichtbar, sind die Dächer hier eine bekletterbare Landschaft und Vogeltränke zugleich. Die überragende Monumentalität der Schulhäuser verschwindet unter den Gummisohlen. Vor einem Gebäude, über das man mit einem grossen Schritt hinwegsteigen kann, braucht man keine Angst zu haben.

Florian Grafs Arbeit spielt seit Langem damit, gebaute Monumente und scheinbare gesellschaftliche Gewissheiten von ihren Sockeln zu holen oder aber anscheinend Alltägliches, Banales oder Funktionales durch eine subtile Überarbeitung aufzuwerten. Die Verkleinerung und

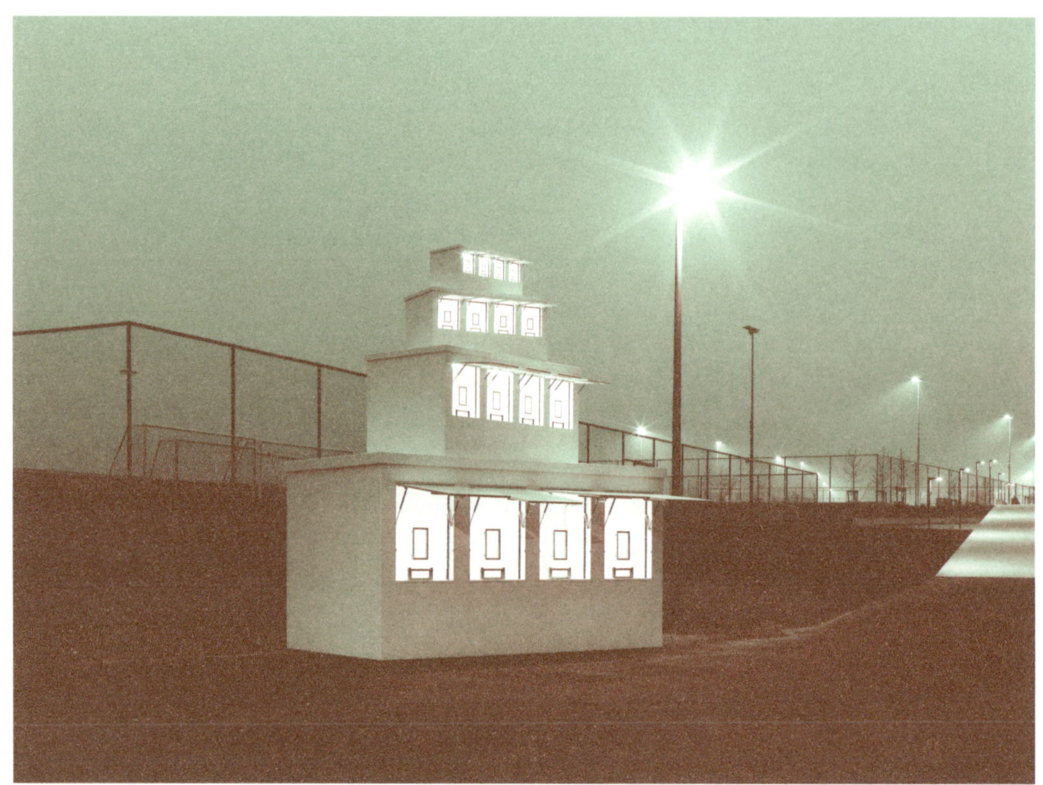

Abb. 1 Florian Graf, *Ticket Pagoda,* 2020, Installationsansicht Fussballstadion La Tulière, Lausanne

der detailgetreue Nachbau sind nicht nur eine Art der Aneignung, sondern öffnen eine Tür in die Welt hinter den Spiegeln. *Ticket Pagoda* (2020) (Abb. 1) vor dem Fussballstadion in Lausanne spielt mit einer matroschkaartigen Vervielfachung der originalen belanglosen Ticketcontainer im Schatten der monumentalen Stadionarchitektur. Minutiös verkleinert und übereinandergestapelt, bilden die zikkurathaften Modelltürme skulpturale Tickettempel. Ihre nächtliche Beleuchtung lässt auf ein ungekanntes, jedoch massstabsgetreues Innenleben schliessen.

Die amerikanische Schriftstellerin Susan Stewart sah in einer solchen unbetretbaren Gulliver-Welt der Modelle eine einsame «Insel».[1] Die meisten Miniaturen besitzen eine solche unsichtbare Barriere zwischen der Welt, in der sich die Betrachter*innen bewegen können, und der Welt, zu der die Modelle selbst gehören. Eine solche Insel mit einem ebenso rätselhaften Innenleben kündigte das Signallicht des schwimmenden Leuchtturms *Ghost Light Light House* (2012) (Abb. 2) an, mit dem Florian Graf über den Bodensee irrlichterte. Anstatt anderen mithilfe eines Leuchtfeuers dabei zu helfen, ihre Position zu bestimmen, trieb die selbst gebaute hölzerne Pyramide orientierungslos im Gewässer zwischen der Schweiz, Österreich und Deutschland umher. Der abstrakte Obelisk, ein weiterer Archetyp der Architekturgeschichte, fügte sich jedoch trotzdem unvermittelt und nahezu nahtlos in die Landschaft ein.

Grafs langjähriges Spiel mit Erwartungen und Gewissheiten im Modell fügt sich ebenso nahtlos in die lange Geschichte des Modellbaus als Spiegel der Wirklichkeit ein: Falsche Fassaden, Materialimitationen und ungewohnte Massstäbe können Brücken bauen, die es jeder und jedem erlauben, zumindest temporär in eine andere Welt einzutauchen und mit den Bausteinen für eine neue Realität zu spielen.

1 Susan Stewart, *On Longing. Narratives of the Miniature, the Gigantic, the Souvenir, the Collection.* Durham, NC 1992.

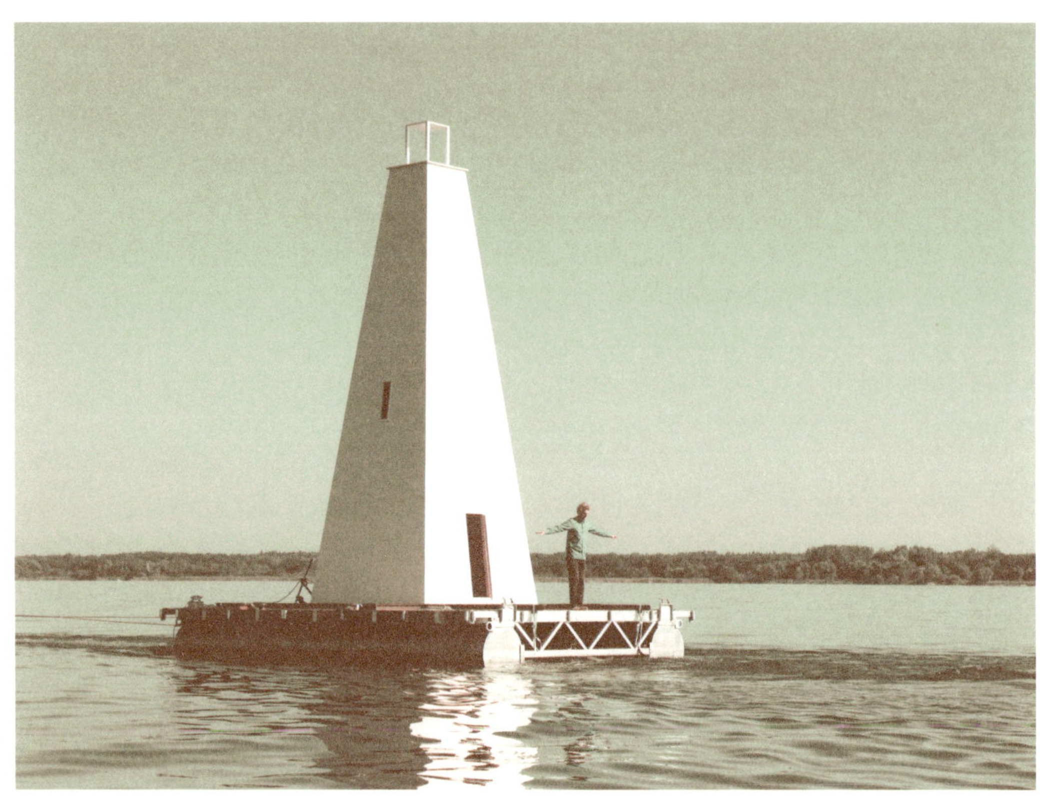

Abb. 2 Florian Graf, *Ghost Light Light House,* 2012, Installationsansicht Bodensee, Zeppelin Museum Friedrichshafen

Archetypal Games

Teresa
Fankhänel

Teresa Fankhänel is an architecture curator, writer, and editor-in-chief of the *Architectural Exhibition Review*. Her recent exhibitions include *African Mobilities* (2018), *The Architecture Machine* (2020/21), *Built Together* (2021), *Shouldn't You Be Working?* (2023), and *Andrea Canepa: As We Dwell in the Fold* (2023/24). Since 2024, she has been interim professor of architecture theory at KIT in Karlsruhe.

As a schoolboy, Florian Graf was initially intimidated by his schoolhouse. He felt he was being overpowered by the imposing building, swallowed up by it. His *School Models* (2023), sculpted in Muschelkalk limestone, overcome this architectural specter by means of a simple yet consequential trick: when reduced in size to scale models, the three stone school sculptures allow absolutely everyone to "occupy" the real buildings surrounding the schoolyard. On a smaller scale, the students can "grasp" their school as a plaything in the yard.

The miniature versions of the schoolhouses, which are protected as historic monuments, spatially symbolize archetypal educational models, which have undergone constant changes over the last three centuries. They are perched on oversized red and green terrazzo blocks; the orangy red represents the nineteenth-century roof tiles, while the green stands for the historical corridors through which generations of students have traipsed.

Anyone who grew up playing with building blocks knows that every set has its own system, its own world. Whether it's Friedrich Fröbel's Anchor Stone Building Blocks, Meccano, or Lego or even the digital blocks used in Minecraft, the construction kit is what defines the limits of the imagination. And each set has its own rules for how to play with it. Architectural history contains a whole array of childhood master block builders, whose later work can be traced back to playing with models and construction archetypes at an early age. To take two examples, architect Walter Gropius and Ivan Sutherland, the pioneer of computer architecture, both apparently "blocked out" shapes as preschoolers. Just like Le Corbusier, who perceived basic geometrical architectural forms in the buildings of ancient Rome, they reduced the complex constructed world around them to simple building blocks.

Most architects love models, displaying a fascination that combines elements of a material fetish, an almost divine ability to control reality on a small scale, a hands-on approach to the details of the draft design, and a tangible collection of ideas. In a model, scale is always inextricably linked with the degree of detail that can be included. In Graf's sculptures, some of the fine stone ridges on these seat-high schoolhouses have been milled by a laser beam and then sanded. Whenever the machine reached the limits of what it could do, the work was continued by hand. The fact that some of the oversized blocks now tower over the schoolhouse models is part of the charm inherent in playing around with proportions and scales. The schematic architecture of the blocks and the basic Euclidean shapes of their three-dimensional geometry—pyramids, cylinders, and cuboids—almost seem to be a caricature of the architectural theories that underpin the schoolhouses and the educational models that are inherent in them, which invariably seek to standardize. Above all, the fifth facade, namely the building's roofscape, takes on a new significance in these models: from the hipped roof of the past to the modernist flat roof that was so long a source of controversy, and ultimately the—still popular—sculptural interplay of pent roof forms, which allow in light from above via transom windows. Roofs are otherwise seldom visible to a building's inhabitants, but here they assume the twin functions of a landscape to be clambered over and a birdbath. The schoolhouses' formidable monumentality disappears under the children's rubber soles. There's no need to be scared of a building that you can step over in a large stride.

Graf's work has long played around with the idea of knocking built monuments and apparent certainties in society off their pedestals, while also upgrading the value of things that might seem to be quotidian, banal, or functional by subtly reworking them. Reducing their size and then reconstructing them in detail is not merely a kind of appropriation, it also opens up a door into the world behind the looking glass. *Ticket Pagoda* (2020) (fig. 1) in front of the football stadium in Lausanne plays with a matryoshka-style replication of the original inconspicuous ticket booth, situated in the shadow of the

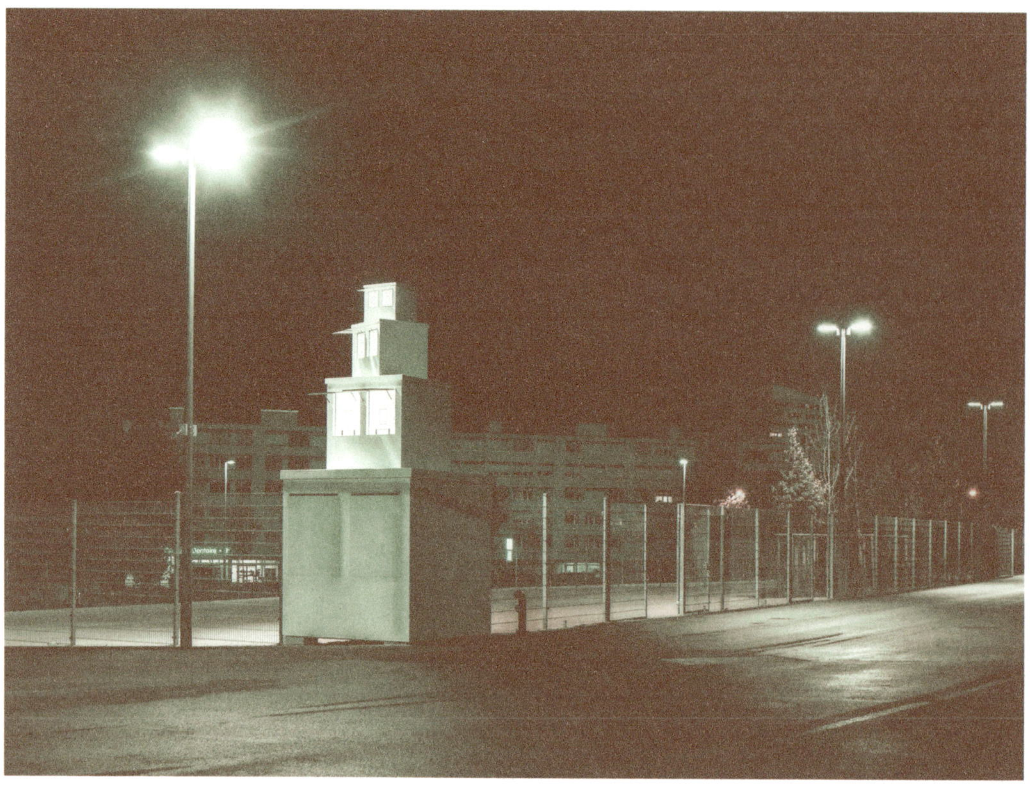

fig. 1 Florian Graf, *Ticket Pagoda,* 2020, installation view, La Tulière football stadium, Lausanne

monumental stadium architecture. Meticulously downsized and stacked one on top of the other, these ziggu-ratesque model towers constitute sculptural ticket temples. Their nighttime illumination suggests inner workings that are unknown but true to scale.

American author Susan Stewart viewed this kind of inaccessible Gulliver's world of models as a lonely "island."[1] Most miniatures are endowed with an invisible barrier between the world the observers occupy and the world that the models themselves belong to. The beam shining from the floating *Ghost Light Light House* (2012) (fig. 2), which Graf cast adrift on Lake Constance, signalized just such an island, with equally puzzling inner workings. Instead of allowing others to determine their position with the help of a beacon, the home-made wooden pyramid drifted aimlessly in the waters between Switzerland, Austria, and Germany. Nonetheless, this abstract obelisk, yet another archetype in architectural history, fitted unexpectedly and virtually seamlessly into the landscape.

The way in which Graf has played with expectations and certainties in models over many years fits just as seamlessly into the long history of building models as a reflection of reality: false facades, material limitations, and unfamiliar proportions can build bridges that allow each and every person to immerse themselves in another world—at least temporarily—and play with the building blocks of a new reality.

1 Susan Stewart, *On Longing: Narratives of the Miniature, the Gigantic, the Souvenir, the Collection*, Durham, NC: Duke University Press, 1992.

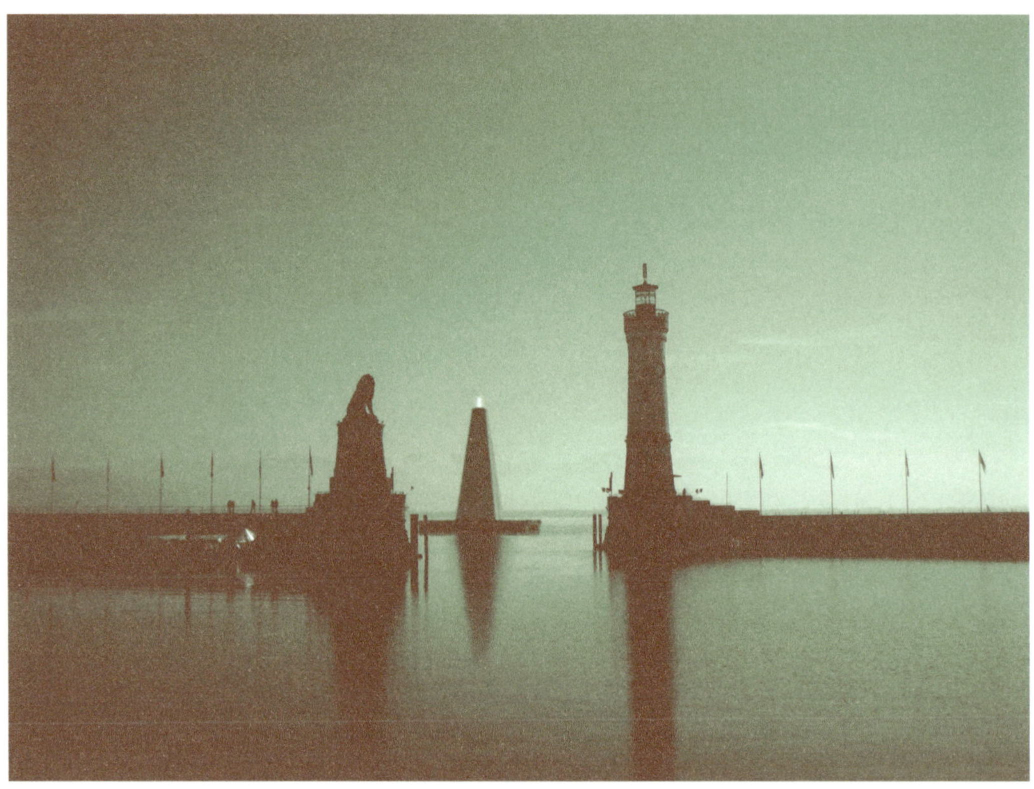

fig. 2 Florian Graf, *Ghost Light Light House,* 2012, installation view on Lake Constance, Lindau

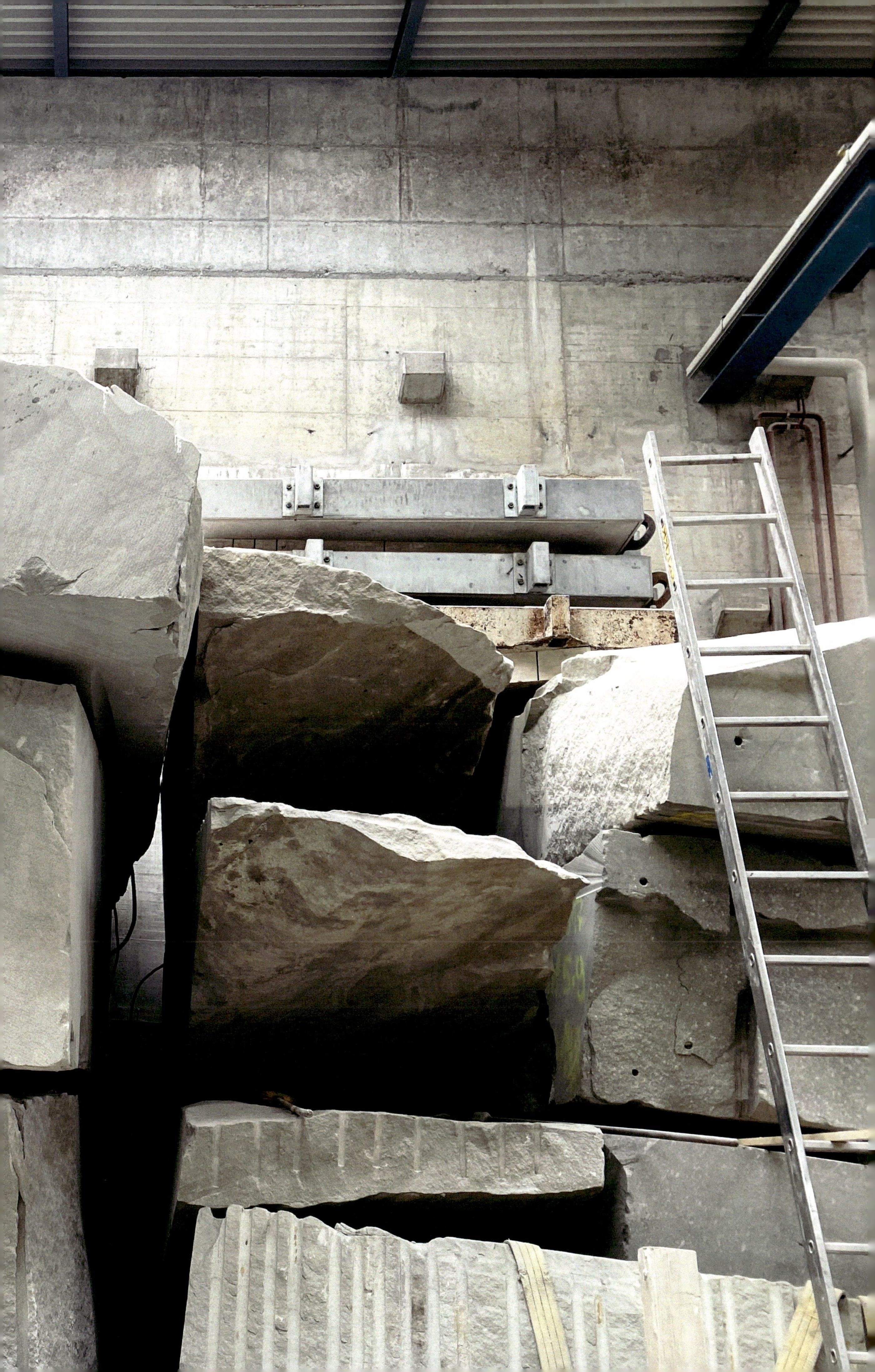

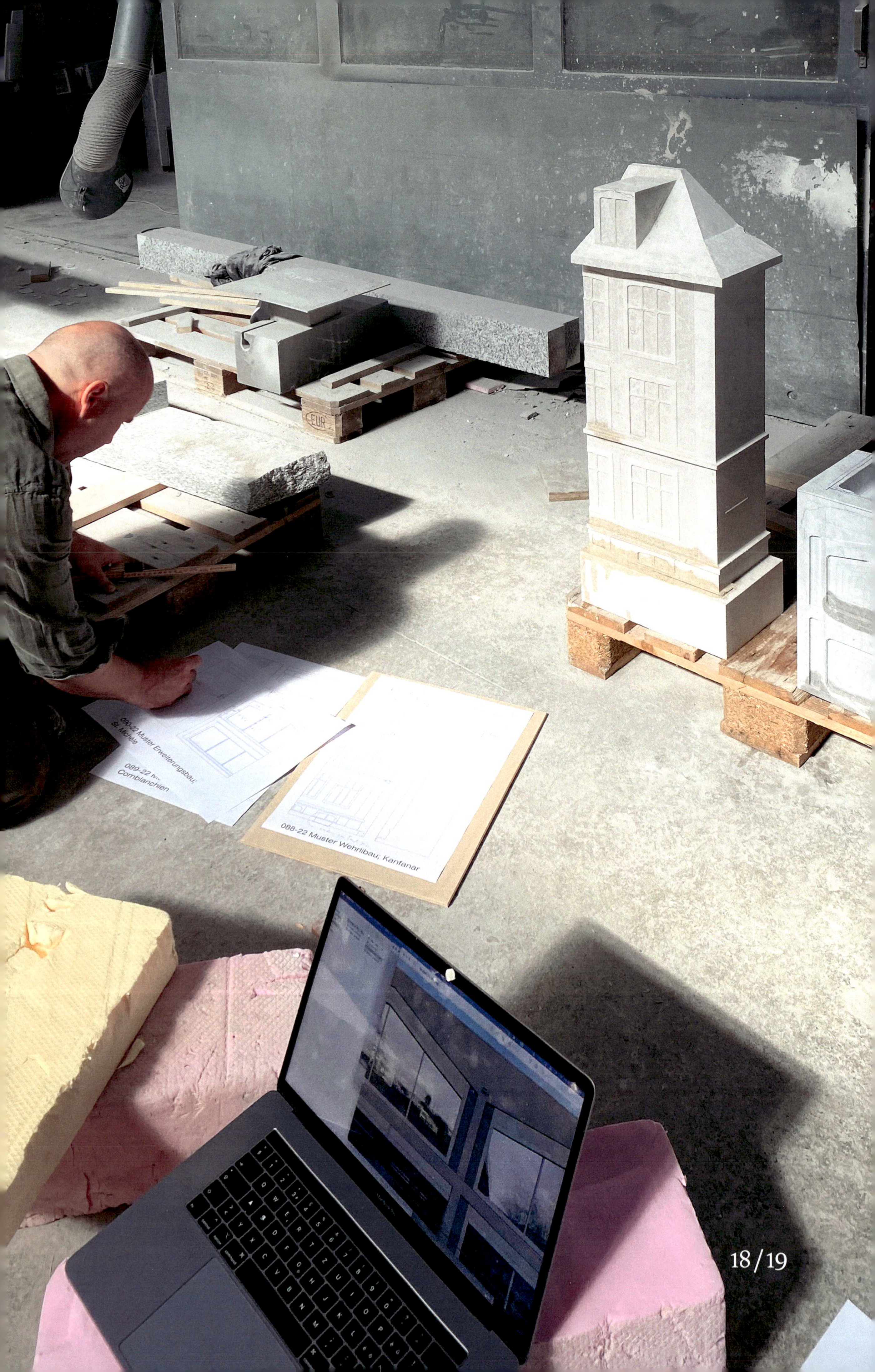
090-22 Muster Erweiterungsbau;
St. Michele
089-22
Comblanchien
088-22 Muster Wehrlibau; Kanfanar

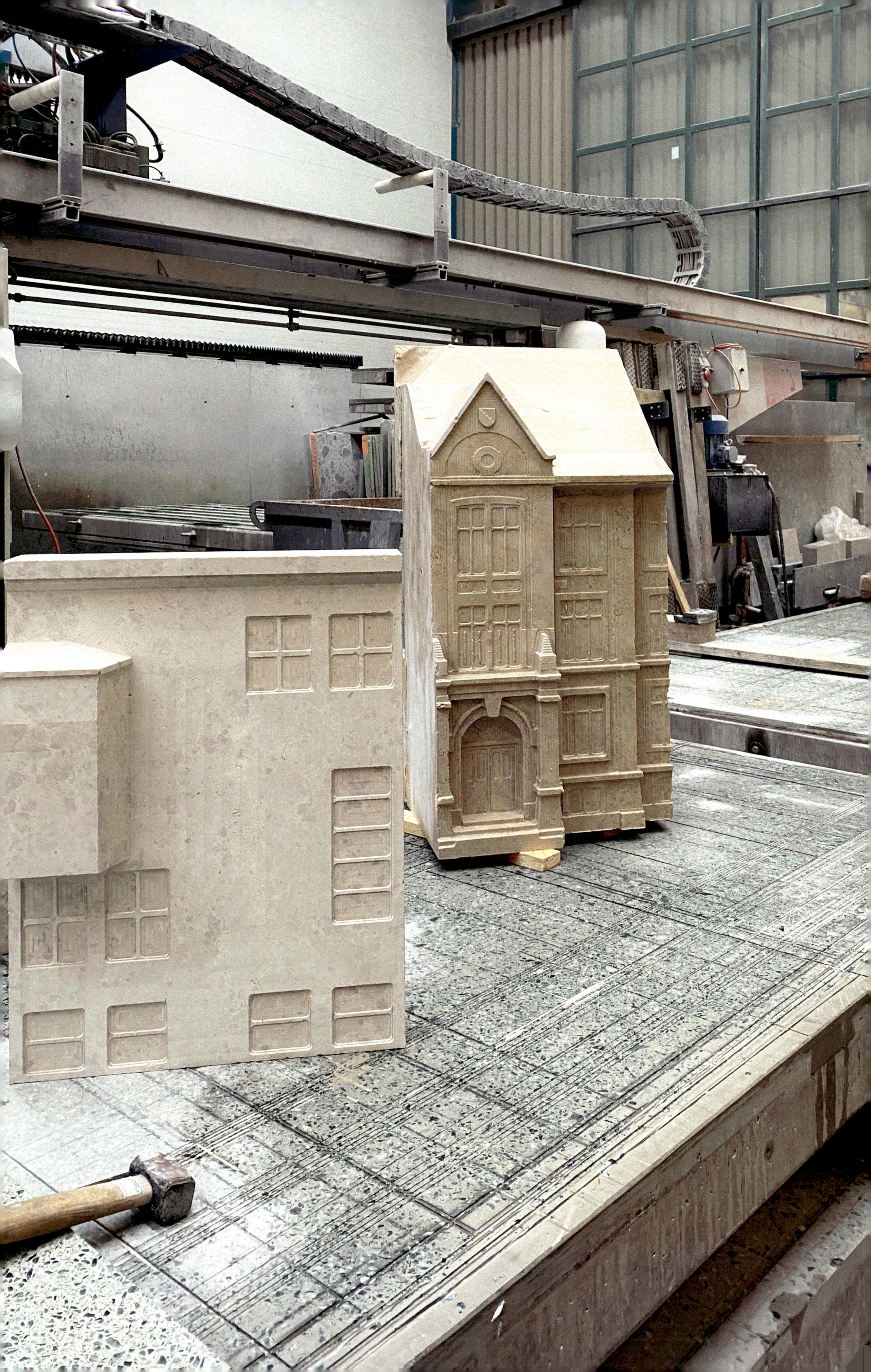

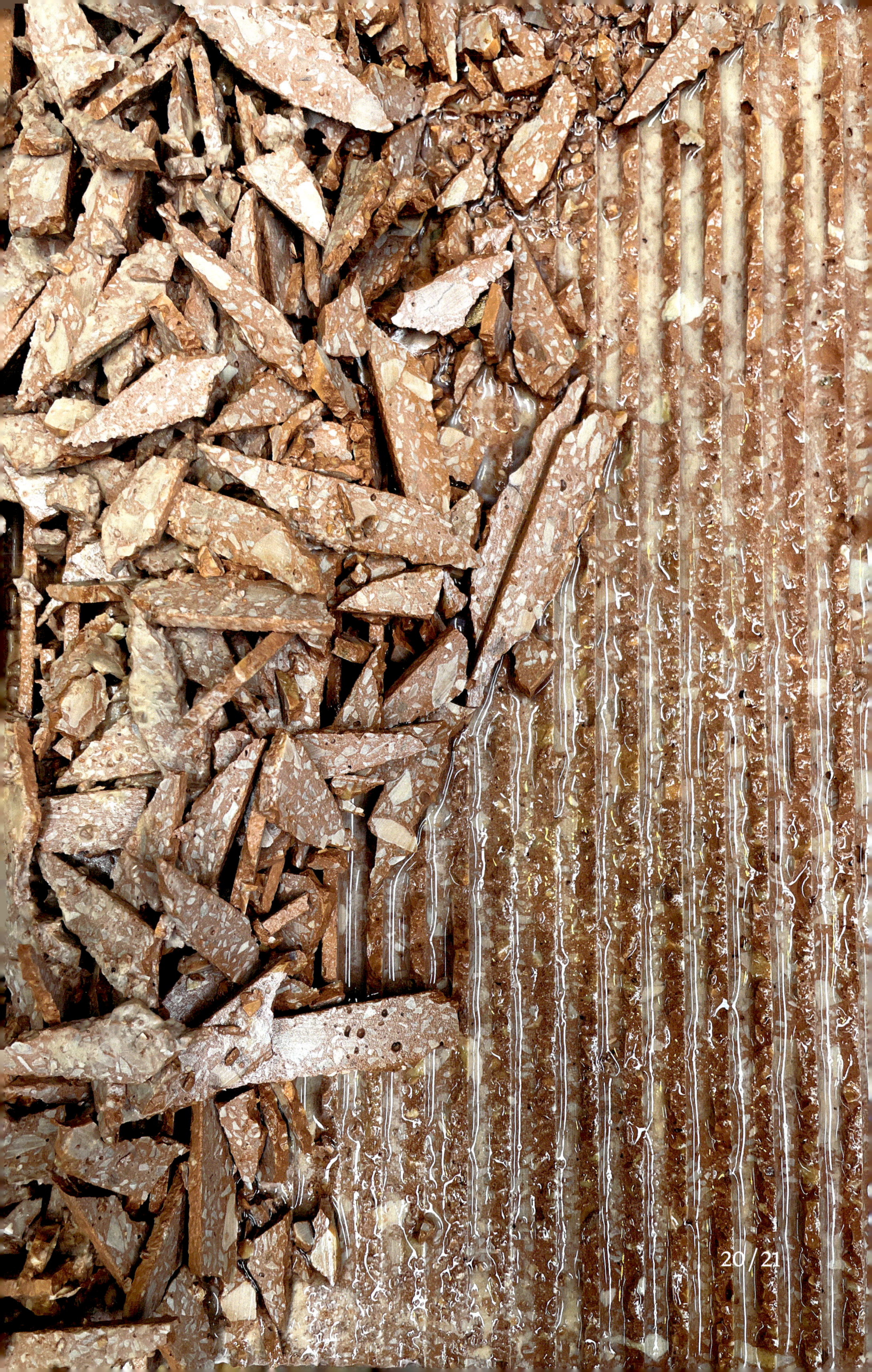

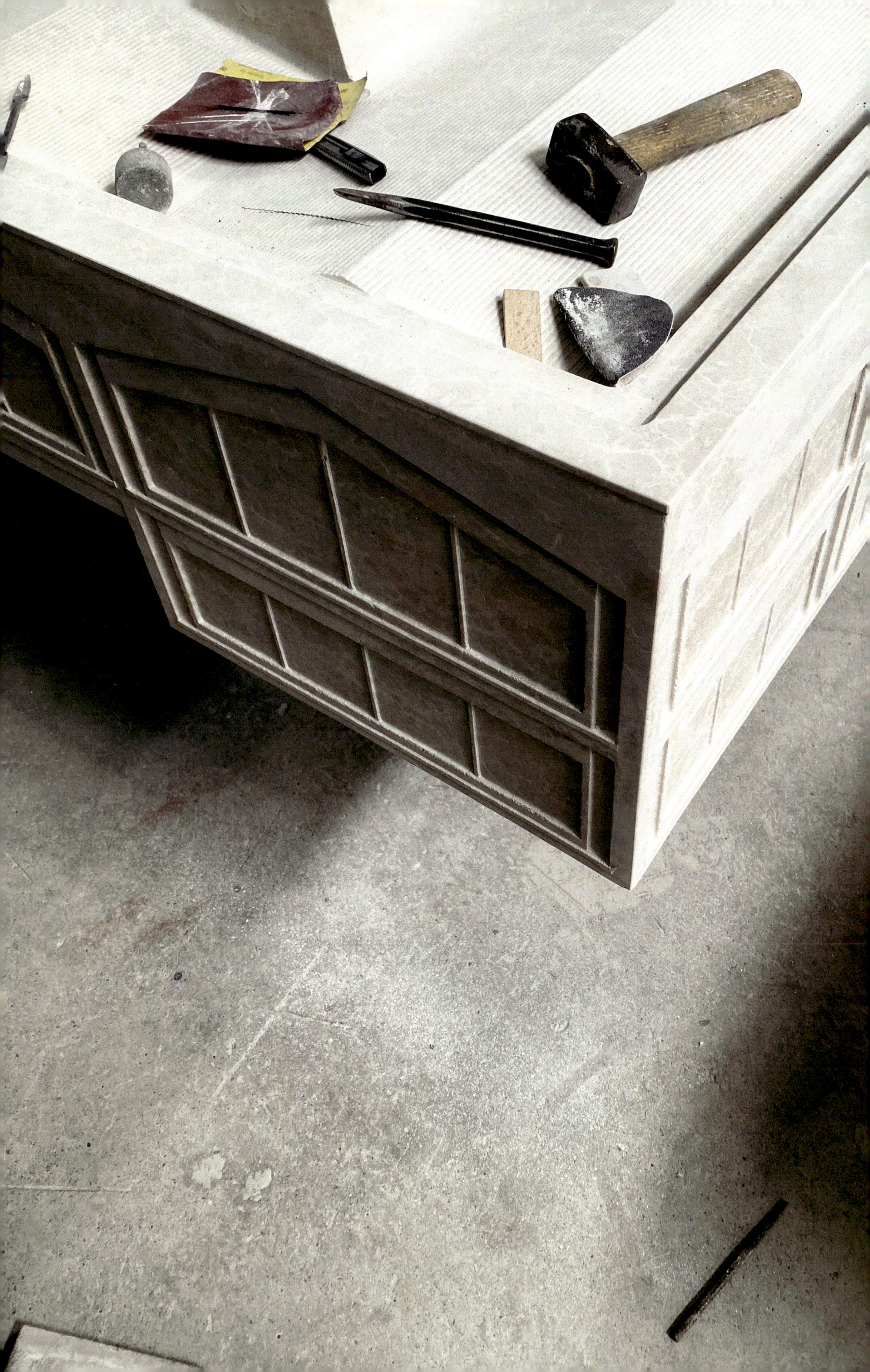

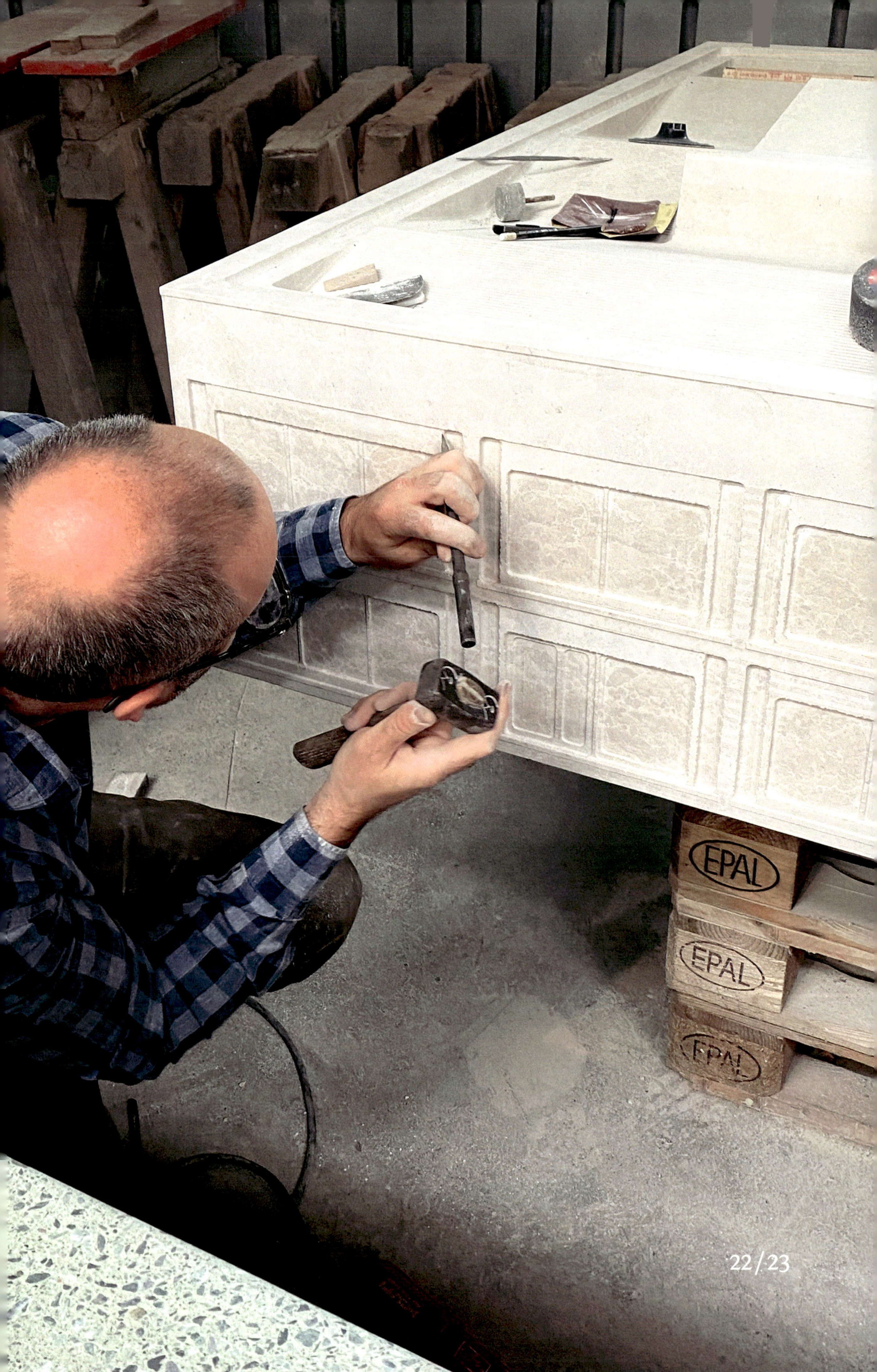
EPAL
EPAL
EPAL

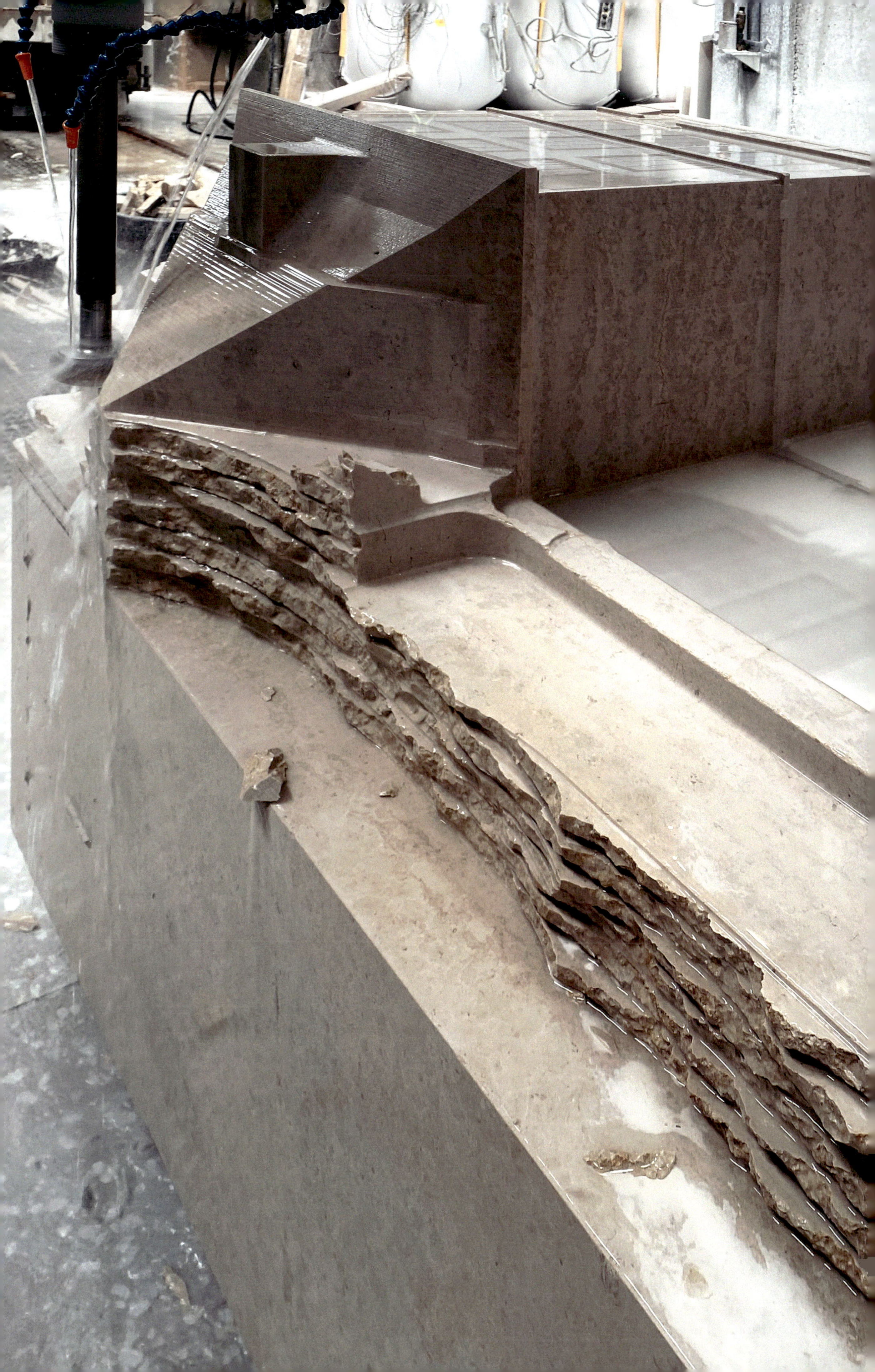

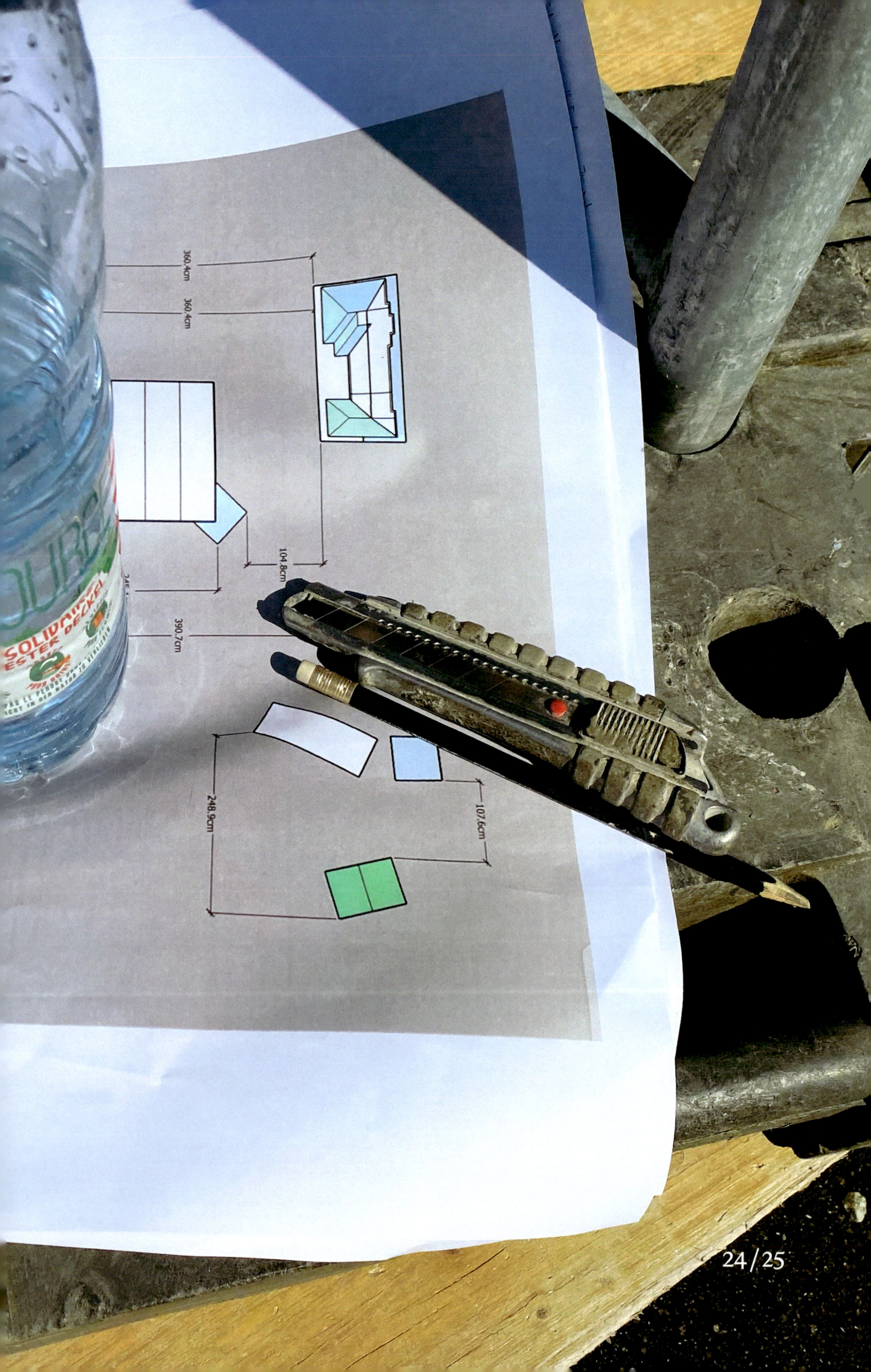

24/25

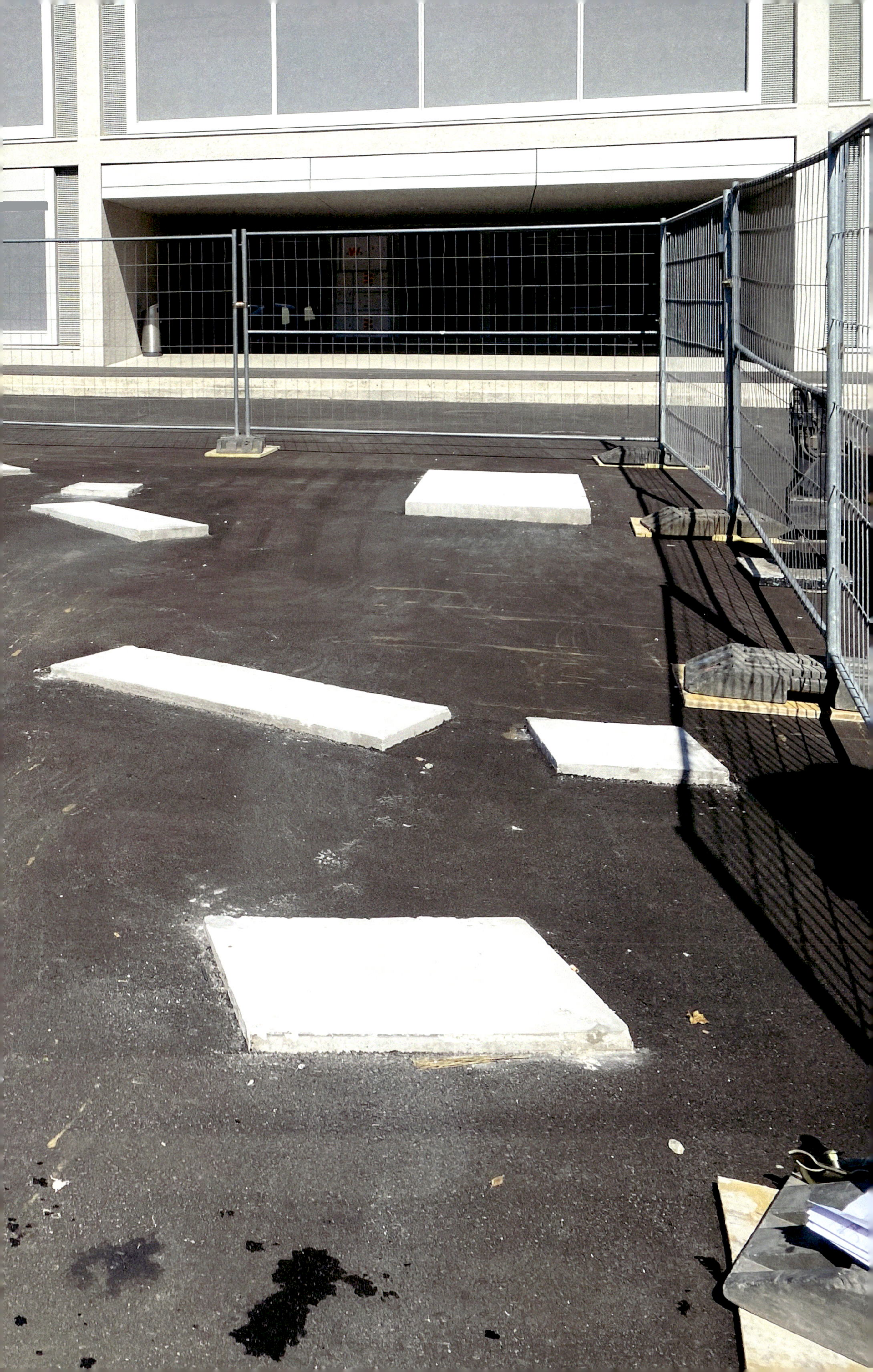

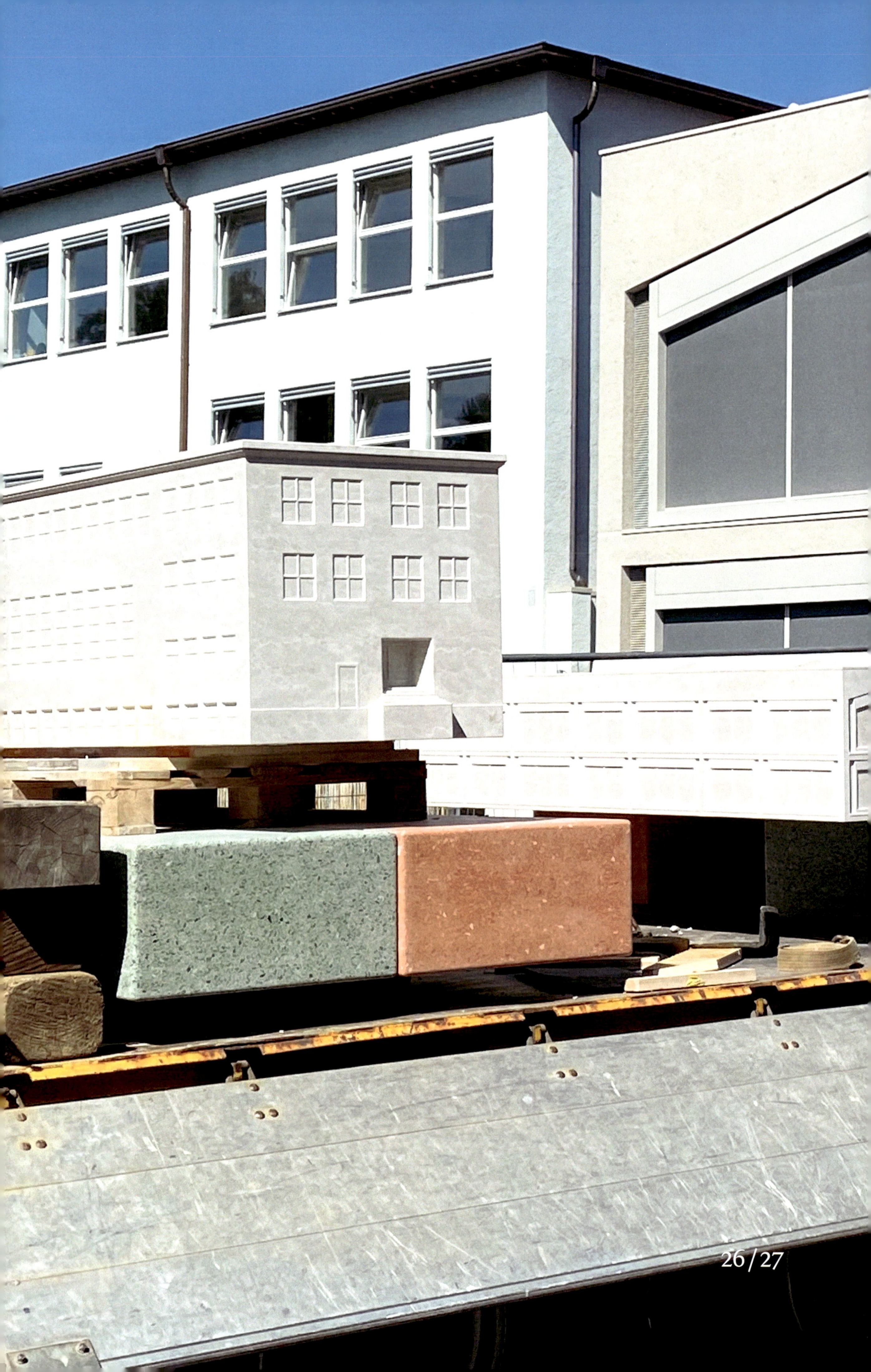

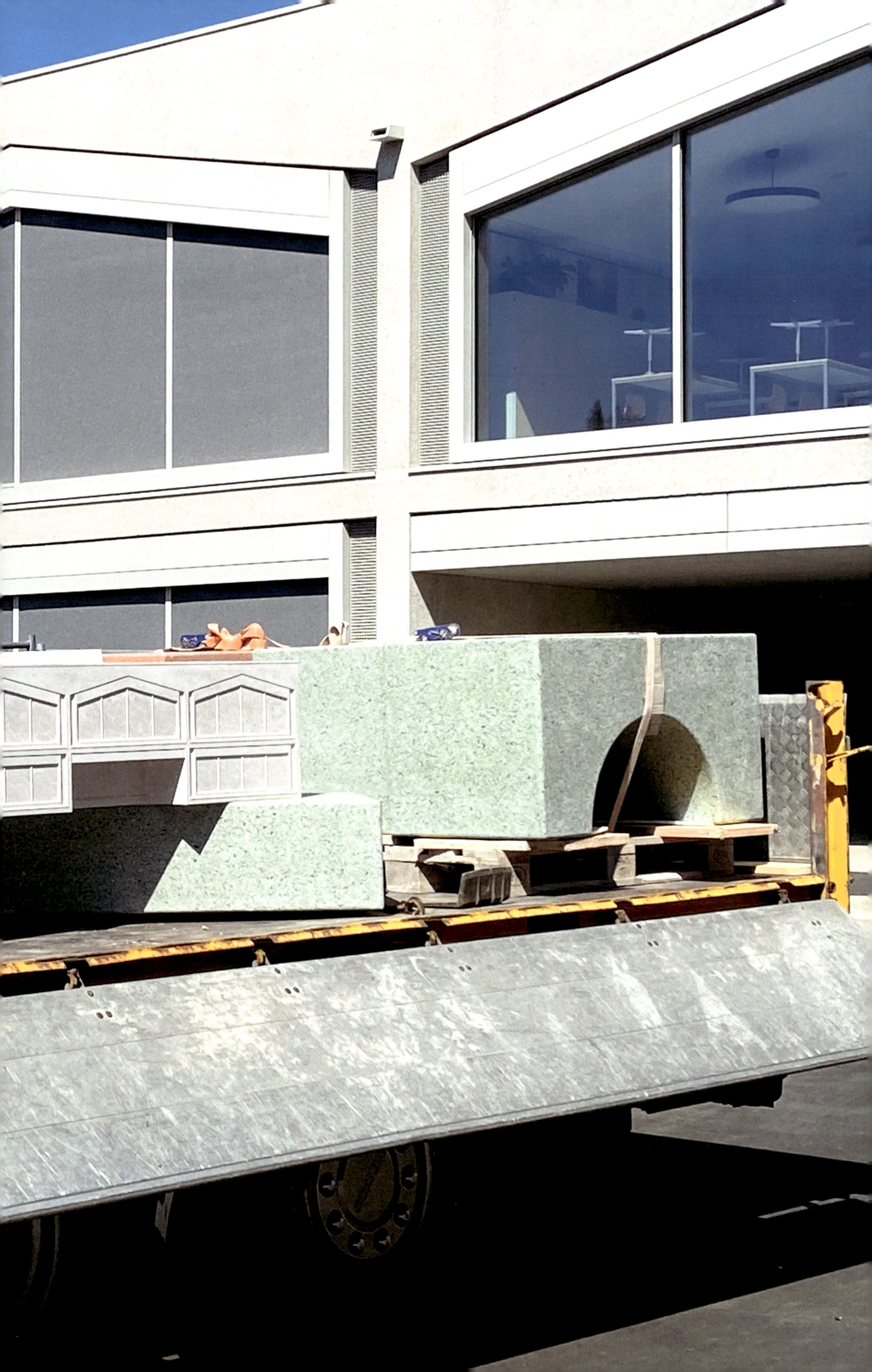

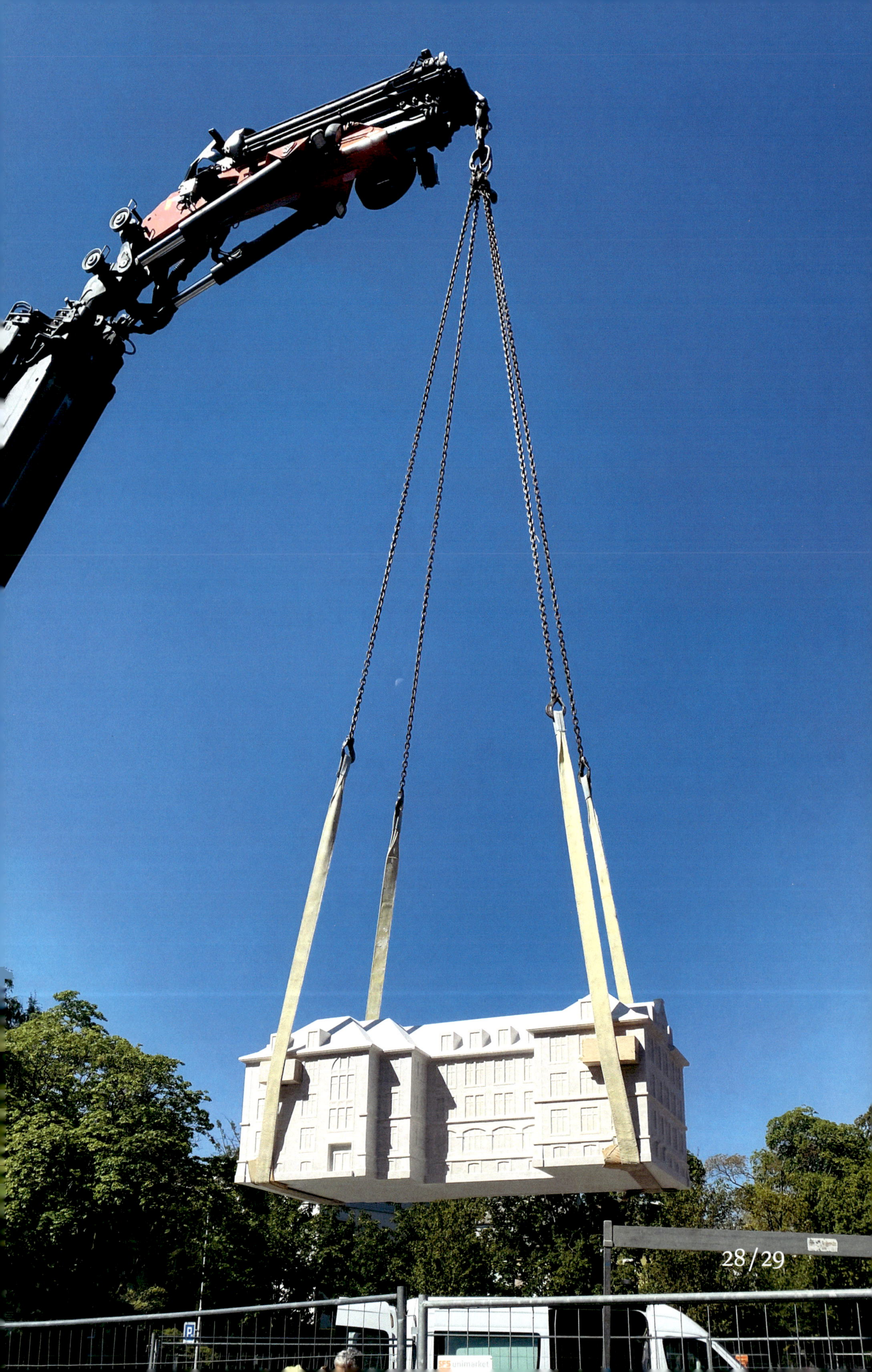
28/29

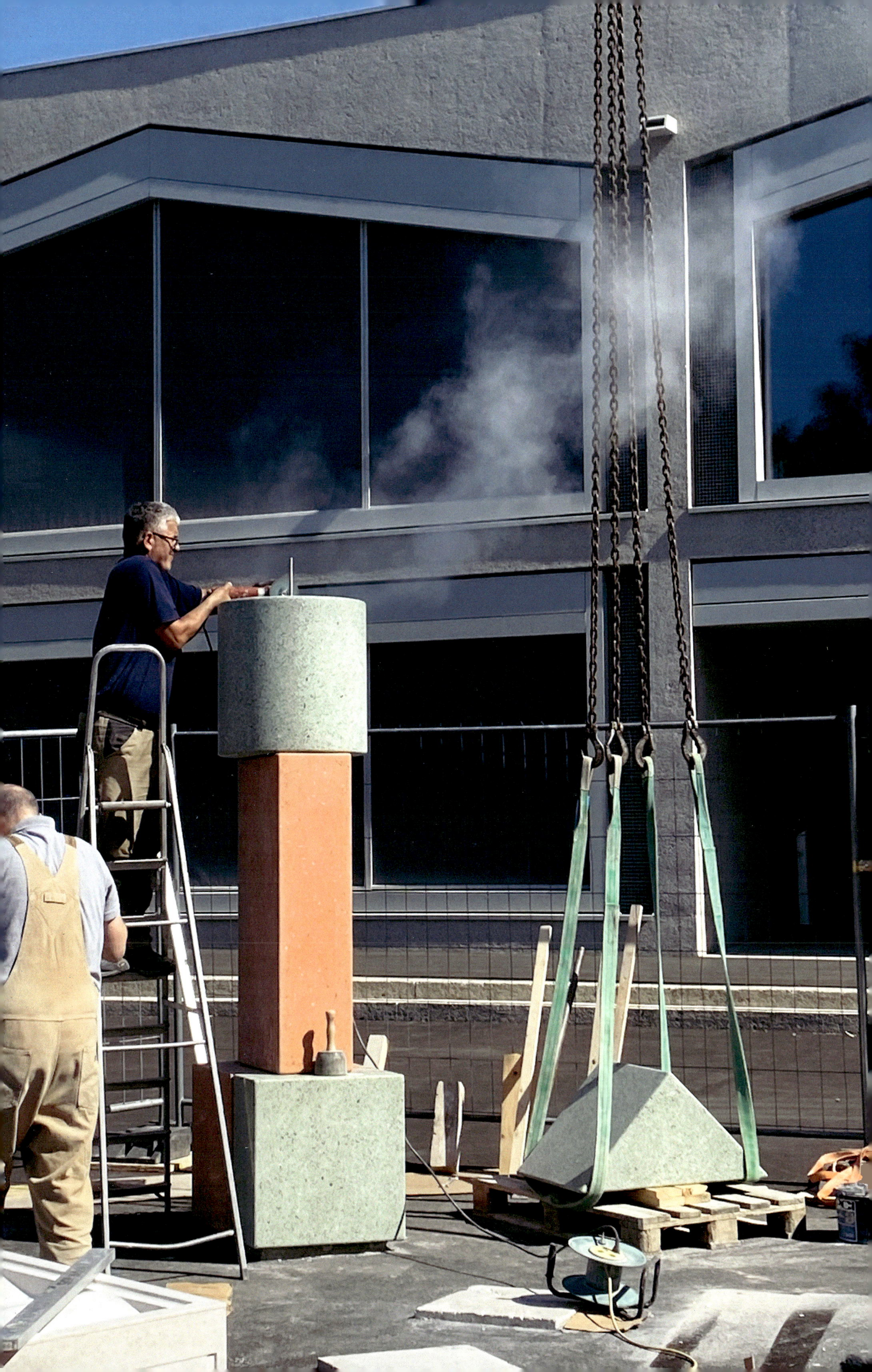

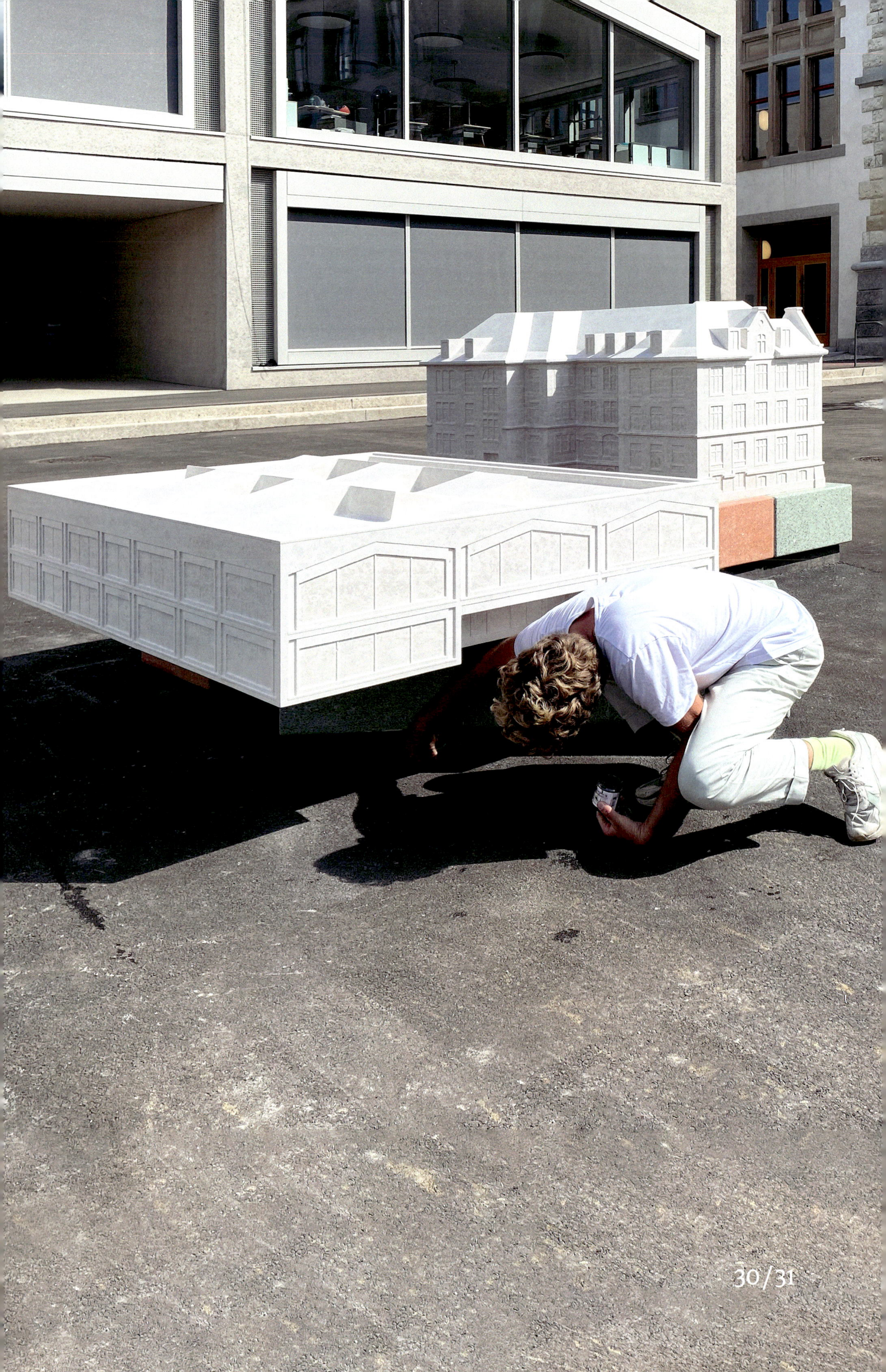

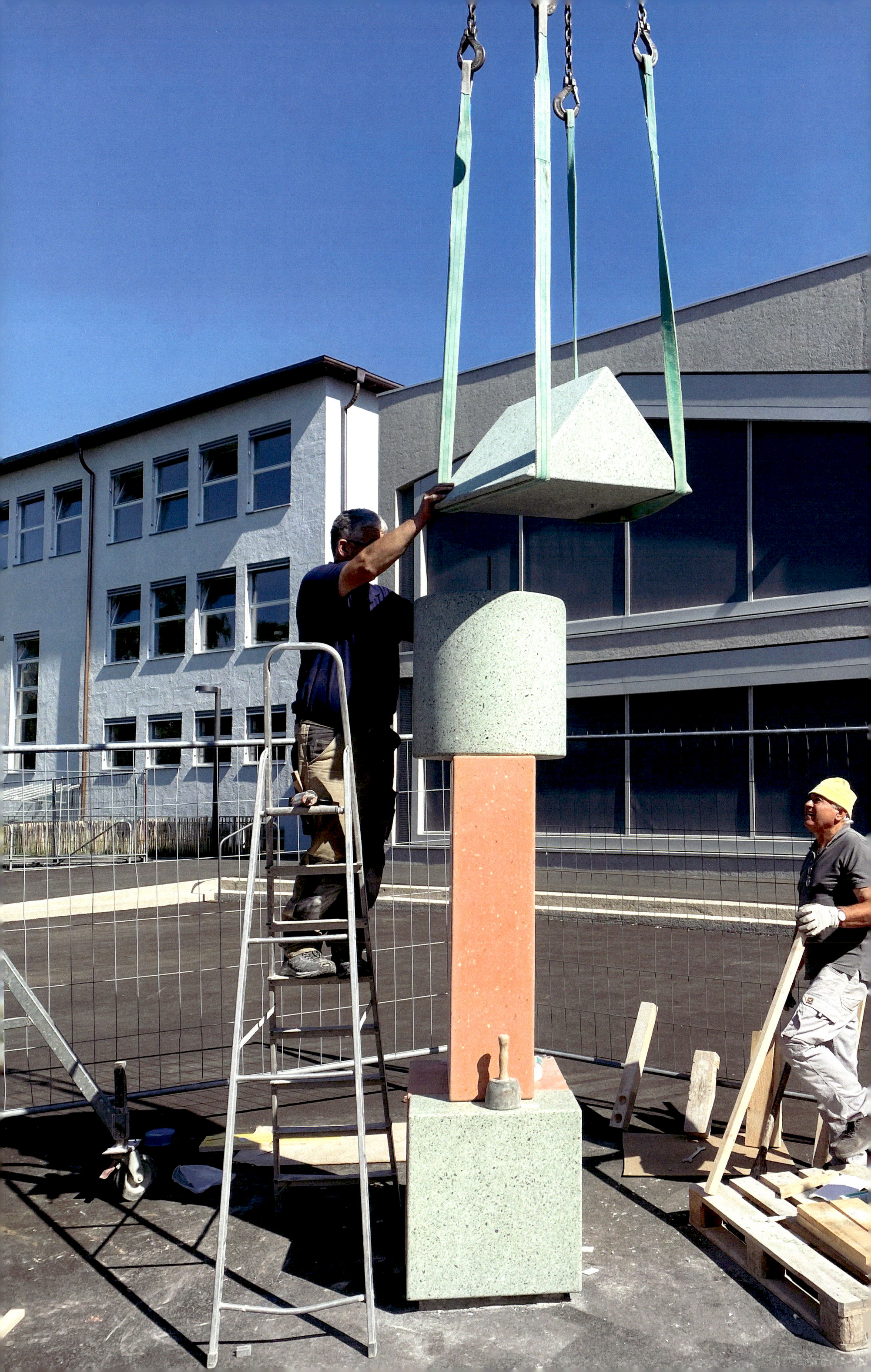

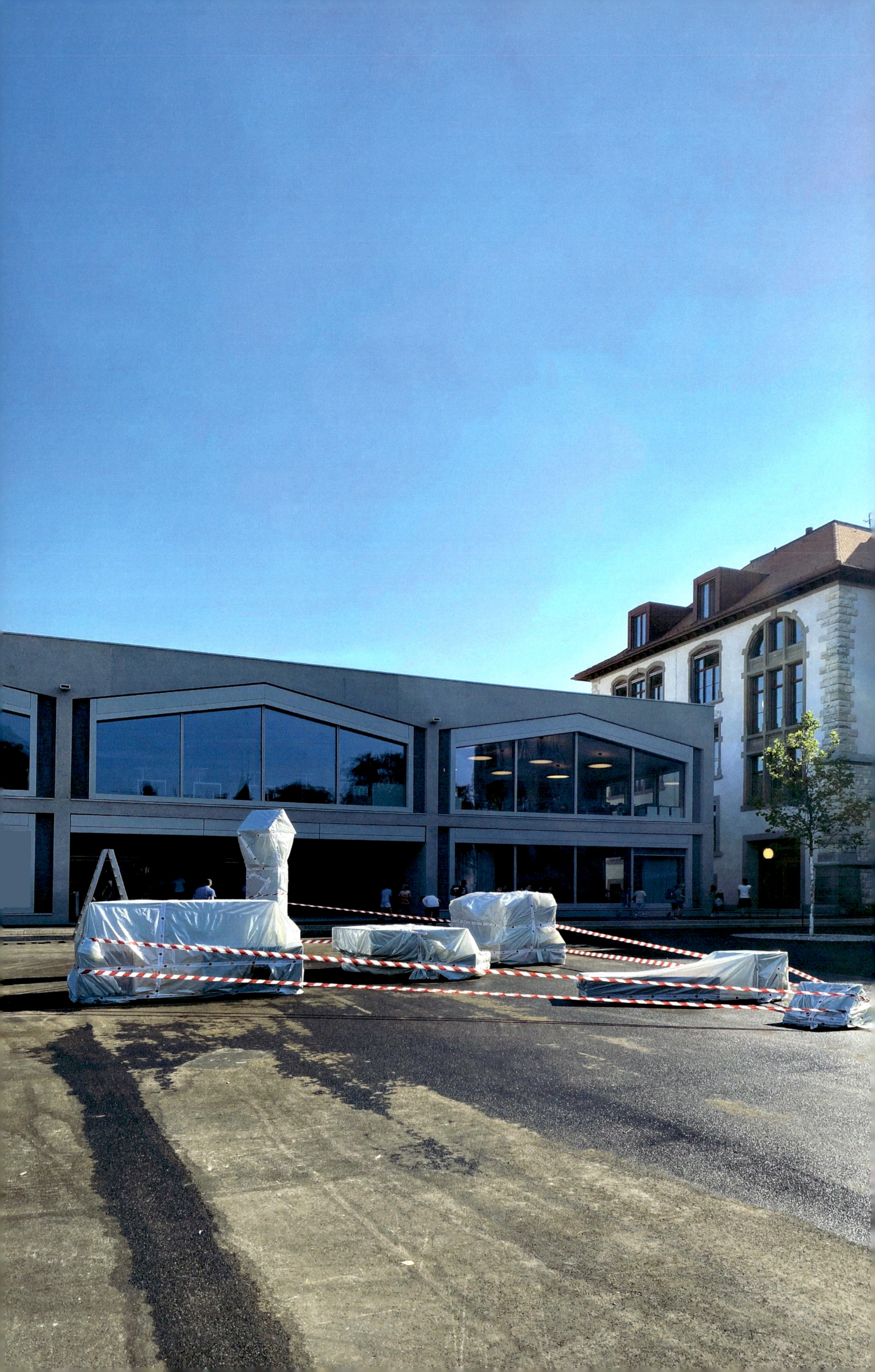

In Beziehung sein: Florian Grafs *School Models* als Resonanzverstärker

Yasmin
Afschar

Yasmin Afschar ist freie Kuratorin und Mediatorin für Nouveaux Commanditaires Suisse, eine internationale Initiative, die zum Ziel hat, der zeitgenössischen Kunst durch Kunstprojekte, die von Bürger*innen in Auftrag gegeben werden, eine neue demokratische Perspektive zu geben. Zuvor leitete sie interimistisch die Kunsthalle Mainz und war von 2018 bis 2021 Kuratorin am Aargauer Kunsthaus in Aarau.

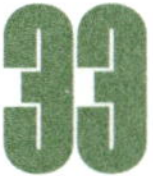

Resonanz sei das Gefühl, mit den Menschen, Dingen und Orten um uns herum eine lebendige Verbindung zu pflegen – mit ihnen in Beziehung zu sein, so der deutsche Soziologe Hartmut Rosa.[1] Resonanz entsteht, wenn gegenseitige Schwingungen erzeugt werden – wenn Geist und Körper, Mensch und Umwelt im Einklang sind. Die Einweihung von Florian Grafs *School Models* in der Schulanlage Hofacker am 15. September 2023 war, so gesehen, eine Übung in Resonanz. Eine Mischung aus Kunstfestival und Quartierfest war der Anlass, nicht lediglich offizieller Festakt, sondern integraler Teil von Grafs künstlerischem Gesamtkonzept – ein aufwendig orchestriertes Experiment, um den Übergang vom Kunstprozess zum Nutzobjekt rituell zu begleiten. Lehrpersonen, Eltern, Freund*innen, das Quartier und Kunstinteressierte aus der ganzen Stadt waren eingeladen, zusammen mit den Schüler*innen und einer Gruppe von Kunstschaffenden sowie den Kuratorinnen Salome Hohl (Cabaret Voltaire), Christiane Rekade (Fachstelle Kunst und Bau, Stadt Zürich) und Elise Lammer die Kunst-und-Bau-Installation willkommen zu heissen: sie zu betanzen, zu besingen und zu bespielen, sie zu ver- und enthüllen, zu zweckentfremden und zu behausen; sie in Schwingung zu versetzen und so die Basis zu legen für künftige Interaktionen.

1 Zu Rosas Resonanztheorie vgl. Hartmut Rosa, *Resonanz: Eine Soziologie der Weltbeziehung*. Berlin 2016.

Veranschaulicht wurde diese Idee, Widerhall und Wechselwirkungen anzuregen, in Nina Emges und Nils Amadeus Langes Beitrag *School Bell 1*. Über die Dauer der Veranstaltung tauchte immer wieder eine Performerin auf, die, mit unterschiedlich grossen und verschieden arrangierten Schellen behängt, als wandelndes Instrument sich selbst spielte oder spielen liess. Die Intervention funktionierte als freie Interpretation der Pausenglocke, inspiriert von Rosas Resonanztheorie. Nicht der Stundenplan gab den Takt vor und nicht das Tonband den Klang, sondern die Interaktion und die Beziehungen zwischen den Objekten, der Performerin und den Schüler*innen und Gäst*innen.

Hartmut Rosa sieht in seinem Resonanzkonzept eine Antwort auf «Steigerungszwang» und «Beschleunigungsimperativ» moderner kapitalistischer Gesellschaften, die zu Entfremdung und distanzierten, mechanistischen Beziehungen führten. Stattdessen seien aktive offene Beziehungen nötig, um Widerhall zu erzeugen.[2] Florian Grafs materialbedingt statisches, aber in der Nutzung sehr bewegliches Ensemble nimmt das auf: Es ist interaktiv in einem analogen Sinne und motiviert zu neuen Auf- und Einsichten. In einer Art Scharnierfunktion zwischen der Architektur aus unterschiedlichen Epochen, dem Sozialraum Schule und der Realität des Schüler*in-Seins handelt die Kunst hier ganz explizit vom Sich-in-Beziehung-Setzen mit der Umgebung, ihren Dingen und Menschen. Sie spielt dabei gerne verkehrte Welt – für uns Erwachsene zumindest. Für die Fantasie eines Kindes hingegen sind die zu grossen Bauklötze und zu kleinen Schulhäuser vielleicht gar nicht so ungewöhnlich.

2 Vgl. ebd., Kap. 5, S. 246–330.

Wunderte ich mich damals arg über Alice im Wunderland, wie sie innert kürzester Zeit erst schrumpfte und wieder wuchs? Oder über Gullivers Reisen von Liliput, einem Land mit klein gewachsenen Fabelwesen, nach Brobdingnag, dem Land der Riesen? Jonathan Swift, der Erfinder von Gulliver, nutzte übrigens die Länder, die er Gulliver bereisen liess, um auf politische Missstände seiner Zeit aufmerksam zu machen. Er übte Kritik an den Klassenunterschieden, an der europäischen Kolonialpolitik oder der Wissenschaft, die sich zu weit von den wahren menschlichen Bedürfnissen entfernt habe. Swift schrieb *Gullivers Reisen* 1726, noch lange bevor auch nur das erste Gebäude der Schulanlage zu stehen kam. Zweieinviertel Jahrhunderte später sprachen Guy Debord und die Situationistische Internationale von *détournement* als revolutionärer Praxis.[3] Sie «entführten» Bedeutungen und Kontexte und arrangierten sie neu, um Gedanken anzuregen und Machtstrukturen und Ideologien infrage zu stellen.

3 Zum Begriff *détournement* vgl. Guy Debord / Gil J. Wolman, «A User's Guide to Détournement», in: *Internationale Situationniste*, Nr. 1, 1956, S. 2–5; Guy Debord, *Die Gesellschaft des Spektakels*. Berlin 1967.

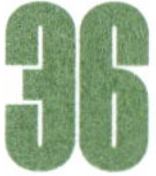

Beide, Swift und Debord, agierten mit Gesten des Verkehrens und Verschiebens, die wir auch bei Florian Graf wiederfinden. Er schrumpft die Schule auf eine Grösse, die sie von den Kindern und Jugendlichen, den «Kleinen» der Gesellschaft, «regierbar» macht. Umgekehrt betont er die Bedeutung kindlichen Spielens und Denkens, indem er die modularen Bauklötze vergrössert. Mehr noch: Florian Graf konzipierte im Vorfeld einen Workshop, für den er die Künstlerin Monster Chetwynd einlud, um zusammen mit den Schüler*innen Puppen als ihr verkleinertes Selbst zu entwerfen. Die imaginativen Bewohner*innen der Modellhäuser durften dann – wir sind wieder beim Eröffnungsprogramm – in einem rituellen Akt «einziehen» (und später weiterziehen, in eine dem Projekt gewidmete Ausstellung im Cabaret Voltaire). Zuvor hatte Yorgos Sapountzis in einer Enthüllungschoreografie für Florian Grafs Skulpturen ein temporäres Beziehungsnetz zwischen Körper, öffentlichem Raum und Denkmal skizziert. *Delicate balance* (2023) von Raffaela Boss und Charlotte Horn nahm mit Gesang- und Soundelementen den Gedanken der Resonanz wieder auf, wobei sie in ihrer Performance die Grenzen zwischenmenschlicher Beziehungen zum Thema machten. Und da waren diese drei Fantasiefiguren, die da und dort neben und auf den *School Models* auftauchten, mit ihnen und den Gäst*innen still und freundlich interagierten: ein Wesen mit Lippen so gross wie der Kopf und mit Augen an den Händen, ein anderes mit mindestens 20 Paar Händen und eine dritte Figur mit langem Haartüll vor dem Gesicht. Julie Monots gewitzt-surreale *Personas* waren Verkörperungen von Formen, Bildern und Gefühlen, die etwas mit dem Körper zu tun haben.

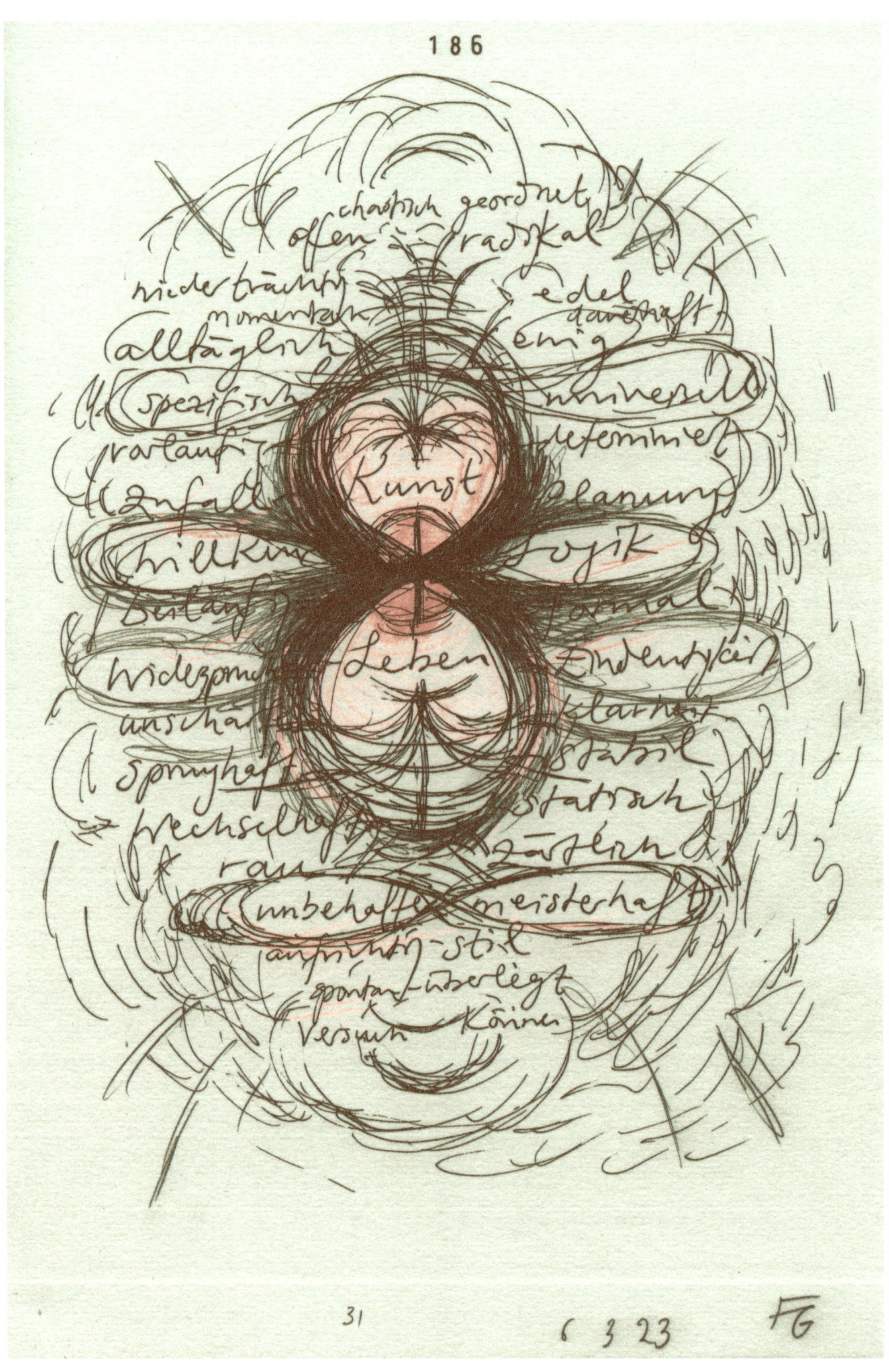

Abb. 1 Florian Graf, *Kunst und Leben*, Skizzenbuch 186, S. 31, 2023, Tinte und Farbstift auf Papier

Das hier beschriebene gemeinsame rituelle Aktivieren des Skulpturenensembles schuf auf dem Pausenplatz einen *Zeit-Ort*. Der Soziologe Bruno Latour sprach einst von «cohabitational time» und meinte damit einerseits die zeitliche Dimension von menschlichem und nicht menschlichem Zusammenleben, andererseits die Bedeutung von Raum als ordnender Grösse in unserer von Gegenwärtigkeit definierten Realität.[4] Erst wenn wir in der öffentlichen Sphäre gemeinsam Zeit verbringen, entstehe «demokratischer Raum». Das gilt auch für die Kunst im öffentlichen Raum. Kunst und Leben liegen hier ganz nahe beieinander – wie in einer Skizze, die Florian Graf während der konzeptuellen Arbeit an *School Models* anfertigte (Abb. 1): Rund um die beiden Begriffe «Kunst» (oben) und «Leben» (unten) setzt ein schneller fortzeichnender Strich bei zwei gespiegelten Herzformen an und setzt sich fort, bis die Wörter von einer 8 umrandet sind, und von da weiter zu Begriffspaaren, die sich rund um Kunst und Leben gruppieren: spezifisch – universell, Widerspruch – Eindeutigkeit, unbeholfen – meisterhaft usw. Bringen wir die 8 in die Horizontale, haben wir das Symbol für Unendlichkeit vorliegen. Die Schlaufe steht dann für den fortwährenden Austausch zwischen Kunst und Leben – für den Resonanzraum, der zwischen Kunst und Leben entstehen kann.

4 Bruno Latour, «Politics of time, politics of space», in: *Domus*, Nr. 876, 2004, unter: domusweb.it/en/from-the-archive/2022/10/13/bruno-latour-politics-of-time-politics-of-space.html (zuletzt aufgerufen: 17.05.2024).

A Sense of Connection: Amplifying Resonance with Florian Graf's *School Models*

Yasmin
Afschar

Yasmin Afschar is an independent curator and mediator for Nouveaux Commanditaires Suisse, an international initiative seeking to give contemporary art a renewed democratic perspective through art projects commissioned by members of the public. Previously, she served as the interim director of Kunsthalle Mainz and was a curator at Aargauer Kunsthaus in Aarau from 2018 to 2021.

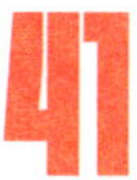

Resonance, according to the German sociologist Hartmut Rosa, is the feeling of nurturing vibrant relationships with the people, things, and places around us, of having a sense of connection with them.[1] Resonance occurs when mutual vibes are generated—when there is harmony between mind and body, between humans and their environment. As such, the inauguration of Florian Graf's *School Models* in the grounds of the Hofacker school on September 15, 2023, might be regarded as an exercise in resonance. A blend of art festival and community fête, the occasion was not simply an official celebration but rather an integral part of Graf's overall artistic concept—an elaborately orchestrated experiment in ritualizing the transition from artistic process to utilitarian object. Teaching staff, parents, friends, the local community, and art aficionados from all over the city were invited to welcome the new art and architecture installation together with the schoolchildren, a group of creatives, and the curators—Salome Hohl (Cabaret Voltaire), Christiane Rekade (Fachstelle Kunst und Bau, City of Zurich), and Elise Lammer. The idea was to celebrate it in song, dance, and play; to veil and unveil it; to use it for unintended purposes and to inhabit it; to set vibes in motion and thus create the basis for future interactions.

1 See Hartmut Rosa, *Resonance: A Sociology of Our Relationship to the World*, trans. by James C. Wagner, Cambridge: Polity, 2019.

The idea of inducing reverberations and reciprocal effects was illustrated in Nina Emge and Nils Amadeus Lange's performance *School Bell 1*. In the course of the inauguration, a performer repeatedly appeared with bells of various sizes draped over her in different arrangements, a changing instrument that could play itself or be played. The intervention functioned as a free interpretation of a recess bell, inspired by Rosa's theory of resonance. But in this case, it was not the school timetable that dictated the rhythm or a prerecorded tape that determined the sound but rather the interaction and the connections between the objects, the performer, and the schoolchildren and guests.

Rosa regards his concept of resonance as a response to the imperatives of "escalation" and "acceleration" in modern capitalist societies, which lead to alienation and to distanced, mechanistic relationships. To generate resonance, active, open relationships are required.[2] Graf's ensemble is, of course, static in a material sense, but its highly versatile uses incorporate this idea. It is interactive in analog terms and motivates the audience to make new discoveries and gain new insights. In its function as a hinge between the architecture of different epochs, the social environment of the school, and the reality of being a student there, the artwork is very explicitly about connecting with one's environment and with the objects and people in it. To do this, the artist playfully constructs a "through-the-looking-glass" world—or so it seems to us adults at least. But in a child's imagination, there may be nothing particularly unusual about the oversized building blocks or the miniature school buildings.

2 See Rosa, *Resonance*, chap. 5.

When I read *Alice in Wonderland* as a child, was I terribly surprised that Alice managed to shrink and then grow again in such a short time? And did I find Gulliver's travels from Lilliput, the land of mythical creatures of small stature, to Brobdingnag, the land of the giants, implausible? In fact, Jonathan Swift, Gulliver's creator, used the countries he had Gulliver travel to as a means to draw attention to the political ills of his time—to criticize class differences, European colonial policy, and the state of science, which had become far removed from real human needs. Swift wrote *Gulliver's Travels* in 1726, long before even the oldest school building here was erected. Two and a quarter centuries later, Guy Debord and the Situationist International spoke of *détournement* as a revolutionary practice.[3] They "hijacked" meanings and contexts and rearranged them in thought-provoking ways to make people question power structures and ideologies.

3 On the term détournement, see Guy Debord and Gil J. Wolman, "A User's Guide to Détournement" (1956), in *Situationist International Anthology*, trans. and ed. by Ken Knabb, Berkeley, CA: Bureau of Public Secrets, 1981; Guy Debord, *Society of the Spectacle*, trans. by Fredy Perlman, Detroit: Black & Red, 1970.

Both Swift and Debord worked with the same gestures of distortion and displacement that we find in Graf's installation. He shrinks the school to a size that allows the children and teenagers, the "little people" in society, to "govern." Conversely, by enlarging the modular building blocks, he emphasizes the importance of children's ways of playing and thinking. In advance of the installation, Graf also set up a workshop to which he invited the artist Monster Chetwynd, who got the children to make dolls as miniaturized versions of themselves. The imaginary inhabitants of the model houses were then—to return to the opening program—allowed to "move in" in a ritual act (and later move on to an exhibition at Cabaret Voltaire devoted to the project). Prior to that, Yorgos Sapountzis had staged an unveiling choreography for Graf's sculptures that sketched a temporary network of relationships between body, public space, and monument. With *delicate balance* (2023), Raffaela Boss and Charlotte Horn returned to the idea of resonance using song and sound elements in a performance that explored the boundaries of interpersonal relationships. And then there were the three fantastical figures who would pop up from time to time, sometimes beside, sometimes on top of the *School Models*, interacting with them and the guests in a quiet and friendly manner: one of them a creature with lips as large as their head and eyes on their hands, another with at least twenty pairs of hands, and a third figure with a long hair net in front of their face. Julie Monot's witty surreal personas were designed to represent forms, images, and feelings that have something to do with the body.

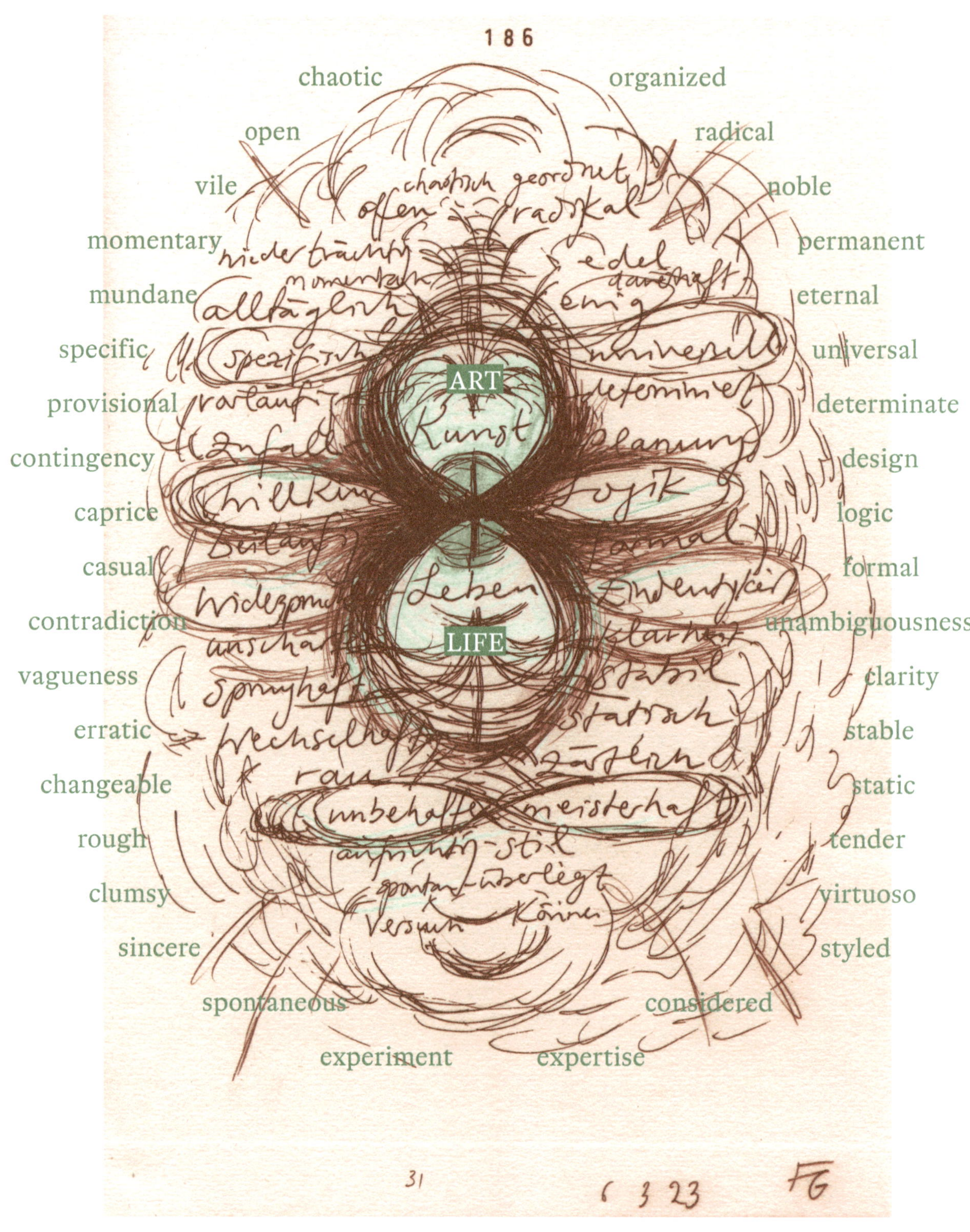

fig. 1 Florian Graf, *Kunst und Leben* (with English translations), Drawing Book 186, p. 31, 2023, ink and colored pencil on paper

The shared ritual activation of the sculptural ensemble described here created a *Zeit-Ort*, a kind of "time space," in the playground. Sociologist Bruno Latour once spoke of "cohabitational time," meaning, on the one hand, the time dimension of cohabitation between the human and the nonhuman, and, on the other, the importance of space as an ordering factor in our reality as defined by the present.[4] Only when we spend time together in the public sphere does "democratic space" emerge. That applies equally to art in public space. Here, art and life are very close together—as Graf illustrated in a sketch that he made while he was working on the concept for his *School Models* (fig. 1). In it, the two terms "art" (at the top) and "life" (at the bottom) are enclosed by a quickly drawn, continuous line that starts as two mirrored heart shapes and continues until the words are framed by an "8." From there, it continues on to pairs of terms that are grouped around art and life: specific/universal, contradiction/unambiguousness clumsy/virtuoso, etc. If we lay the "8" horizontally, we have the symbol for infinity before us. The loop then stands for the continuous process of dialogue between art and life—for the resonating space that can emerge between them.

4 Bruno Latour, "Politics of Time, Politics of Space," *Domus*, 876 (2004), https://www.domusweb.it/en/from-the-archive/2022/10/13/bruno-latour-politics-of-time-politics-of-space.html.

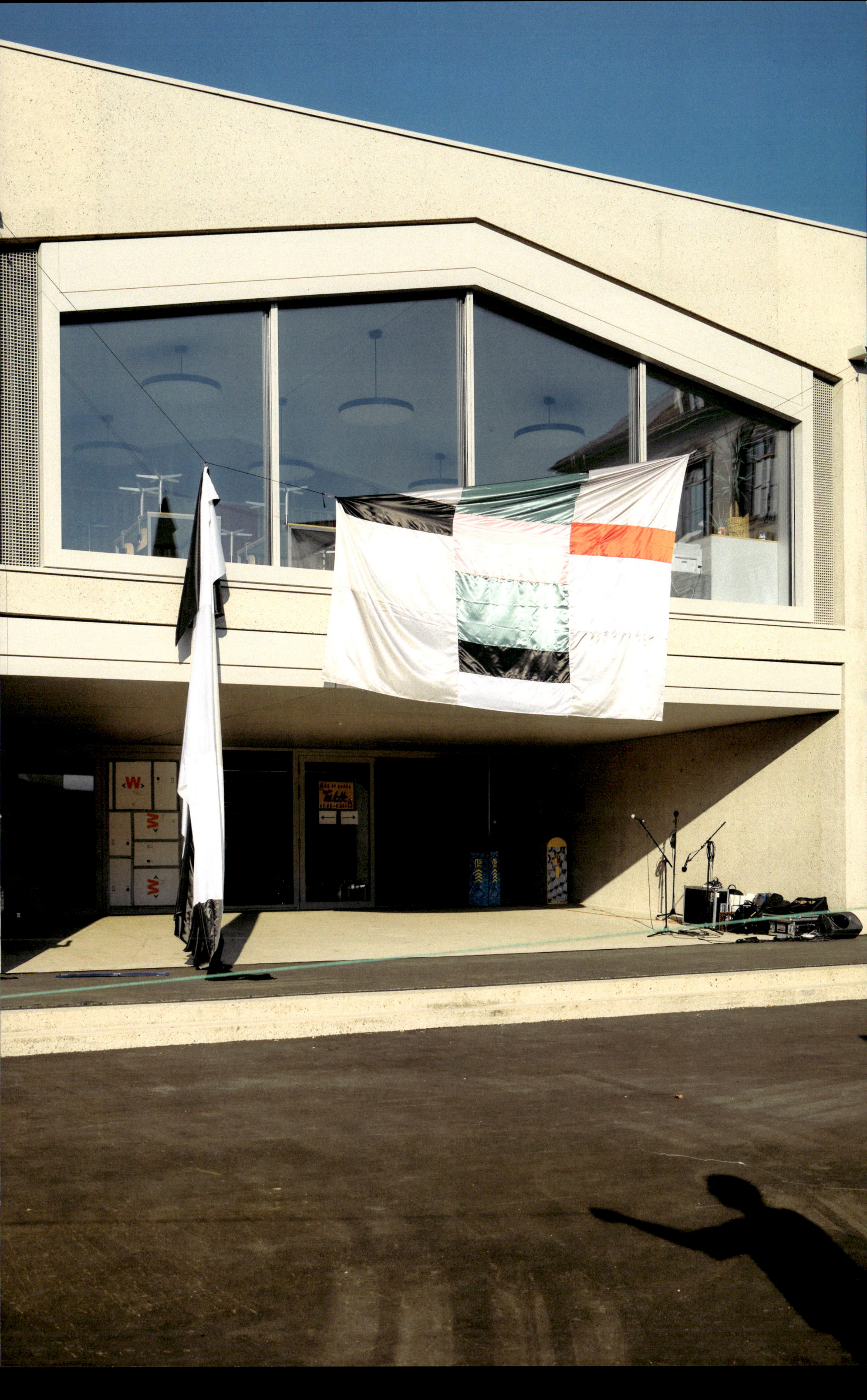

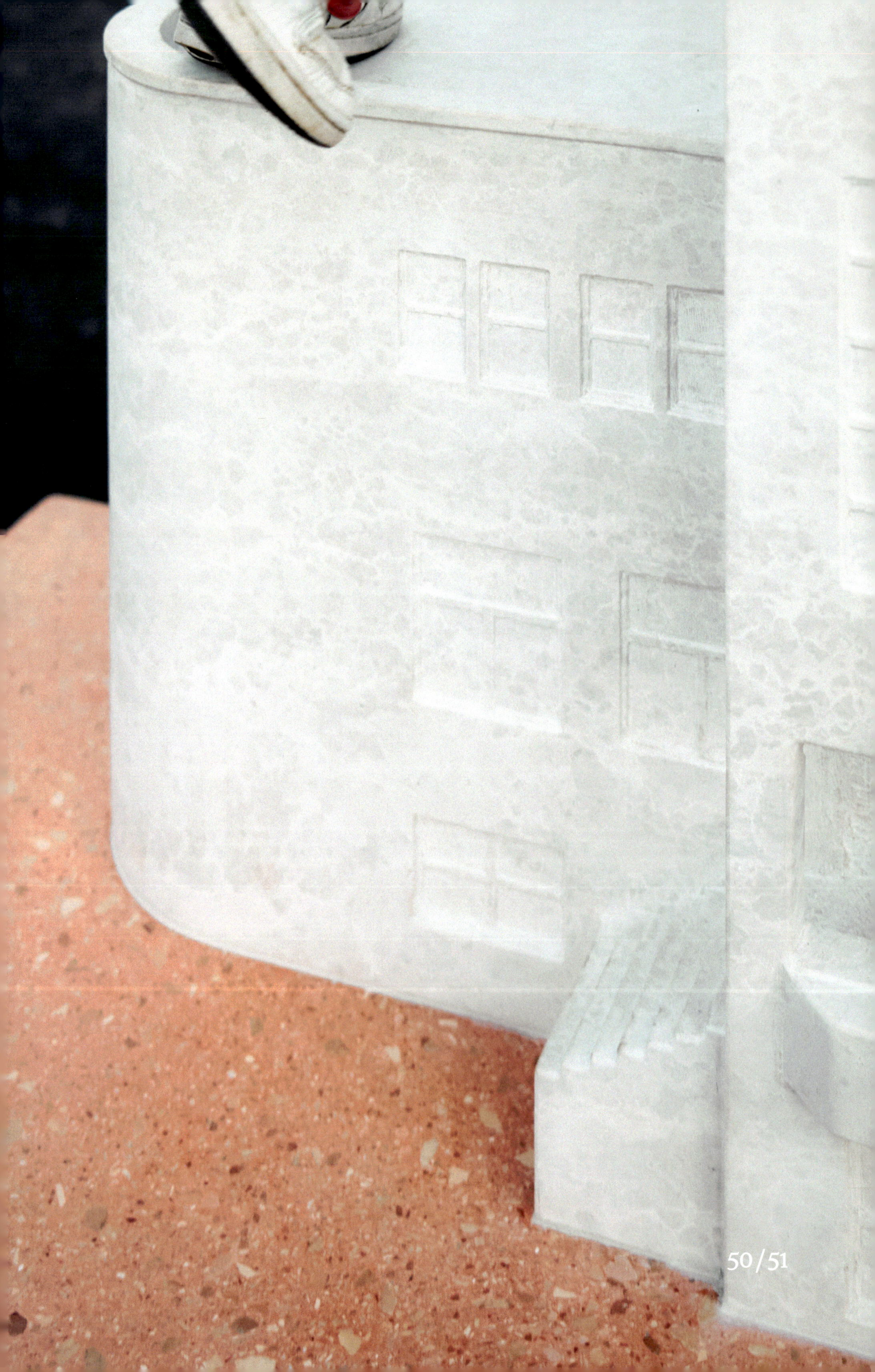

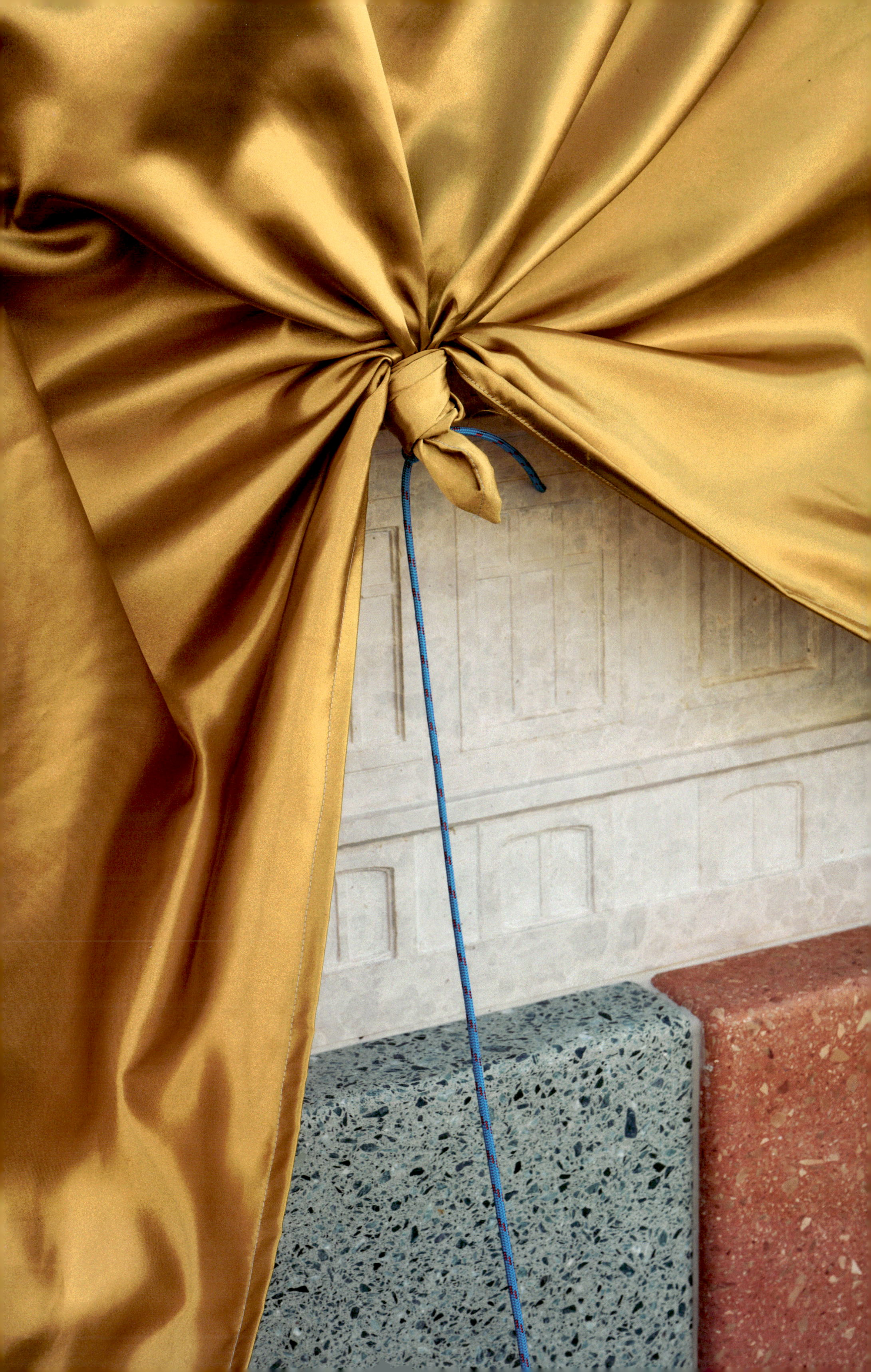

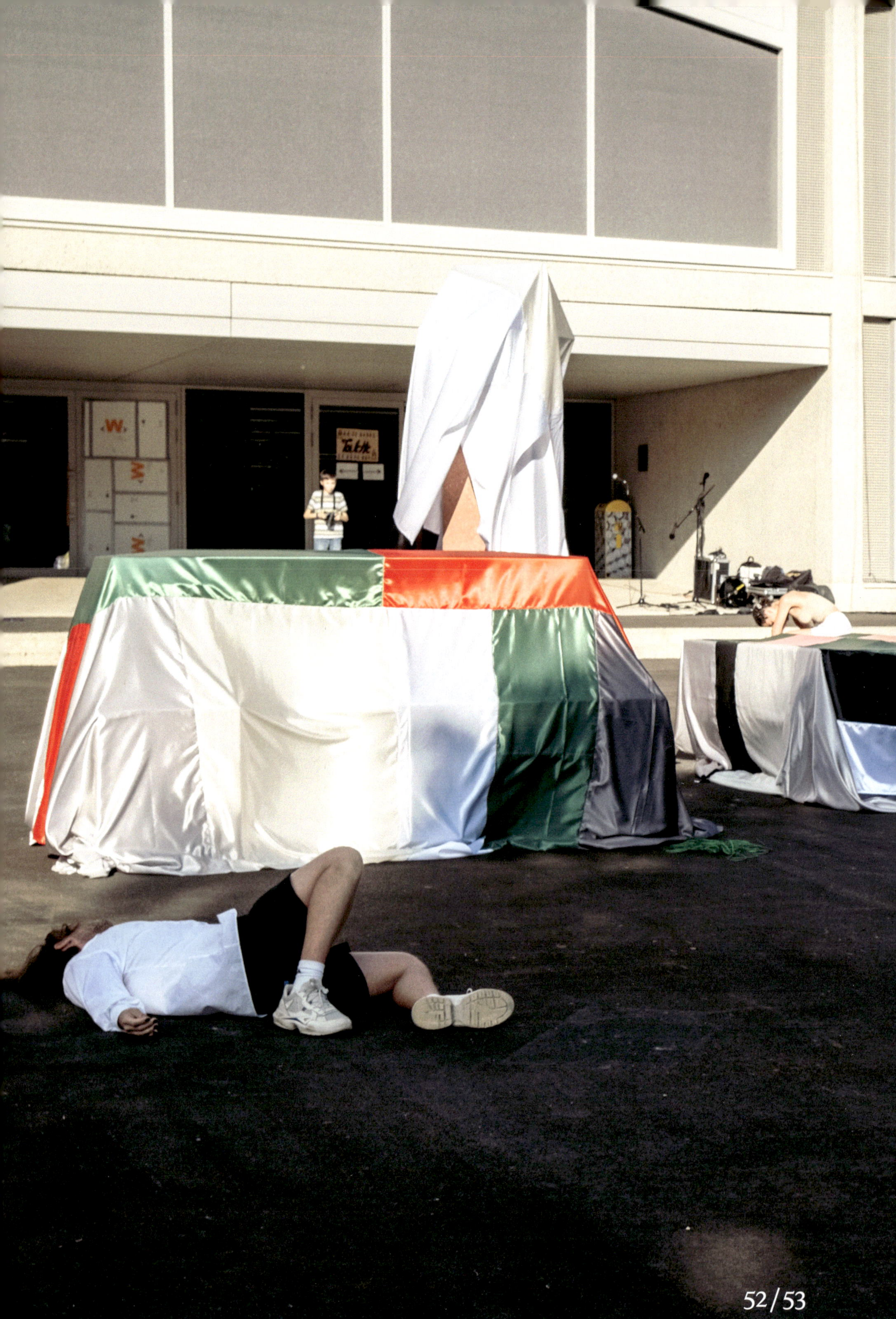

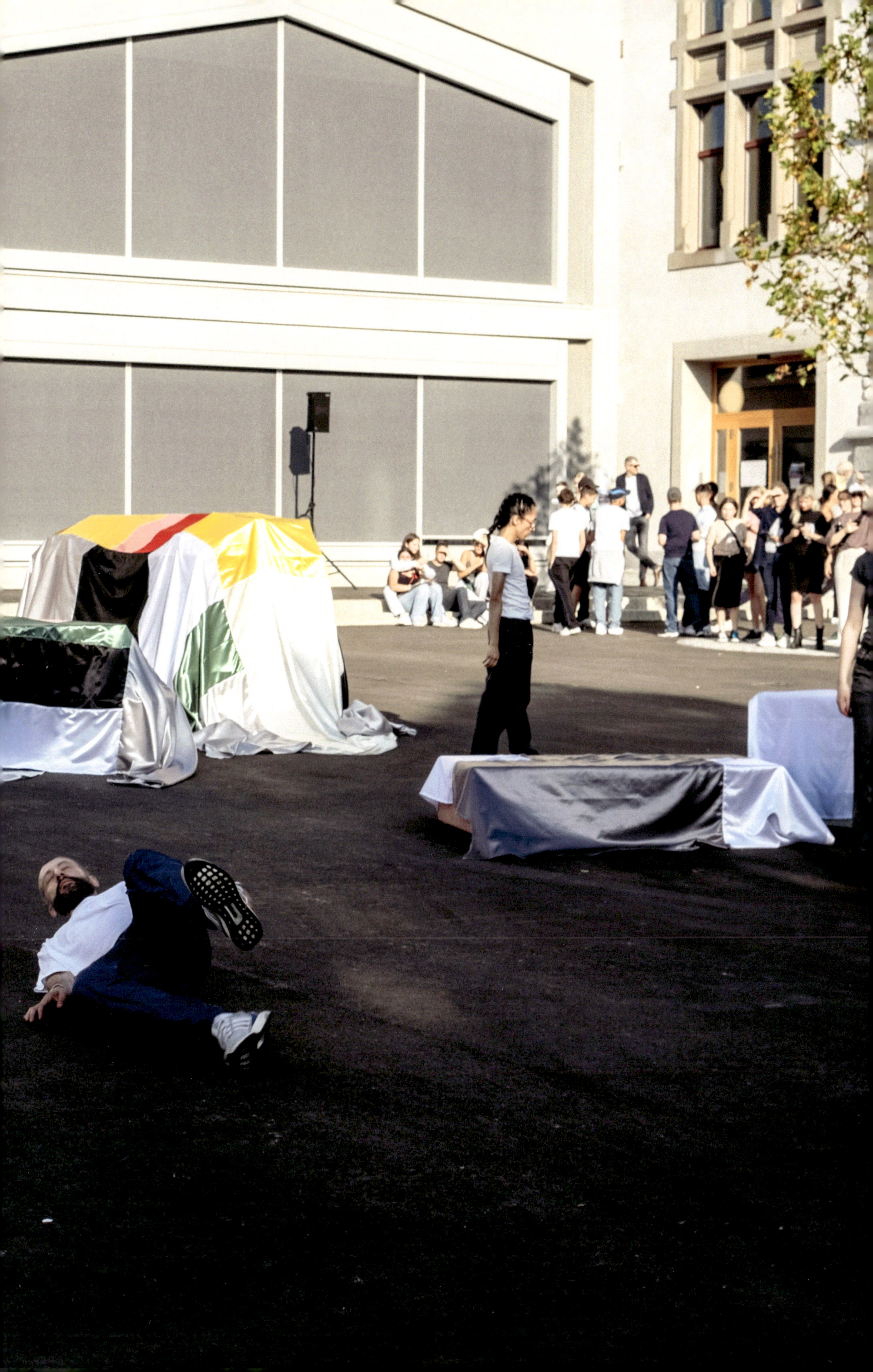

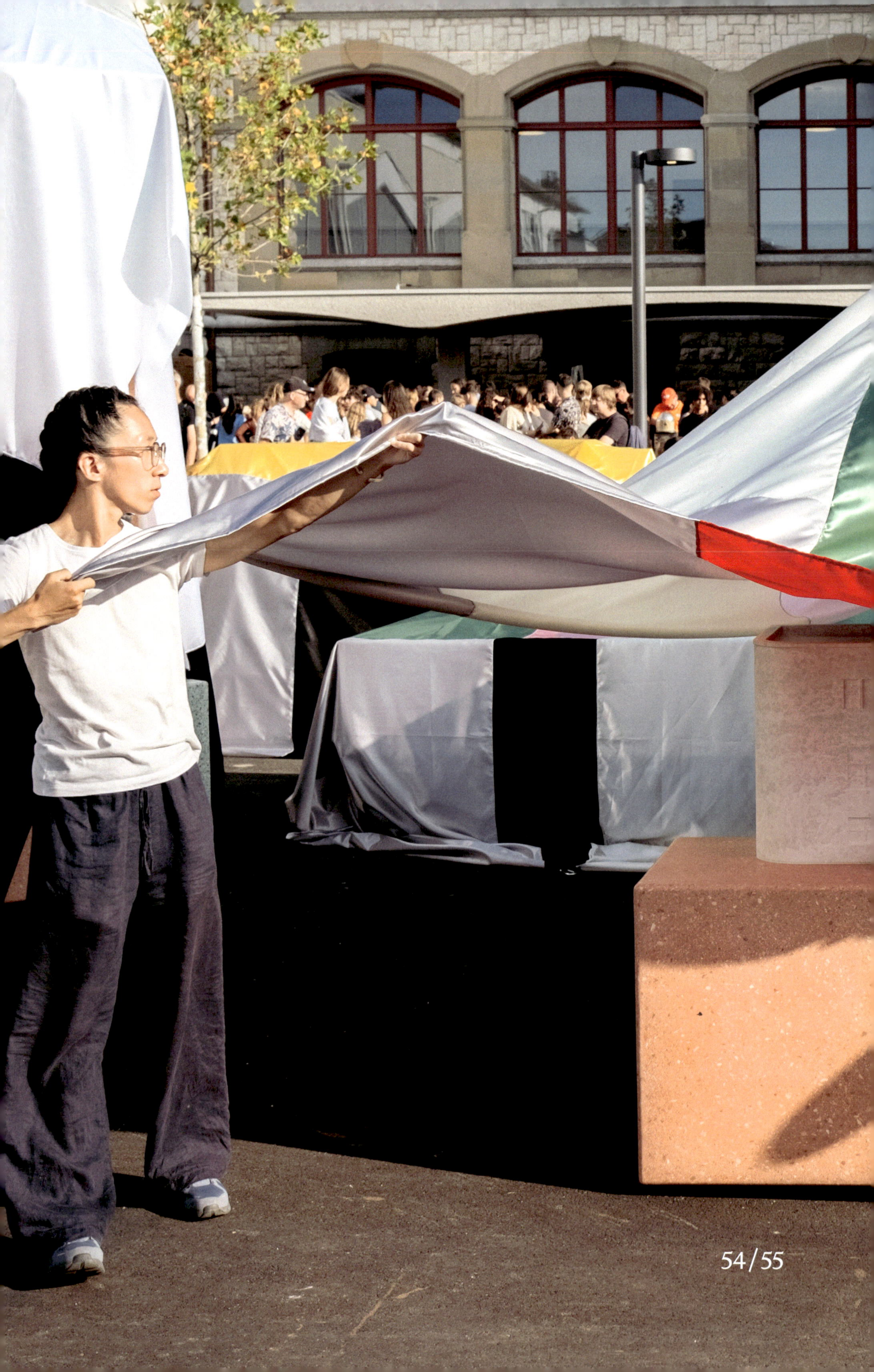

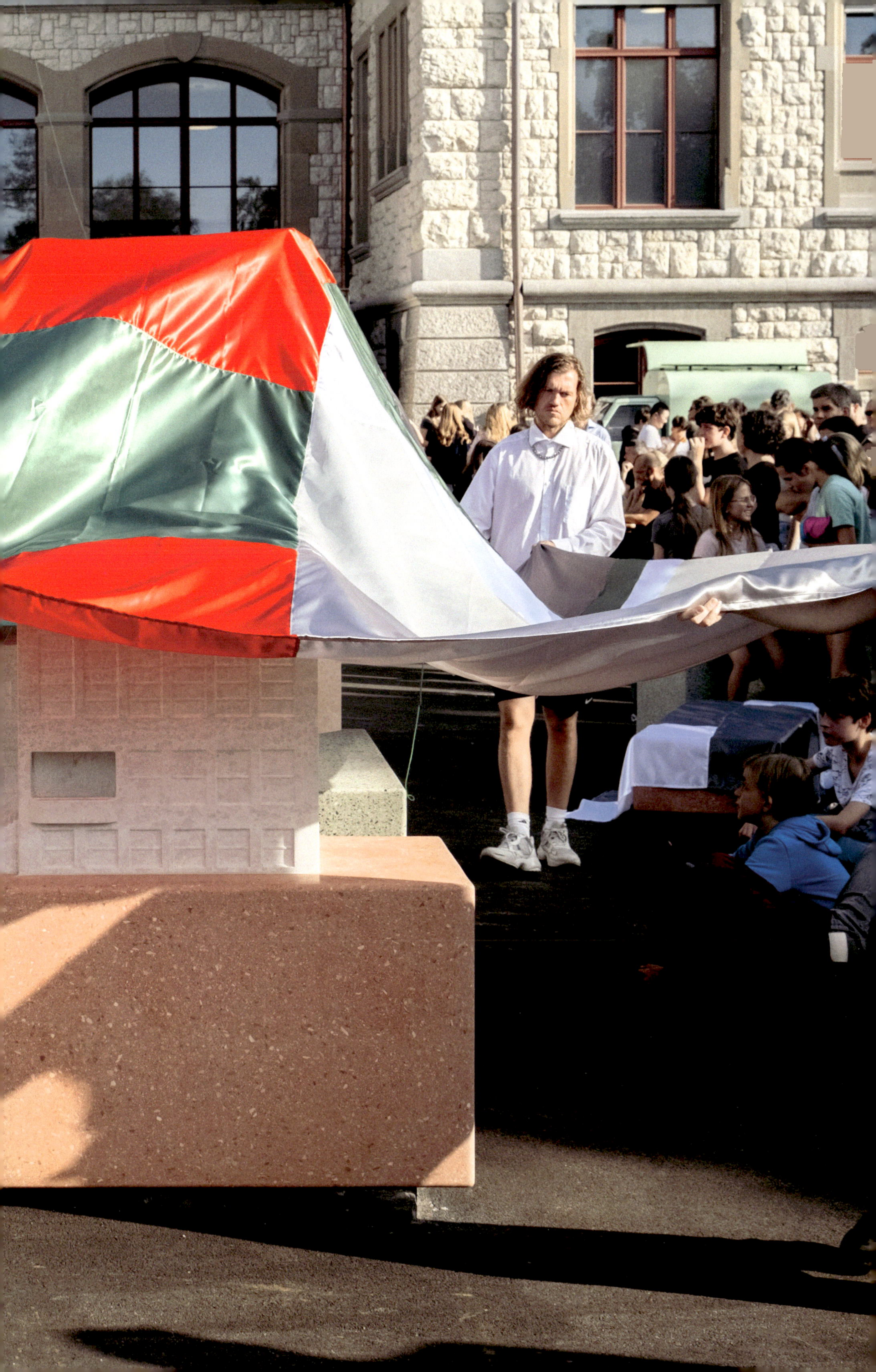

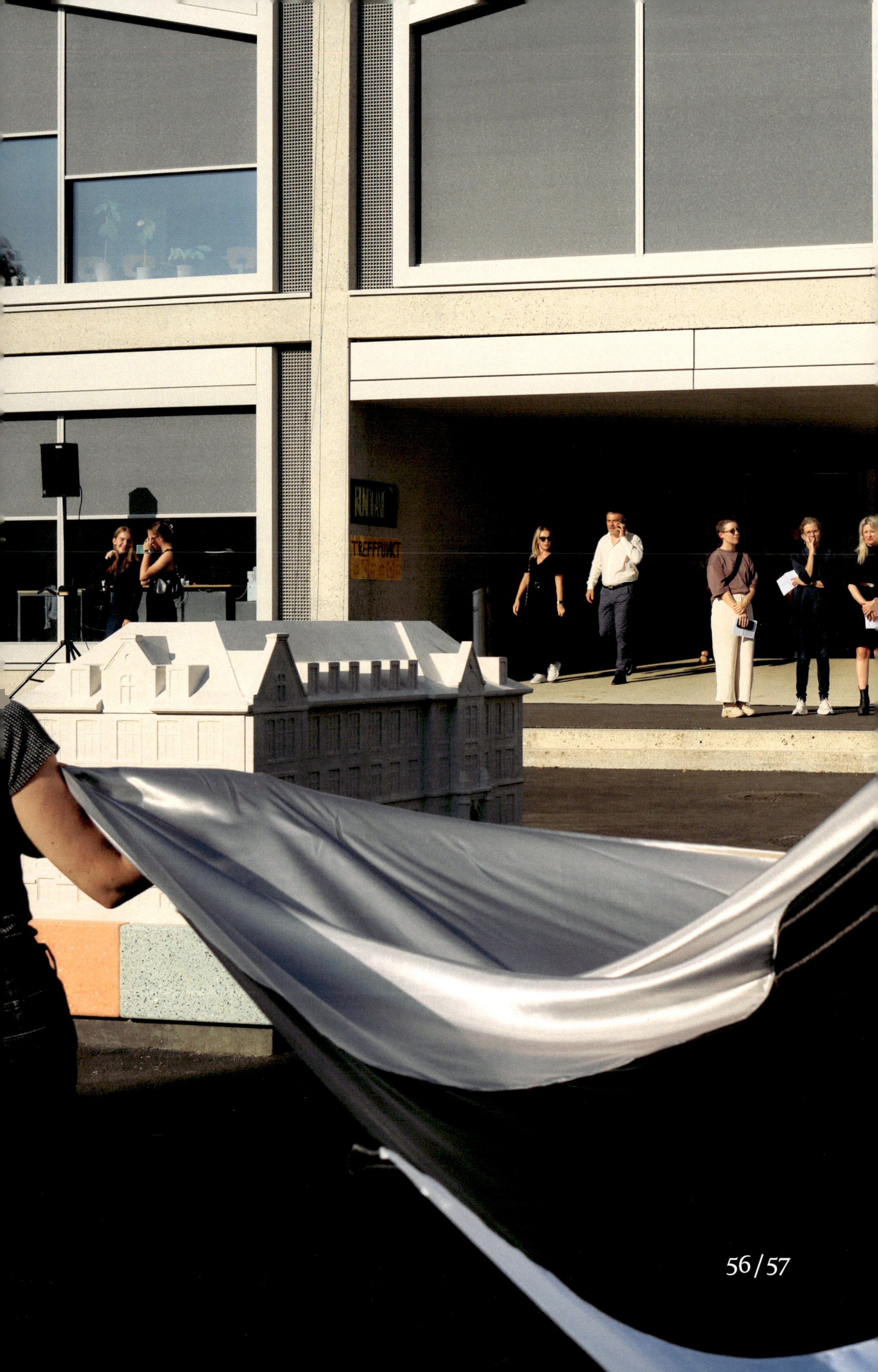
TREFFPUNKT

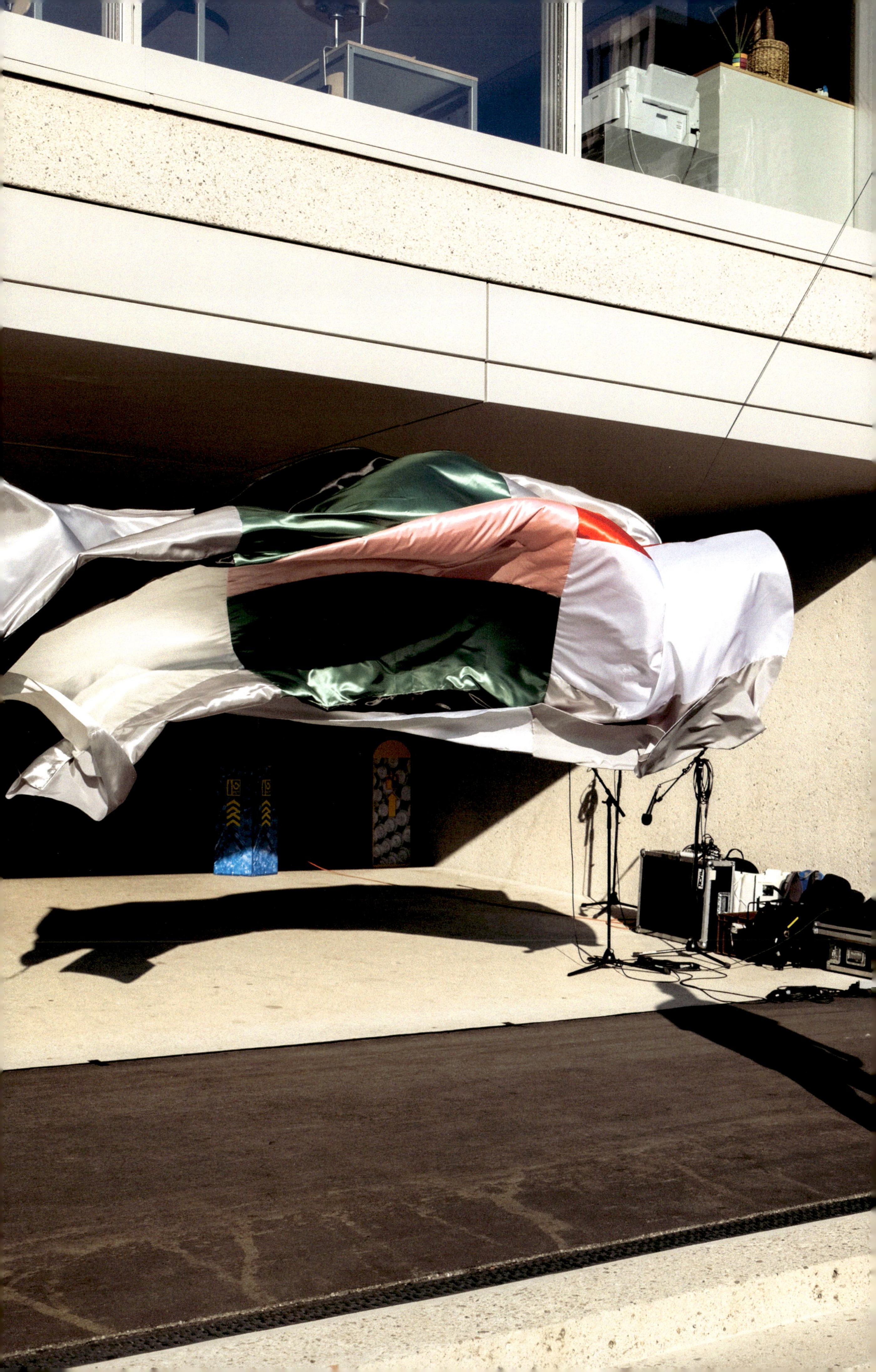

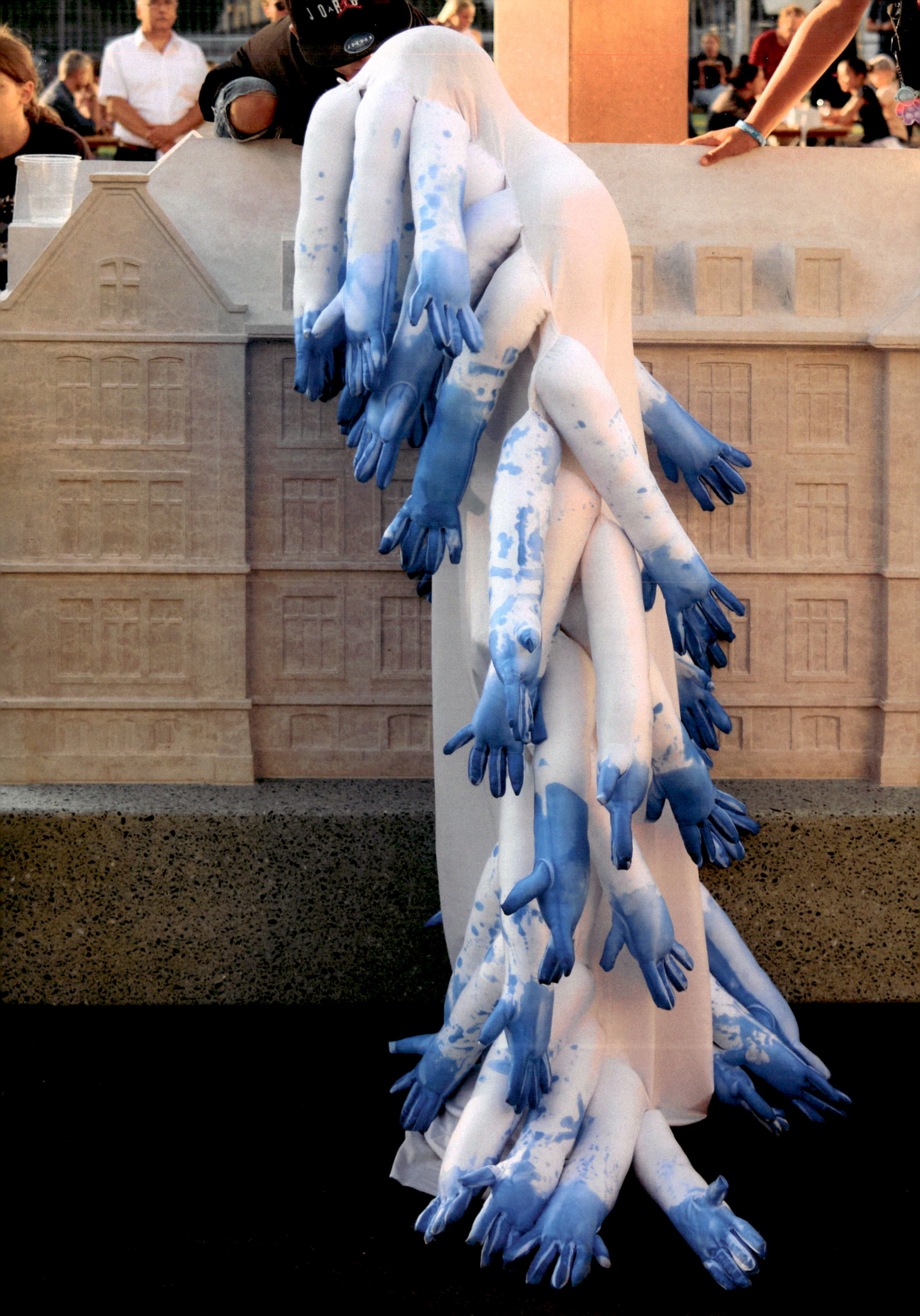

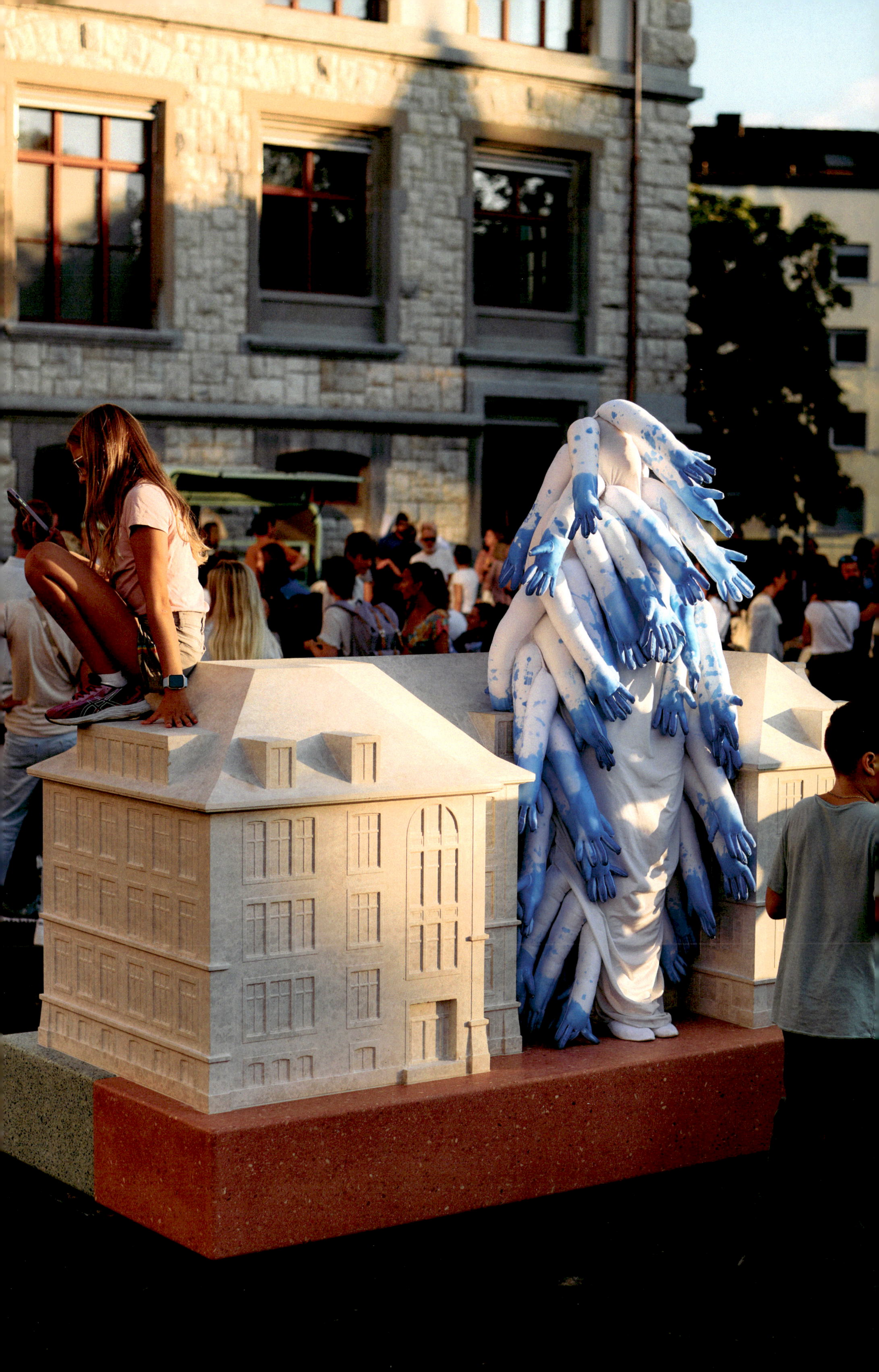

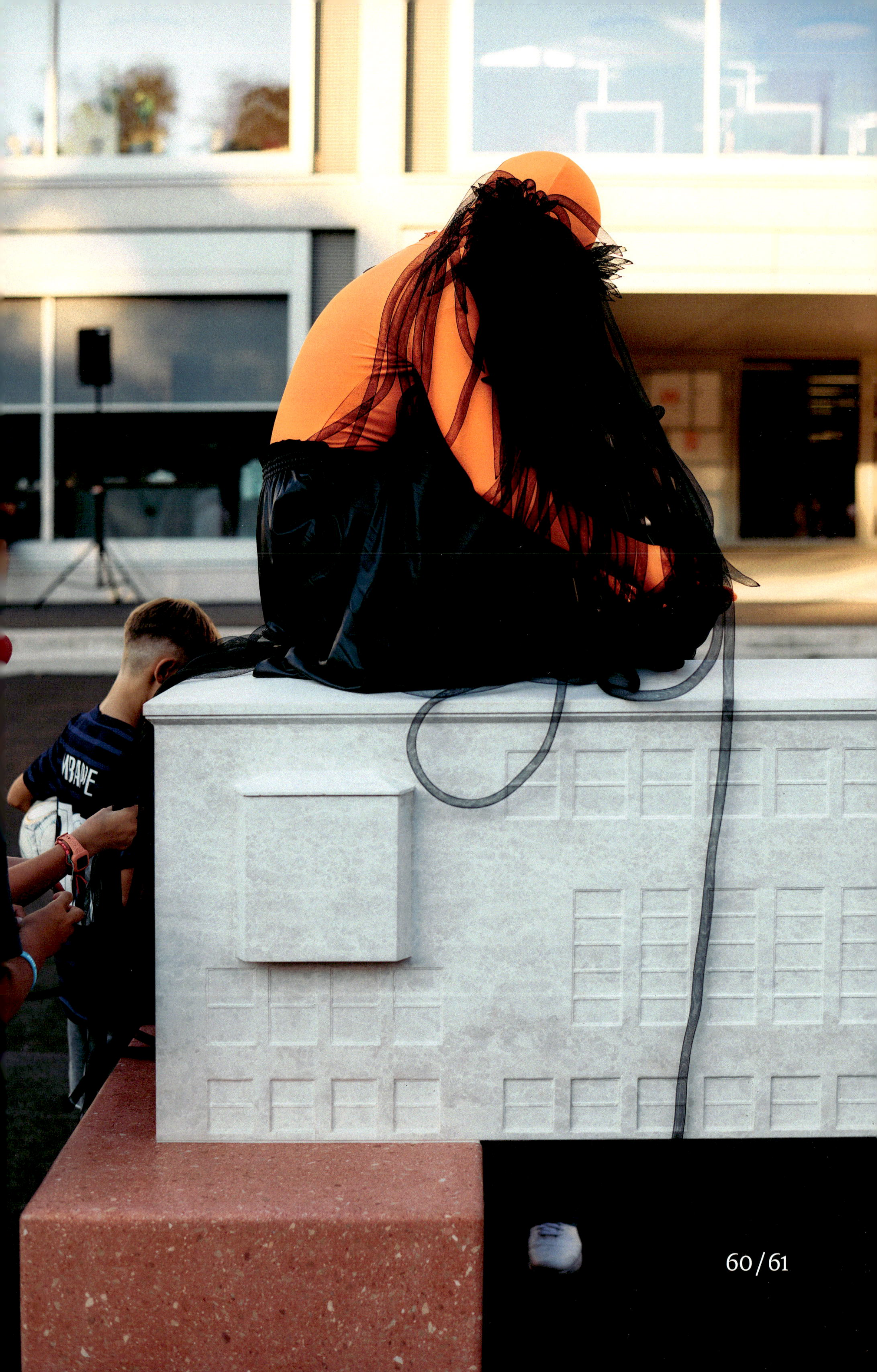
MBAPPE

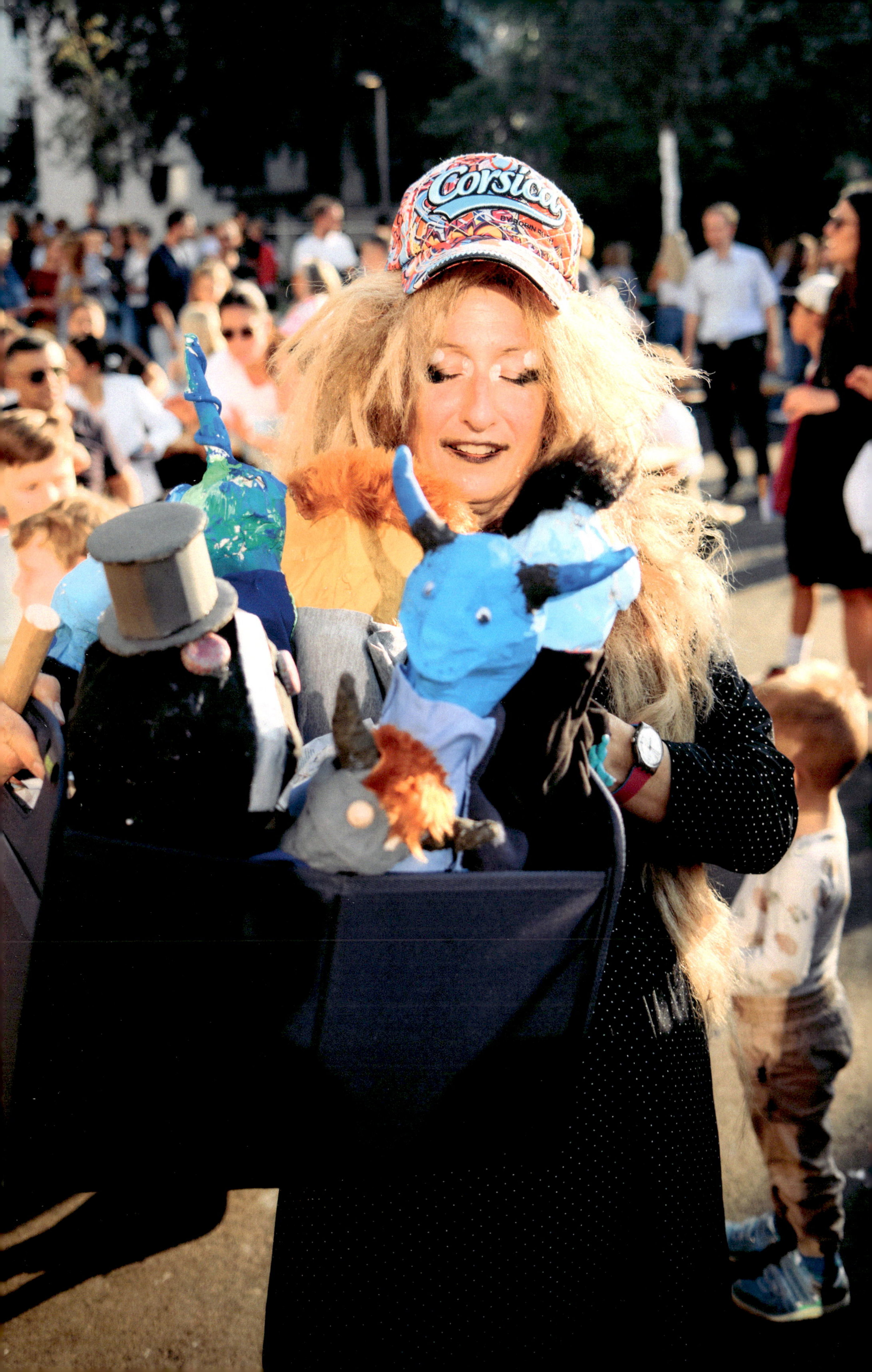
Corsica

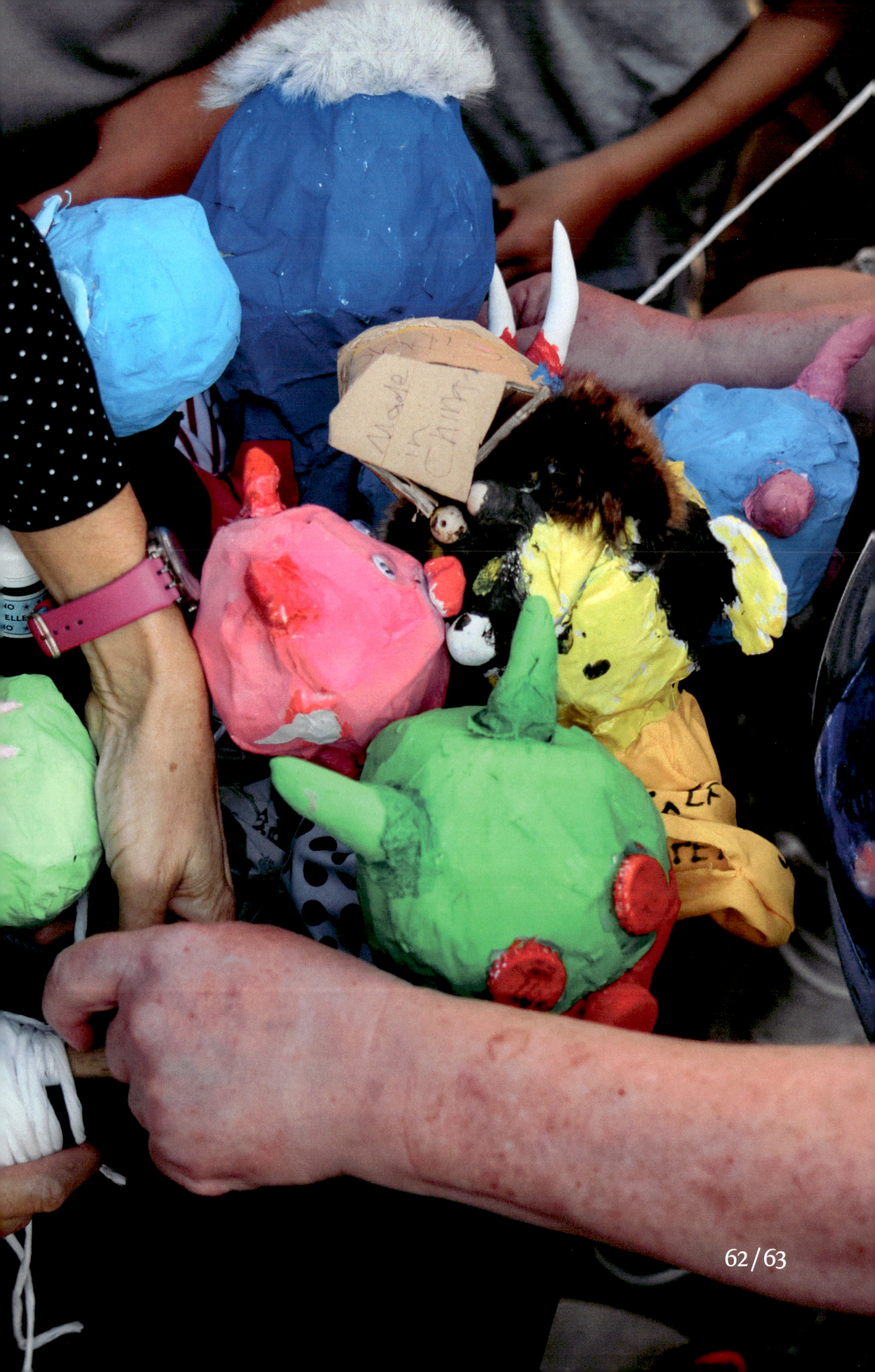
Made in China

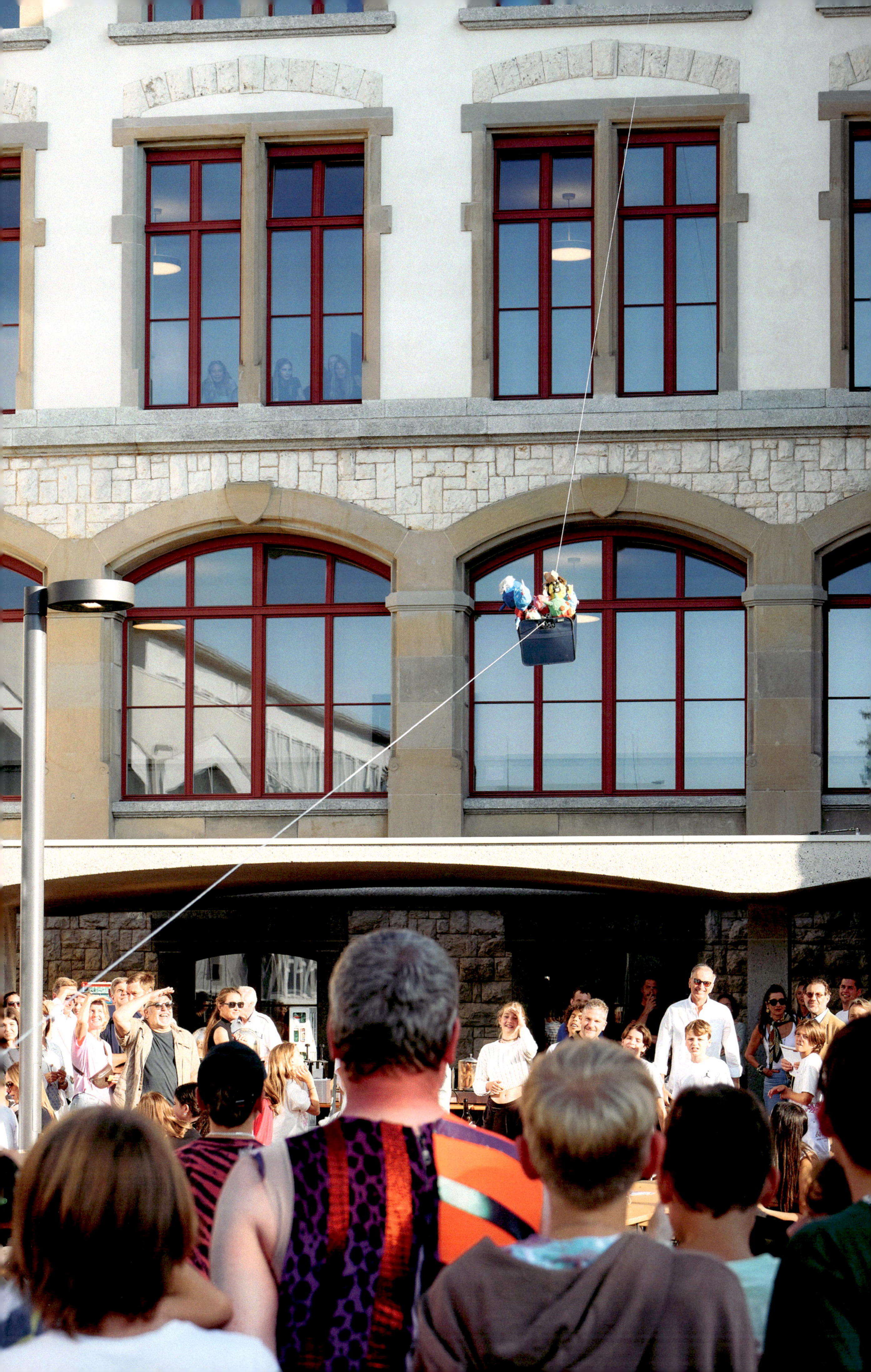

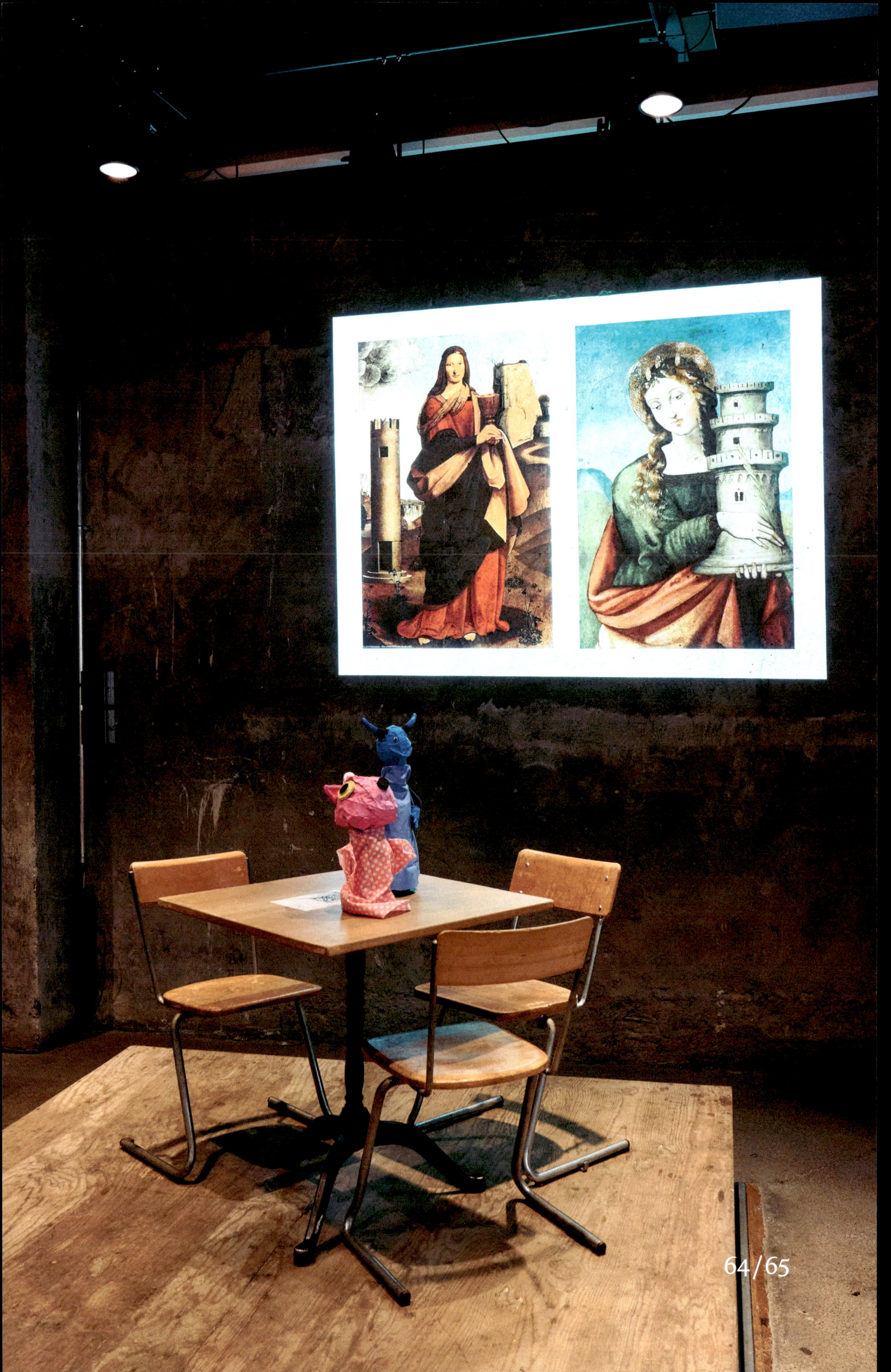

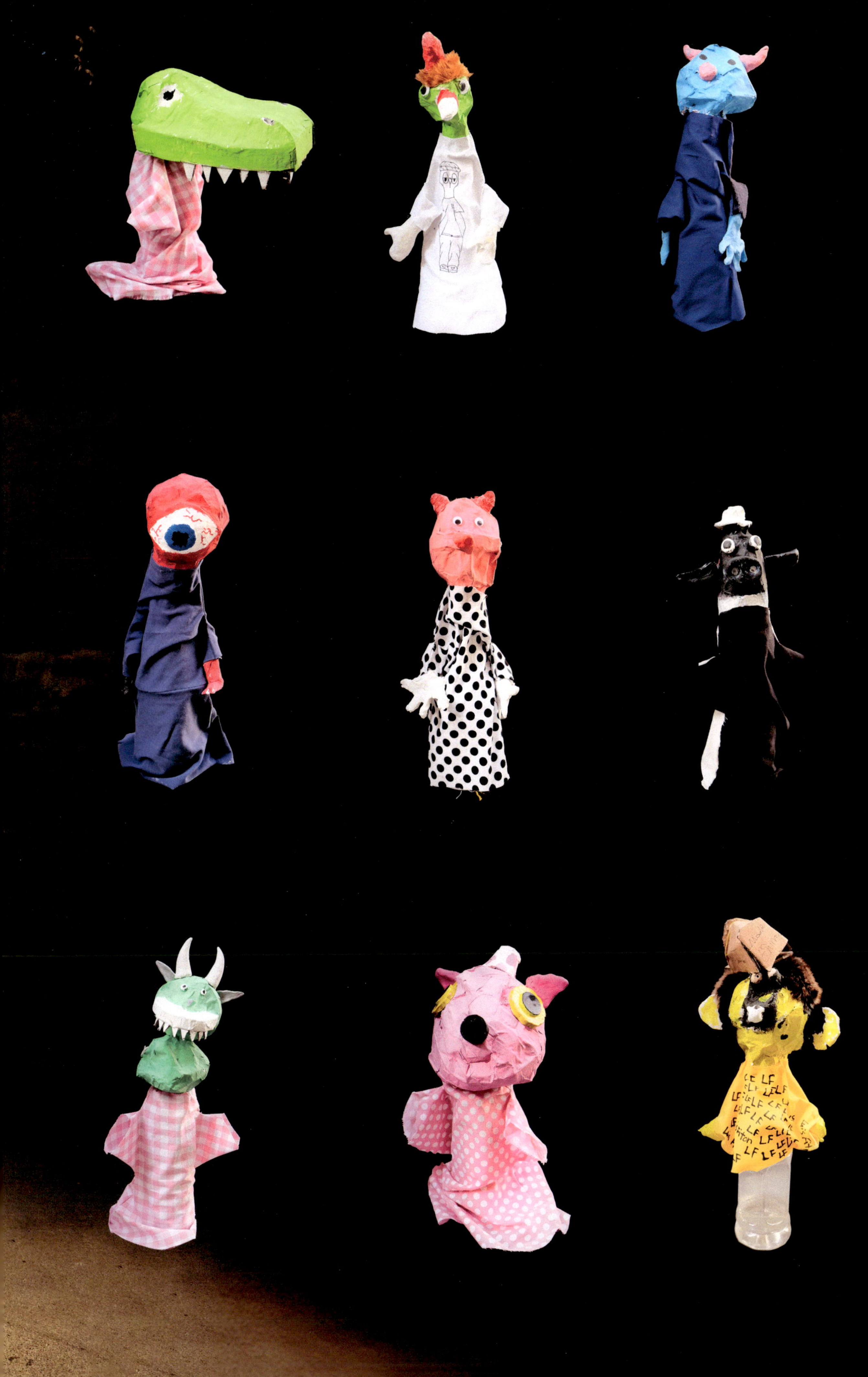

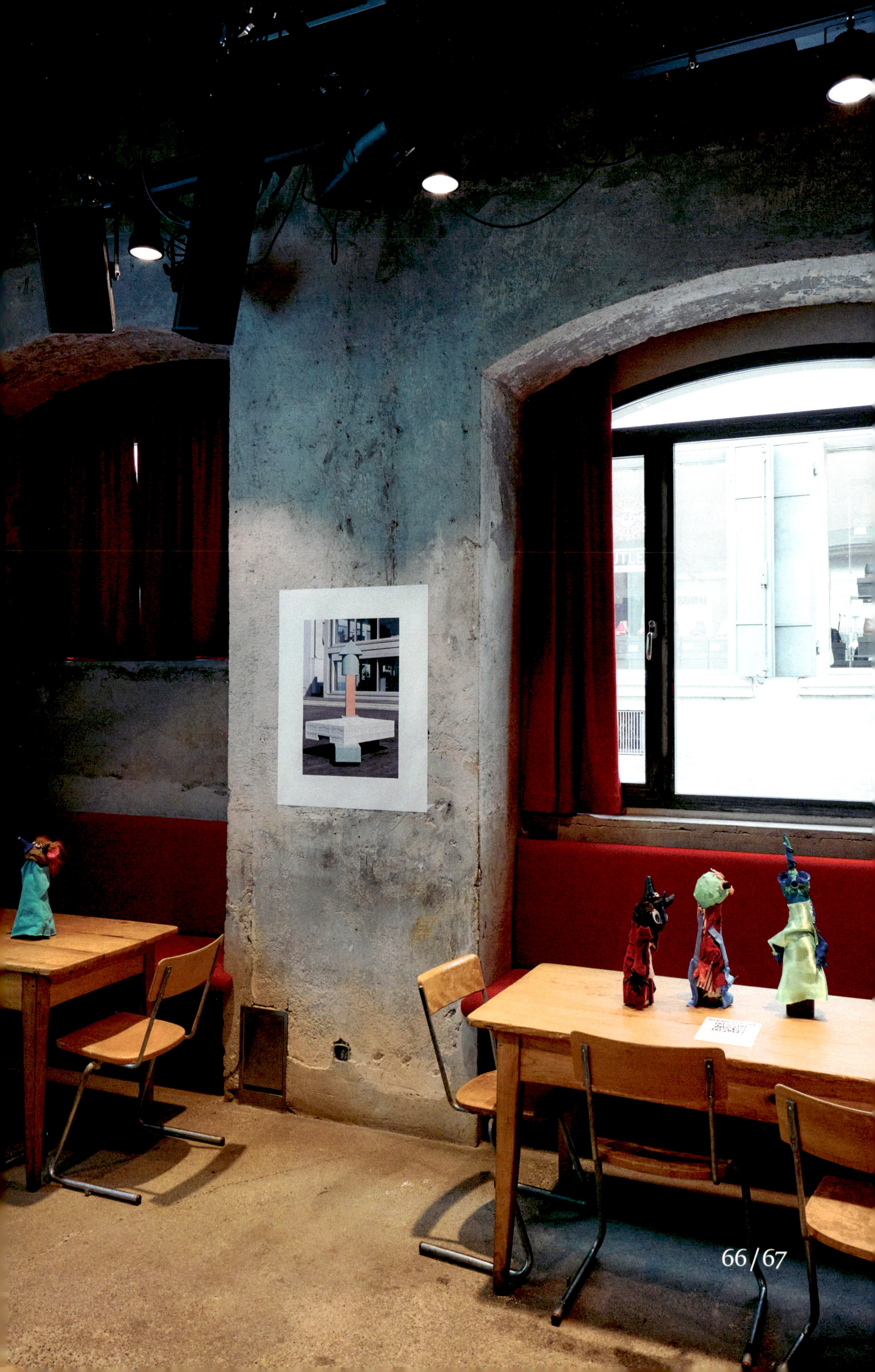

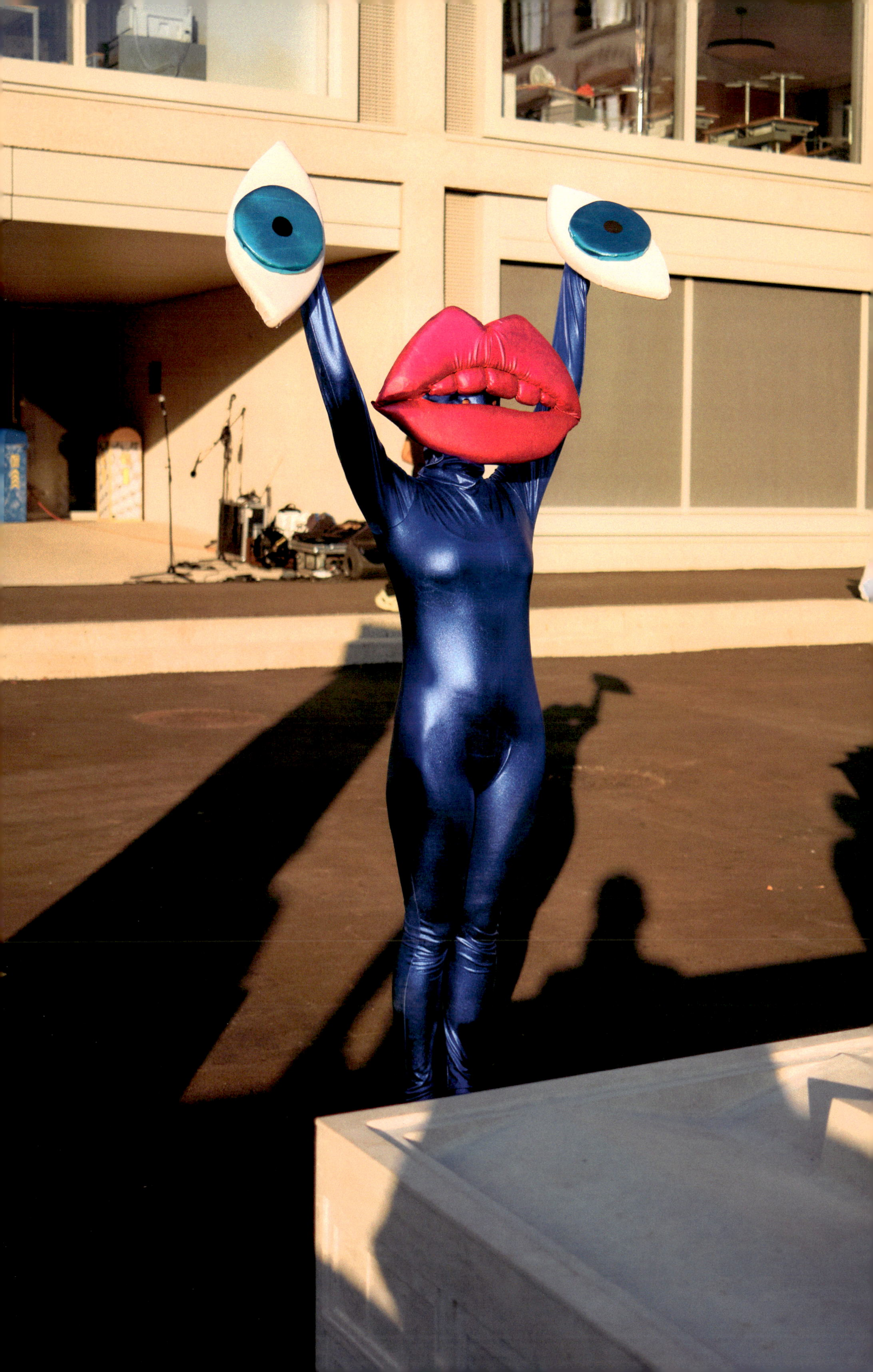

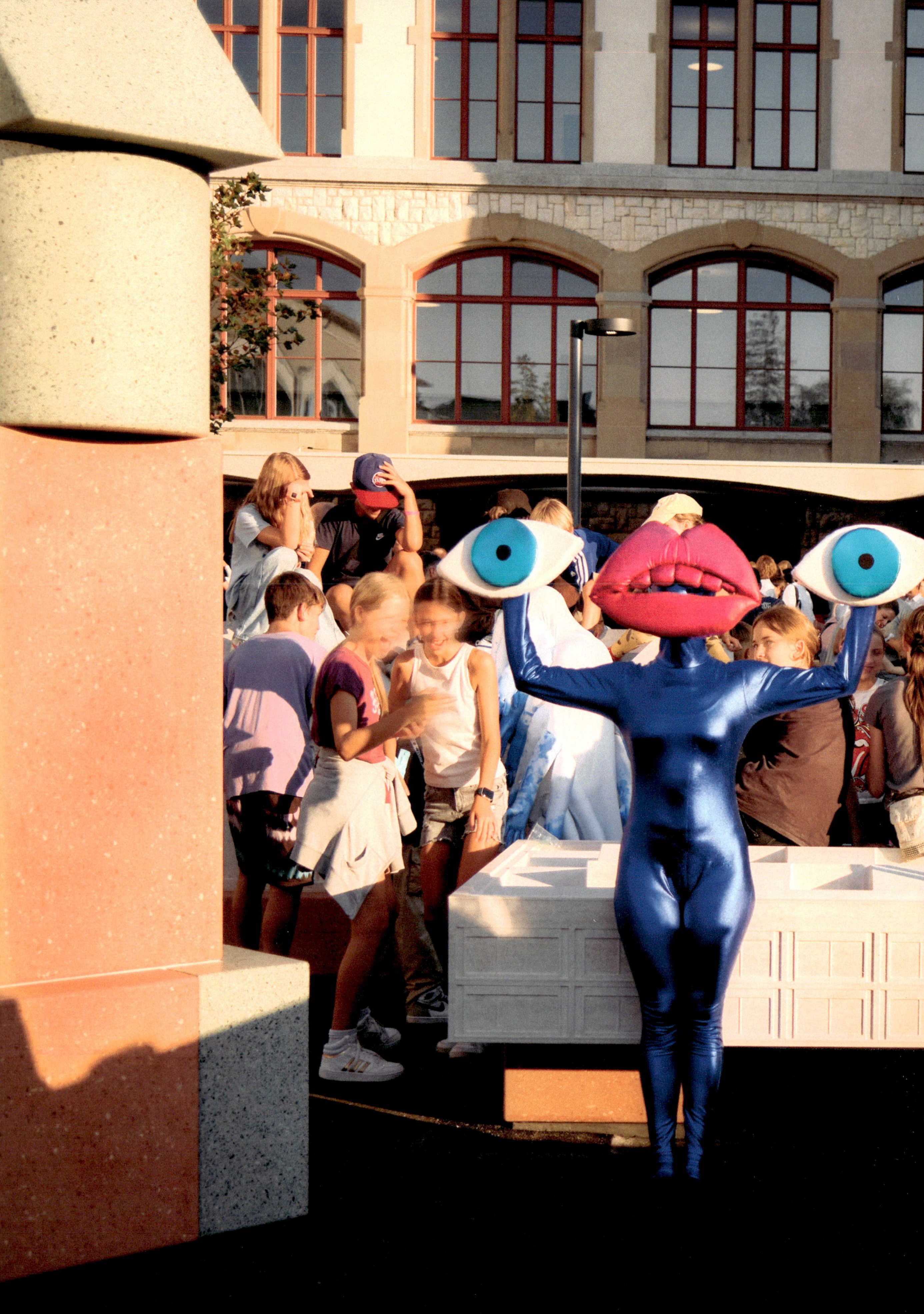

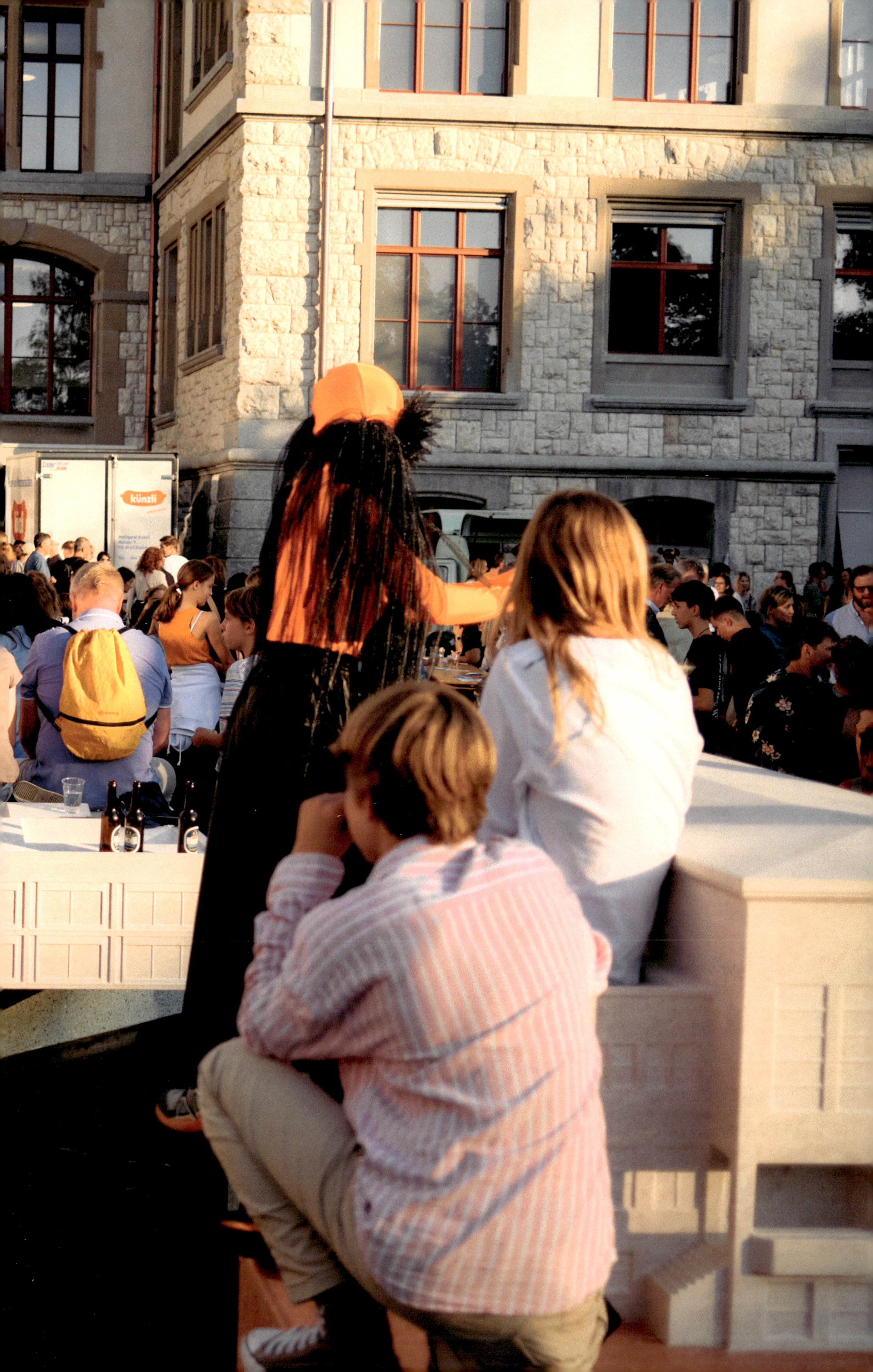
künzli

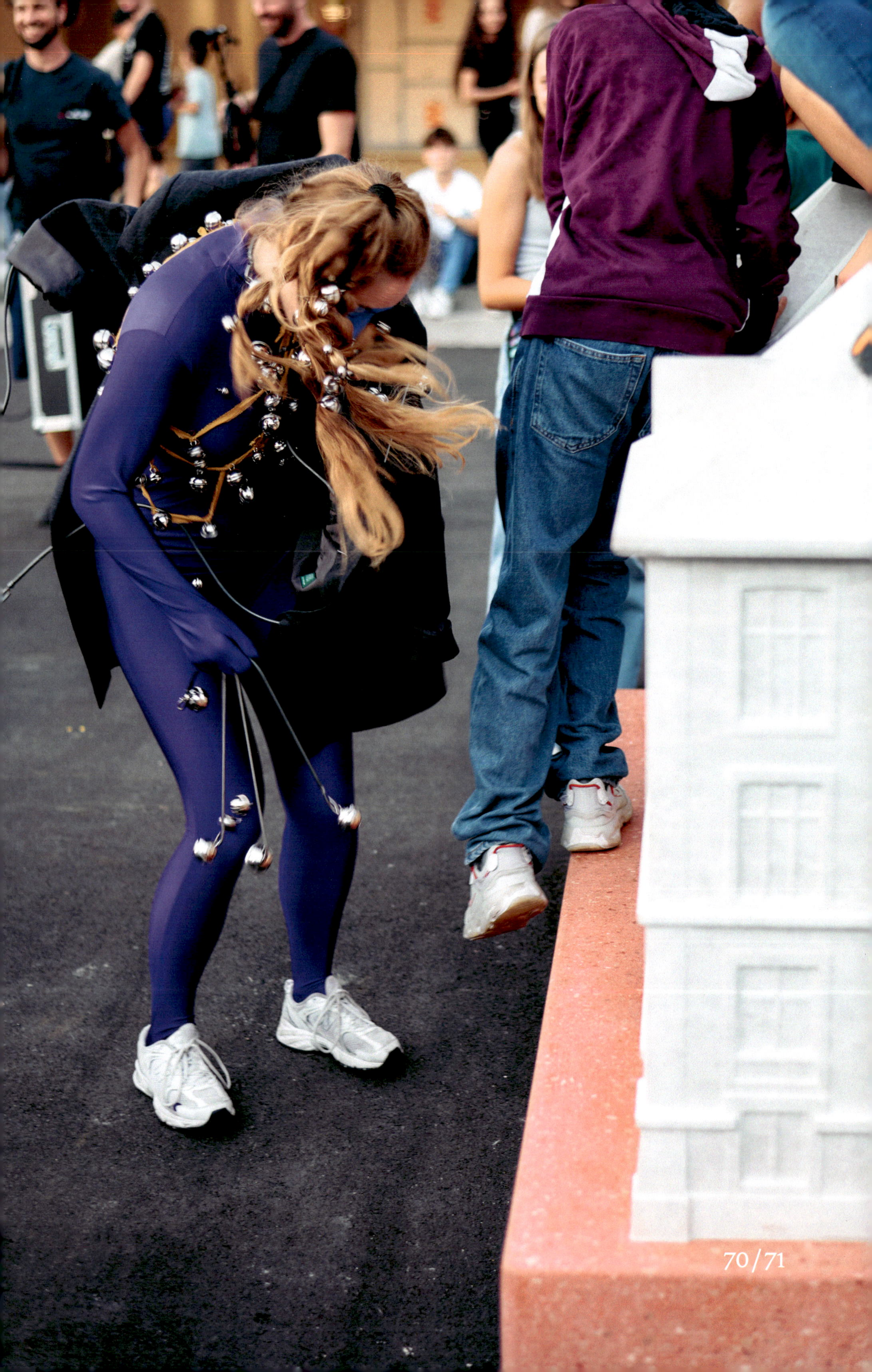

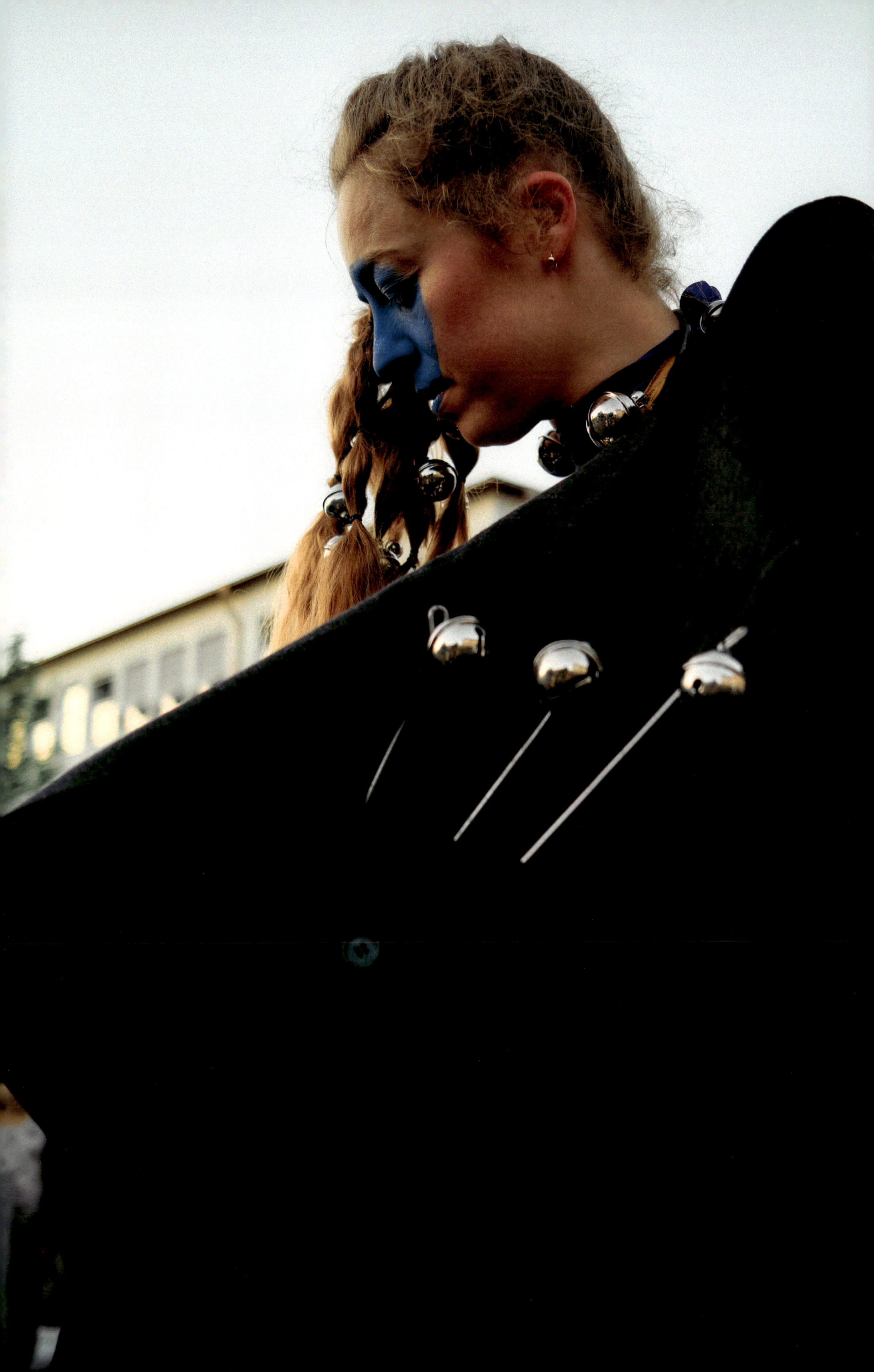

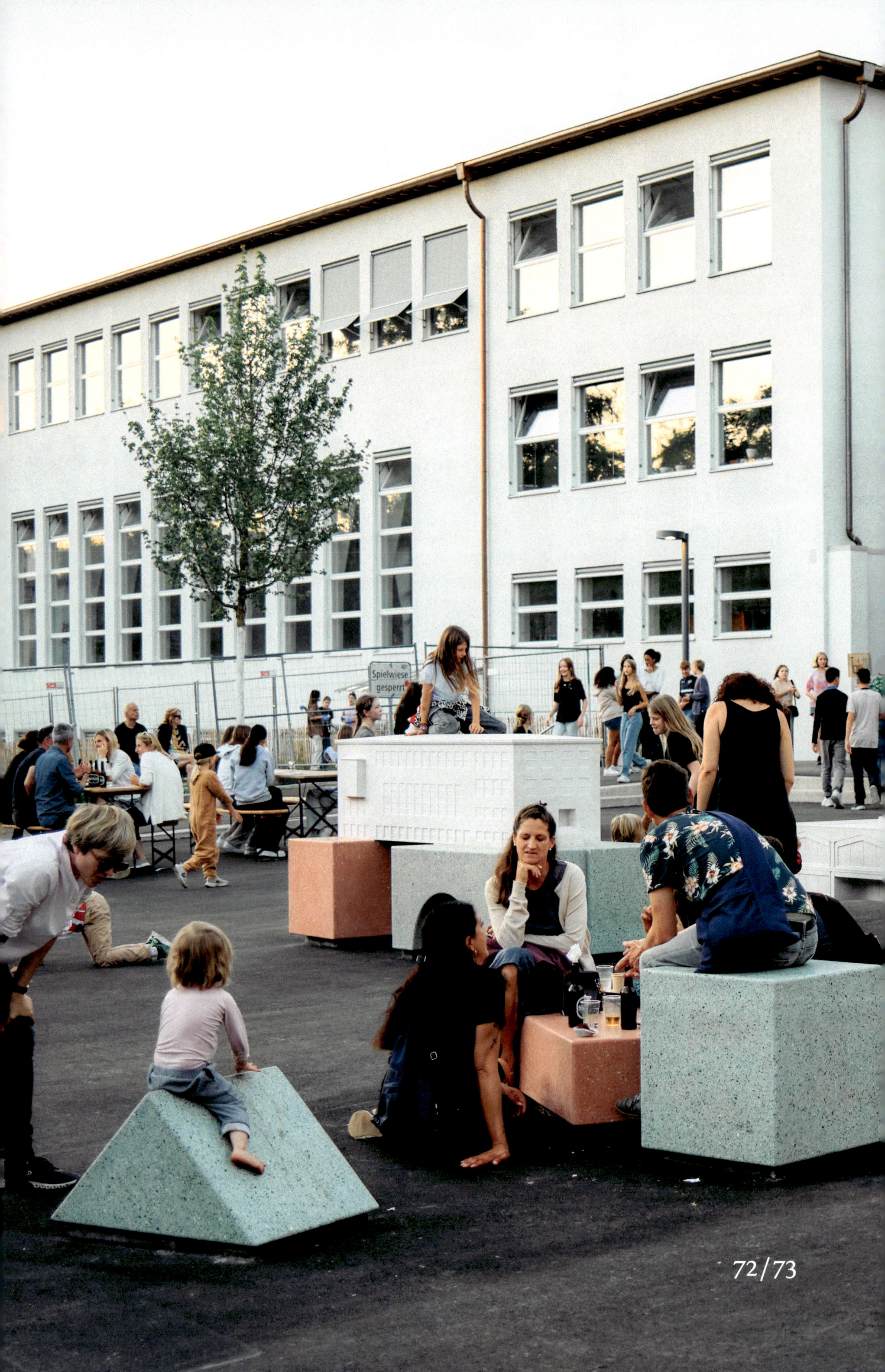
Spielwiese
gesperrt

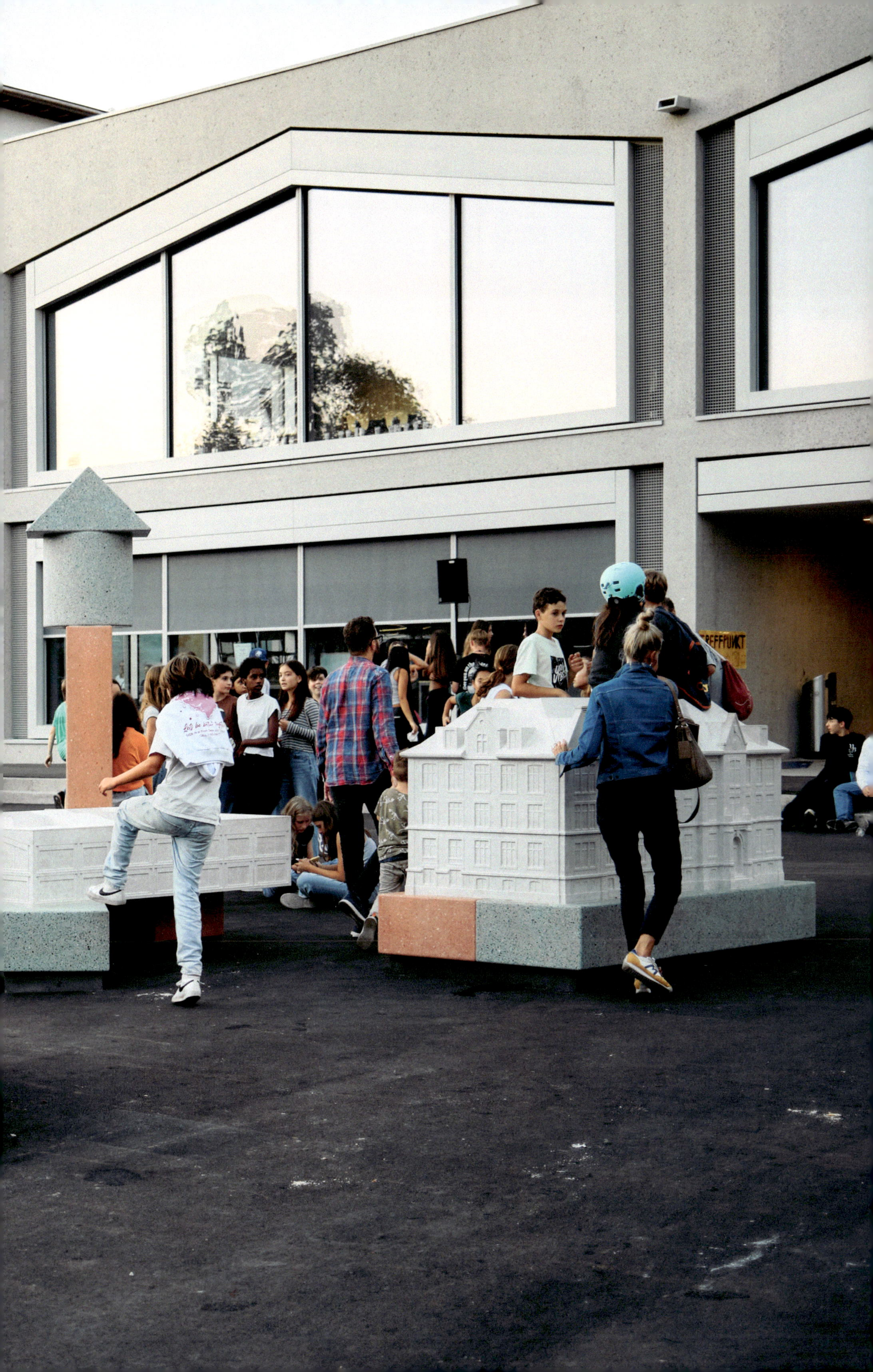

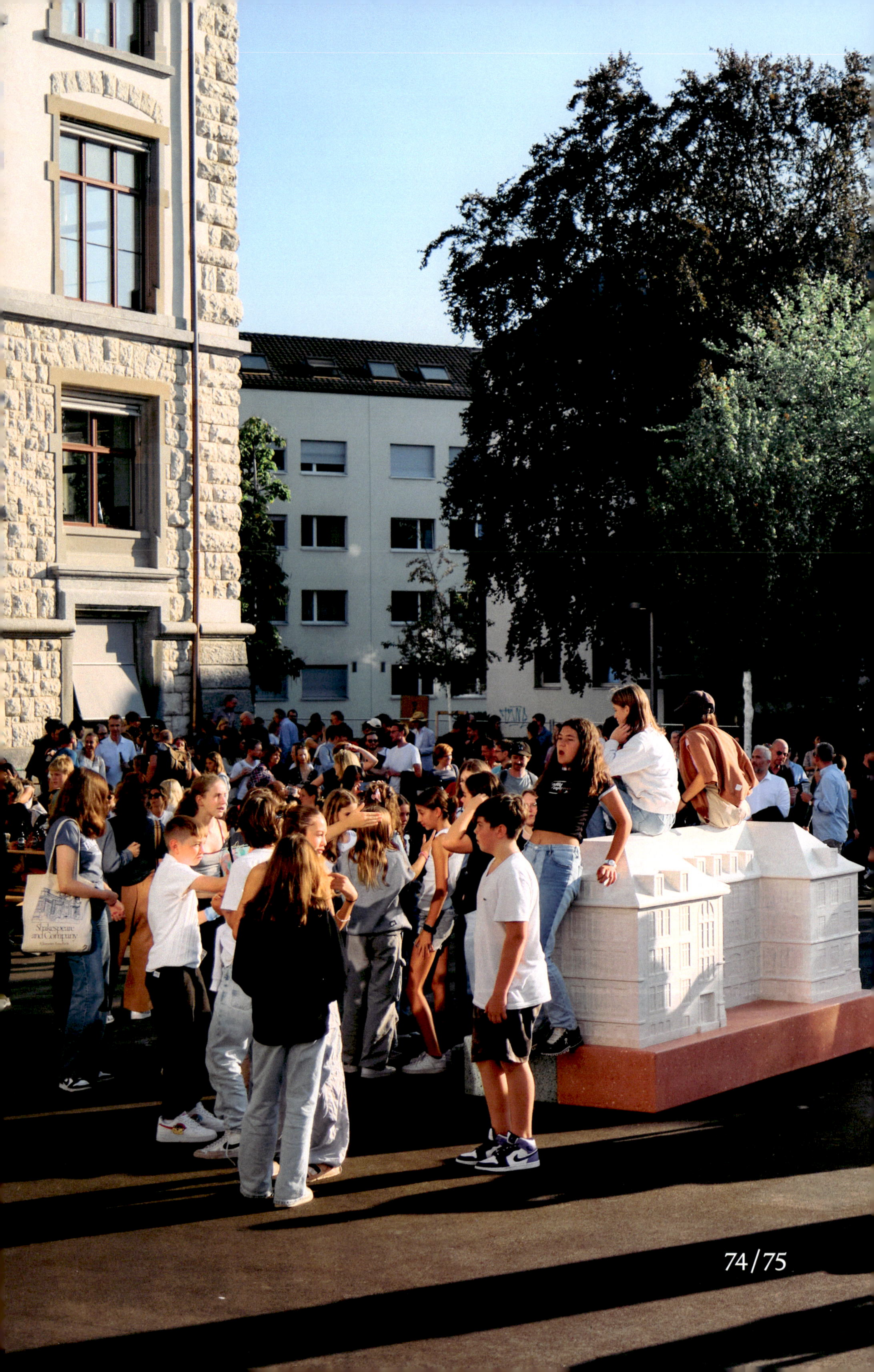
Shakespeare and Company

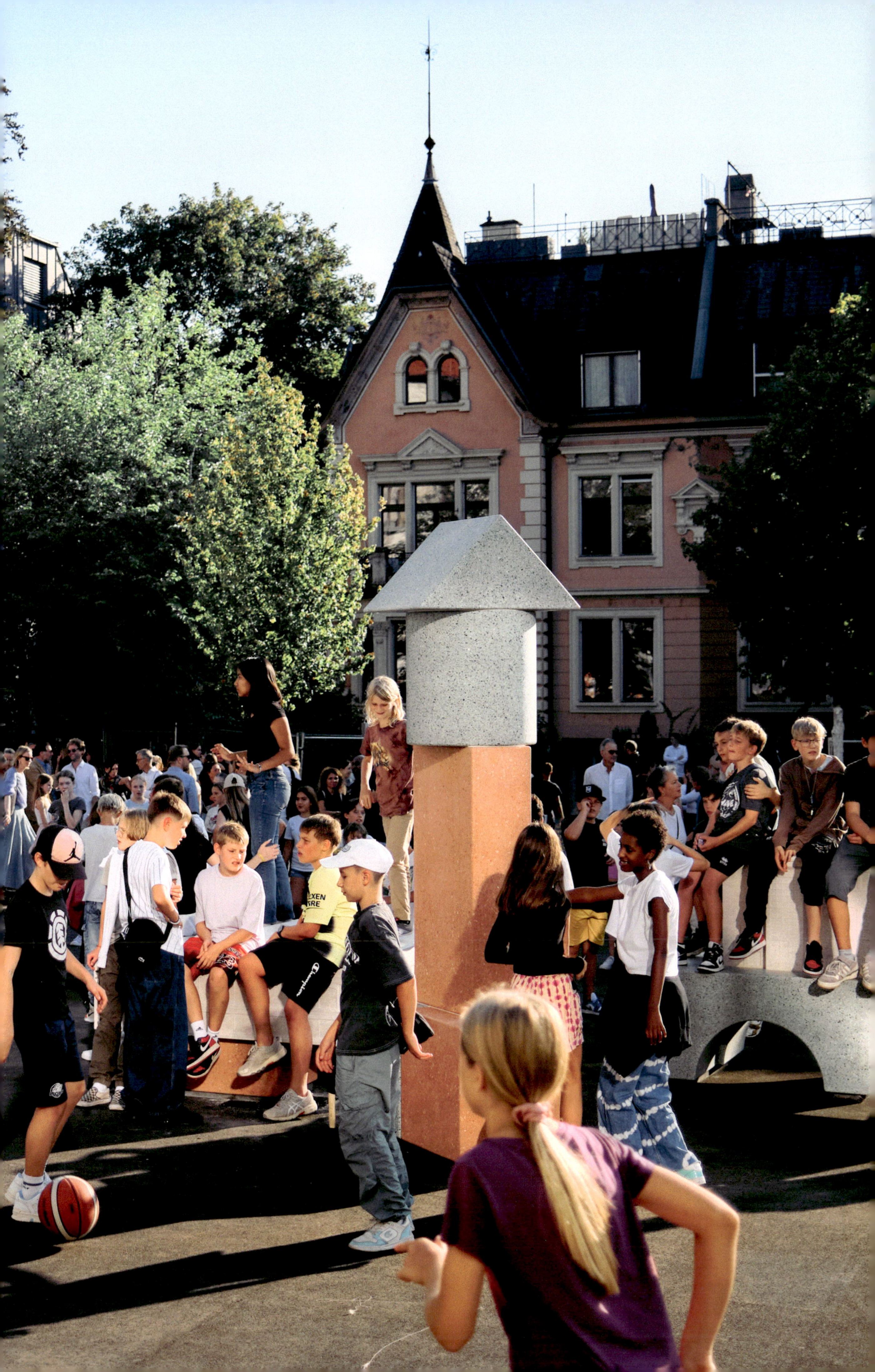

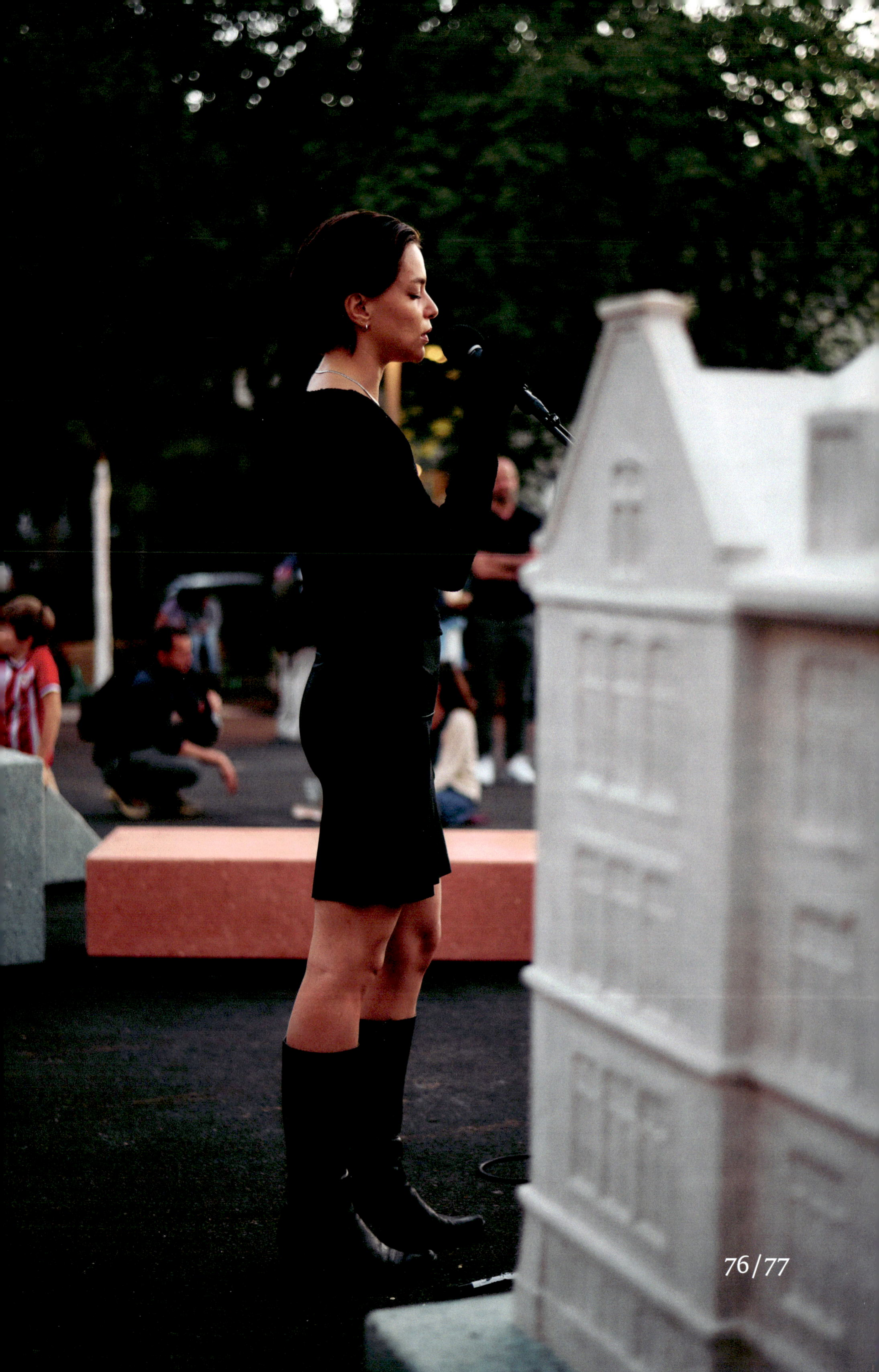

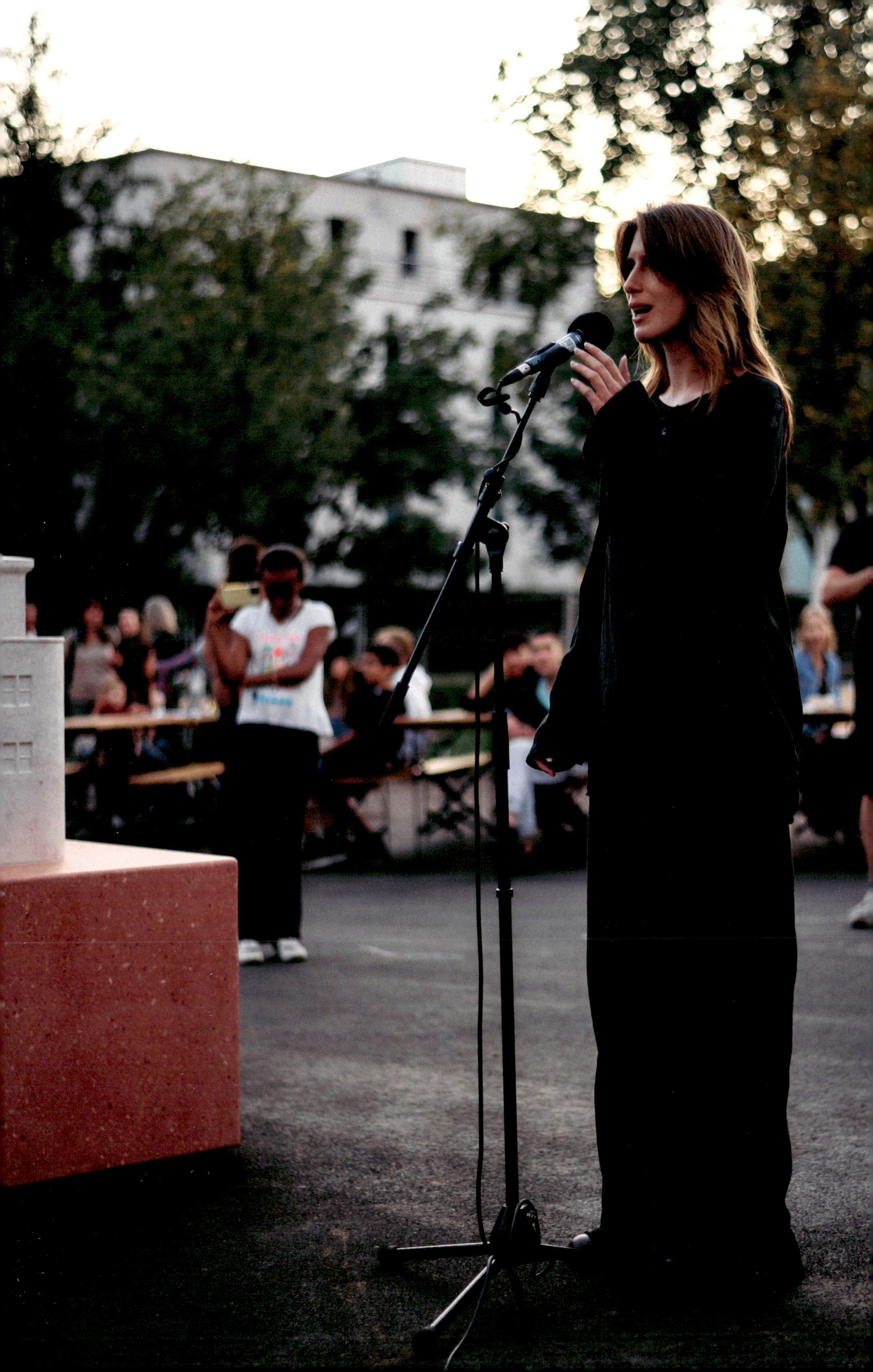

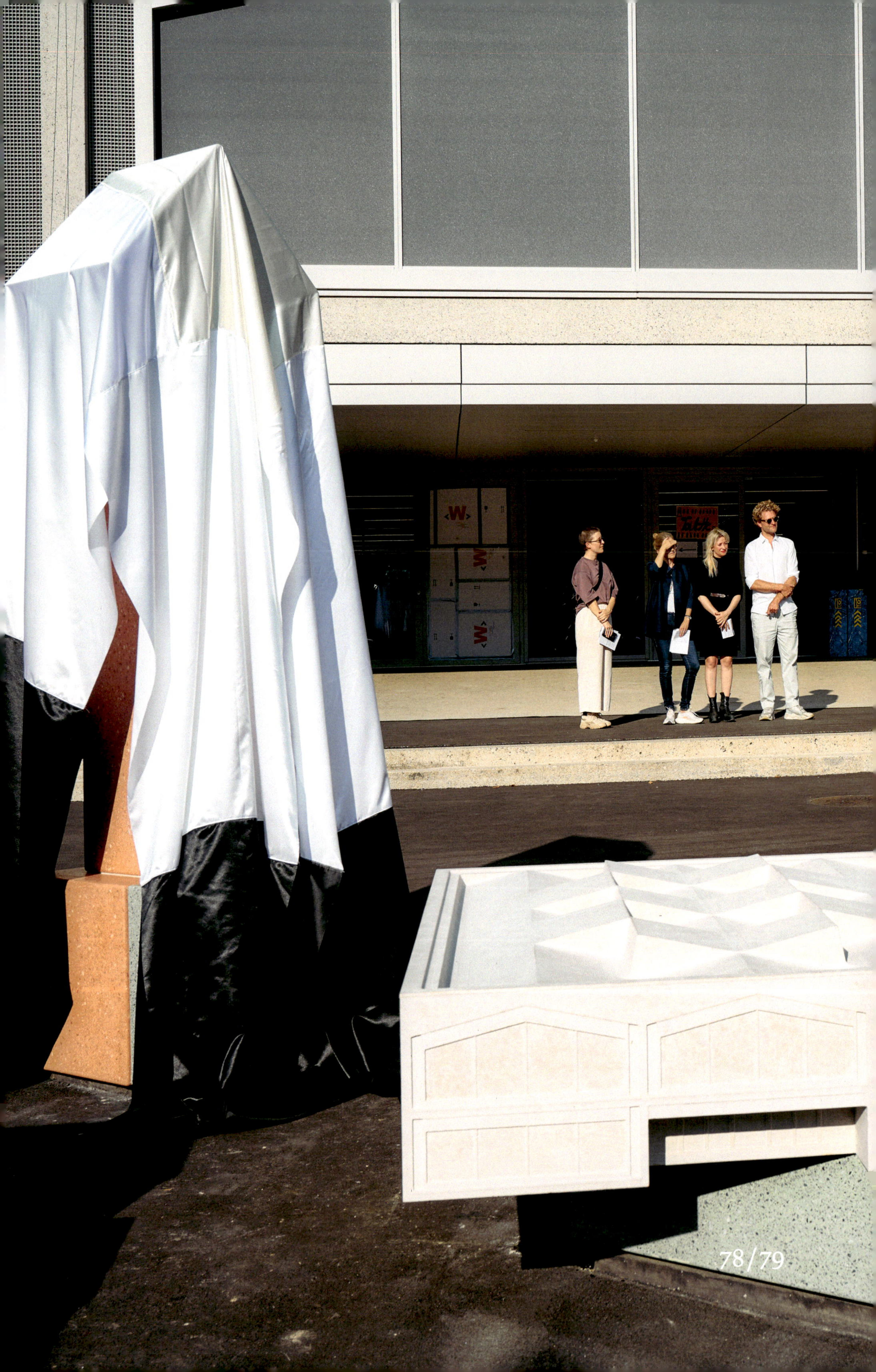

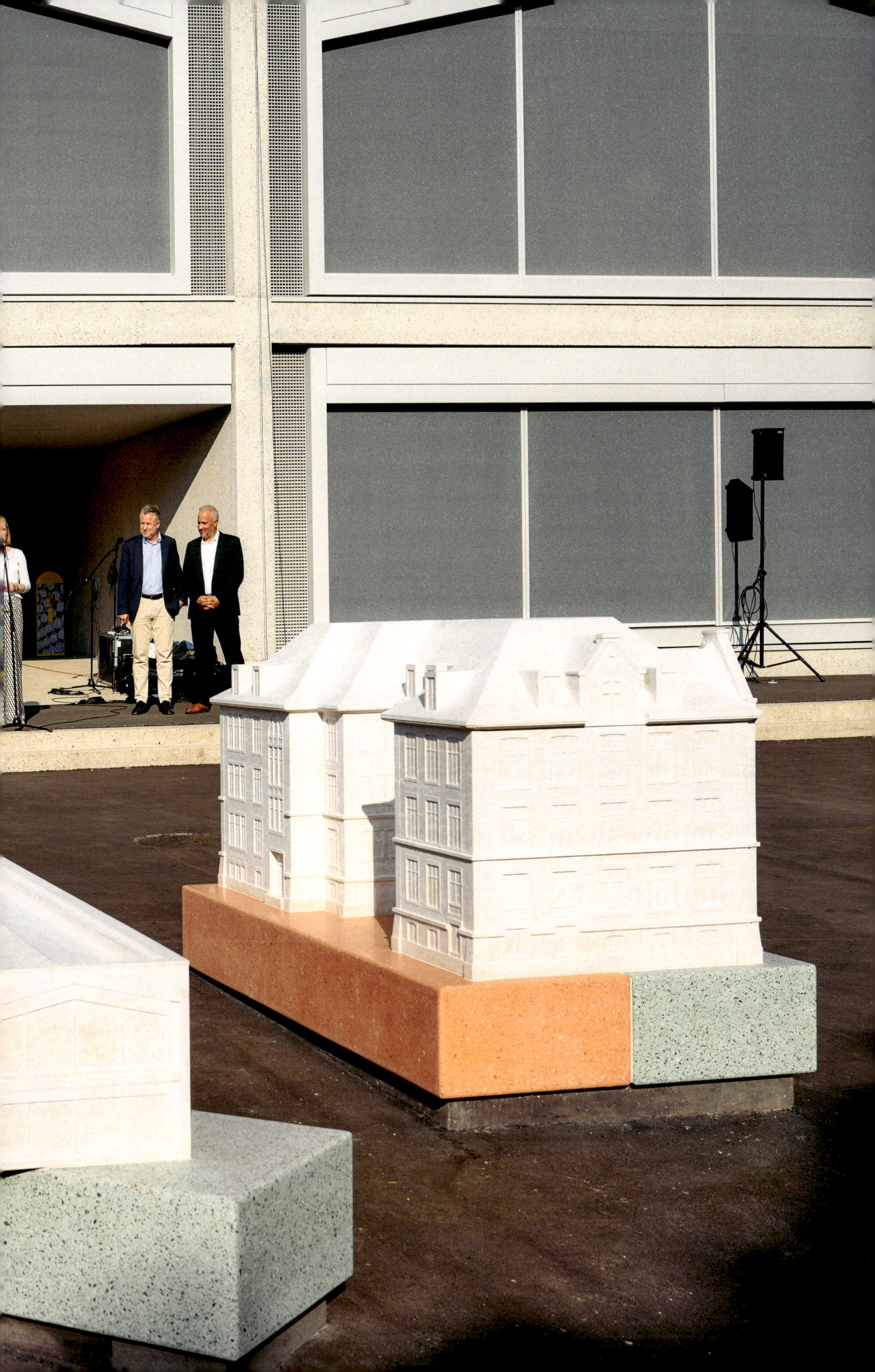

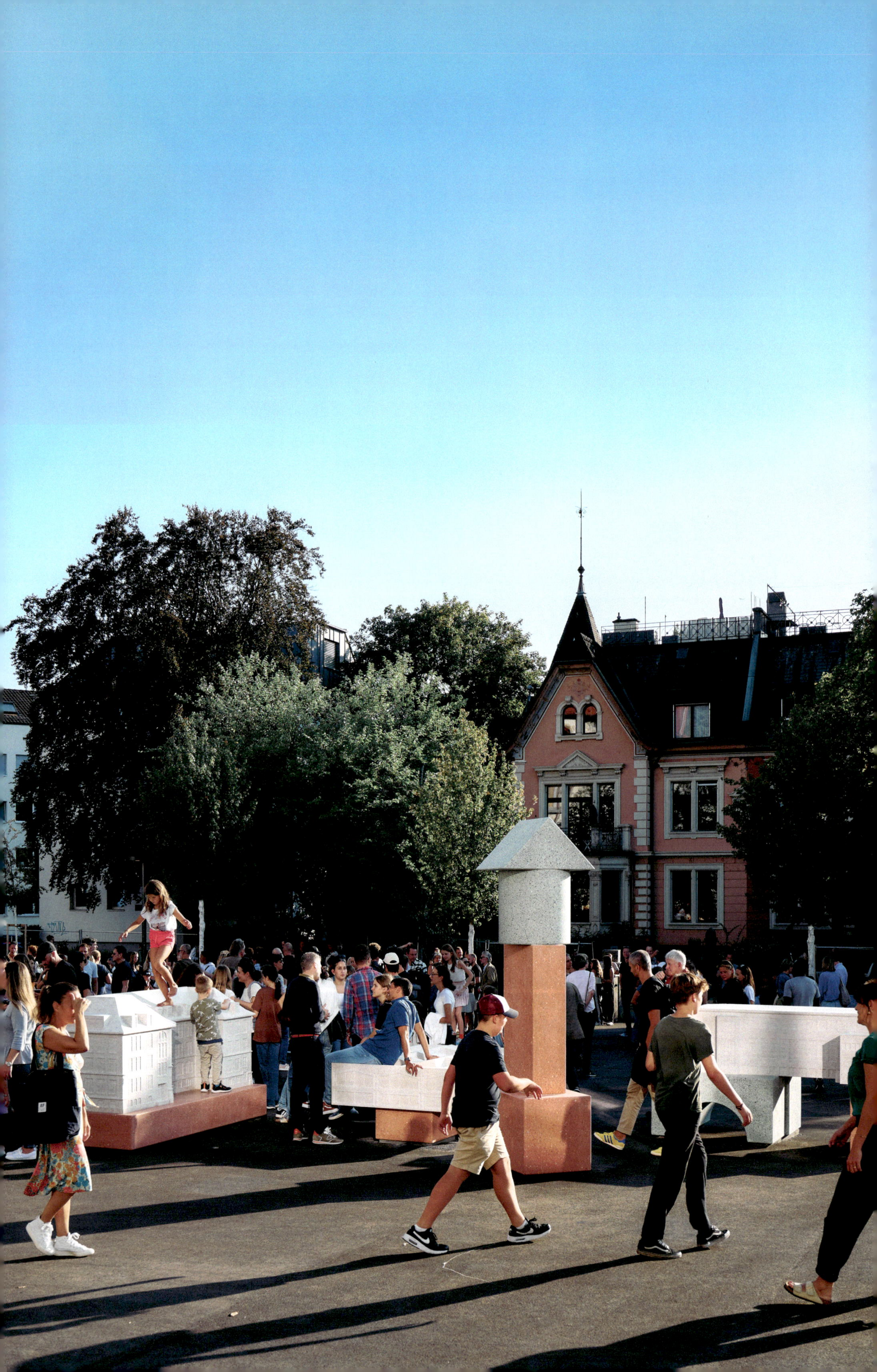

Selbstüberschreitungen: Florian Grafs *School Models* und die Paradoxien der Bildung

Dominique
Laleg

Dominique Laleg ist Senior Lecturer am Institut für Kunstgeschichte der Universität Zürich. Seine Forschung konzentriert sich auf die Theorie und Geschichte der modernen Kunst, die Zusammenhänge zwischen Ästhetik und Politik, sowie das Verhältnis von Kunst, Architektur und Demokratie. Er lehrt unter anderem an der Universität Basel, der Universität Wien und der Fachhochschule Nordwestschweiz.

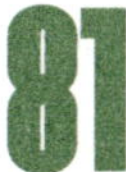

«Zuallererst muss man wissen, dass ein ‹Punkt› ein Zeichen ist, das sich sozusagen überhaupt nicht in Teile zerlegen lässt.»

Leon Battista Alberti[1]

Das obige Zitat aus Leon Battista Albertis kunsttheoretischem Traktat von 1436 beschreibt nicht einfach eine geometrische Sachlage, sondern auch eine menschliche Verfasstheit, denn der zentrale Punkt ist für Alberti ein perspektivischer Fluchtpunkt und damit das Zeichen des subjektiven Blicks, das heisst jener Position im Raum, von der aus die Welt wahrgenommen wird. Alberti bezieht sich auf den Umstand, dass die menschliche Welterschliessung perspektivisch sei, weil der Blick die Welt immer nur von einem isolierten Blickpunkt aus wahrnehmen könne. Diese Perspektivität der menschlichen Weltwahrnehmung wird von Florian Grafs Arbeit *School Models* überschritten.

Auf dem Gelände des Zürcher Schulhauses Hofacker hat Graf sorgfältig drei Modelle aus Muschelkalk positioniert, die das umgebende Architekturensemble abbilden. Platziert auf überdimensionierten, farbigen Terrazzo-Bauklötzen, verkehrt das Werk die perspektivische Beziehung zwischen gebauter Umwelt und Mensch. Während die mehrgeschossigen Gebäude aus der Untersicht erscheinen, die sich mit der Bewegung der Betrachter*innen auf dem Schulhof nur langsam verändern lässt, sind gleichzeitig dieselben Gebäude als Modelle aus der überschaubaren Vogelperspektive sichtbar. Nur wenige Schritte führen dazu, dass der Blick die Gebäude vollständig überfliegt. Den Grenzen der menschlichen Weltwahrnehmung wird damit ein Schnippchen geschlagen, der Blick überschreitet – wenn auch nur imaginär – den isolierten Blickpunkt.

1 Leon Battista Alberti, «De pictura», in: Oskar Bätschmann / Christoph Schäublin (Hg.), *Leon Battista Alberti. Das Standbild. Die Malkunst. Grundlagen der Malerei.* Darmstadt 2000, S. 194–335, hier: S. 194.

Anders als Albertis perspektivischer Fluchtpunkt vollzieht sich die vom Werk ermöglichte Selbstüberschreitung aber nicht im luftleeren Raum. Sie ist nicht auf eine geometrische Sachlage bezogen, sondern auf ein spezifisches Architekturensemble. Seine Spezifik ist zum einen typologisch: Es handelt sich um Schulhäuser. Zum anderen ist sie aber auch historisch: Das Ensemble besteht aus drei Gebäuden aus drei verschiedenen Jahrhunderten. Diese Spezifik verleiht der perspektivischen Überschreitung von *School Models* erst ihre eigentliche Bedeutung und Wirksamkeit. Der Bautyp des Schulhauses verweist auf eine Institution, deren Paradoxie das Kennzeichen des modernen Menschen ist: die paradoxe Beziehung zwischen «Freiheit», dem Kernanliegen liberaldemokratischer Gesellschaft, und der dort obligatorischen «Disziplinierung». Freiheit bedingt notwendigerweise Befähigung, diese ist wiederum nur durch Disziplinierung erreichbar. Die Arbeit *School Models* operiert mit dieser Paradoxie der Volksschule und dem durch sie hervorgebrachten Subjekt, das von Grafs Arbeit in den Fluchtpunkt gesetzt wird.

Im ersten Gebäude, das von *School Models* aufgegriffen wird, ist die historische Konfiguration dieser Paradoxie jene der bürgerlichen Moderne des 19. Jahrhunderts (Abb. 1). Der Bau aus dem Jahr 1898 verrät, dass die damals noch junge Volksschule ihre Bildungsziele seinerzeit durch die Beschäftigung mit der Klassik erreichen möchte. Seit der Einführung der Schulpflicht im Jahre 1874 soll jedes Mitglied der Gesellschaft, wenigstens ansatzweise, diese Bildung des Geistes durchlaufen. Die Überschreitung subjektiver Grenzen ist hier geistiger Art, das Ziel der Bildung ist es, «*in* uns selbst eine freie Existenz [zu] verschaffen»[2]. Die Paradoxie zwischen Freiheit und Disziplinierung erscheint hier folglich als eine zwischen dem Aussen des Subjekts und seiner

2 Johann Heinrich Pestalozzi, *Wie Gertrud ihre Kinder lehrt.* Bern/Zürich 1801, S. 22 [Hervorhebung im Zitat: D.L.].

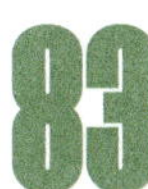

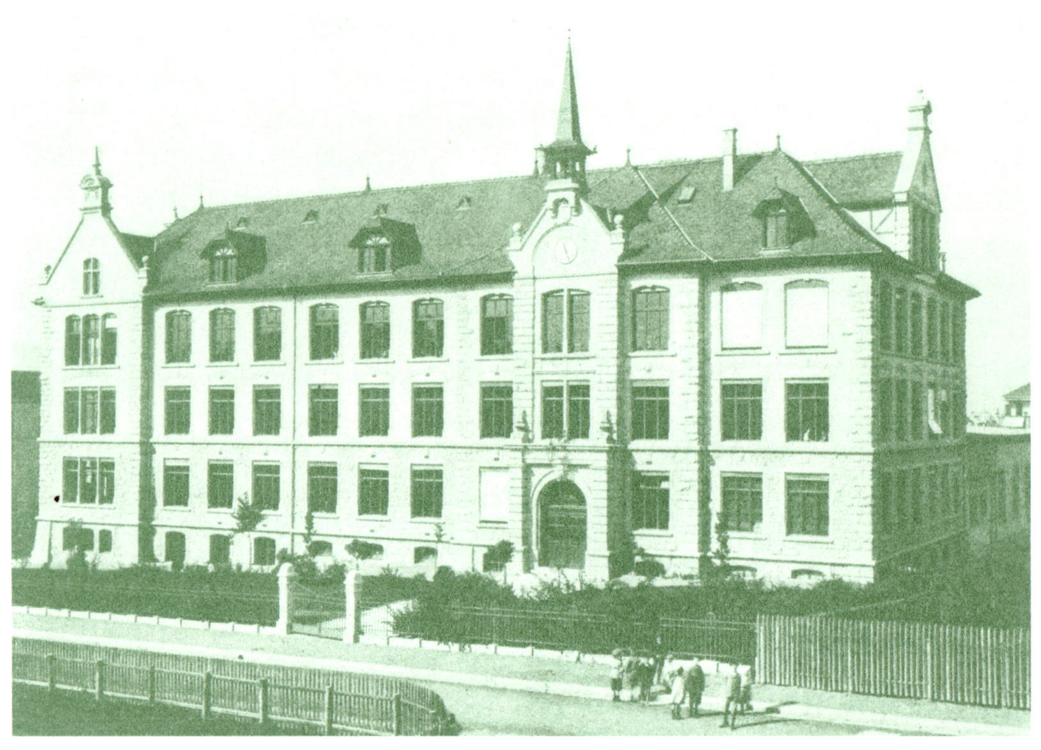

Abb. 1 Schulanlage Hofacker, erstes Gebäude, Friedrich Wehrli, 1898

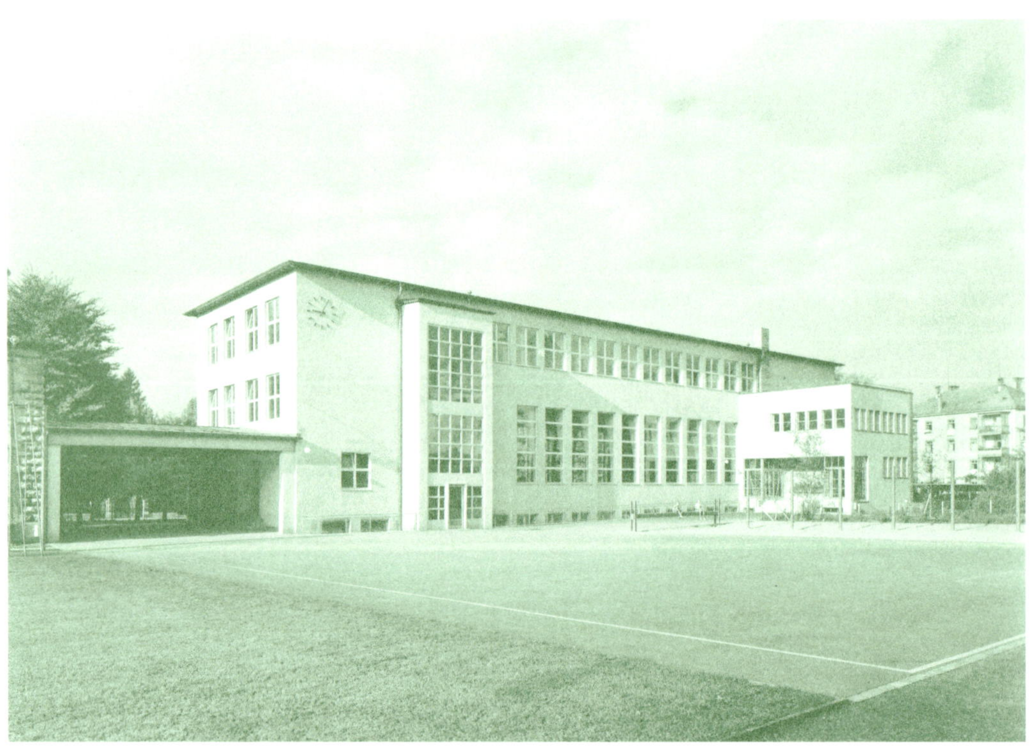

Abb. 2 Schulanlage Hofacker, zweites Gebäude, Hermann Herter, 1938

Innerlichkeit.[3] Der geistige Höhenflug des neuhumanistischen Subjekts ist dabei wesentlich eine Selbstüberschreitung des Körpers und dessen «pathologischen»[4] Neigungen, die eine bürgerliche Disziplinierung notwendig machen: «Es ist der Geist, der sich den Körper baut»[5], schreibt Schiller in *Wallenstein*.

Das zweite Schulgebäude, das Graf in seine Arbeit aufnimmt, ist der 1938 fertiggestellte Nachbarbau (Abb. 2), dessen pragmatischer Funktionalismus mit seinen Referenzen der modernen Industrie die Reminiszenzen an die Klassik fast vollständig abgelöst hat. Diese Ablösung ist symptomatisch für den Modernismus der Zwischenkriegszeit, der das neuhumanistische Bildungsideal aufgibt. Auf ihn folgt ein fortschrittsverliebter Technizismus, bei dem die rationale Beherrschbarkeit von Mensch und Natur im Zentrum steht.[6] Die Schule wird in diesem Kontext zu einem Reproduktionsort benötigter Fähigkeiten im Zeichen der kapitalistischen Produktion, was Louis Althusser später dazu bringen wird, sie als Ort zu bezeichnen, der «die Unterwerfung unter die herrschende Ideologie»[7] sichere. Die Paradoxie zwischen Freiheit

3 Diese Spannung ist in der idealistischen Systemphilosophie Immanuel Kants sowie Georg W. F. Hegels wirkmächtig vorgezeichnet und wird im 19. Jahrhundert in den Schriften Friedrich Schillers und Johann Heinrich Pestalozzis pädagogisch wirksam.
4 Immanuel Kant, *Kritik der Urteilskraft* [1790]. Hamburg 2006, B14.
5 Friedrich Schiller, *Wallenstein. Ein dramatisches Gedicht* [1800]. Berlin 1869, S. 253.
6 Die damit einhergehende Krise zeichnet sich etwa in den Schriften von Max Horkheimer, Karl Jaspers, Martin Heidegger oder Edmund Husserl ab. Exemplarisch dafür: Max Horkheimer, «Bemerkungen über Wissenschaft und Krise», in: *Zeitschrift für Sozialforschung*, Nr. 1, 1932, S. 1–7; Karl Jaspers, *Die geistige Situation der Zeit*. Leipzig/Berlin 1932.
7 Louis Althusser, *Ideologie und ideologische Staatsapparate* [1969], in: ders., *Ideologie und ideologische Staatsapparate. Aufsätze zur marxistischen Theorie*. Hamburg/Westberlin 1977, S. 108–153, hier: S. 112.

und Disziplinierung ist hier eine zwischen technischem Fortschritt und dessen Kehrseite, der gleichzeitigen Entfremdung des modernen Subjekts.[8]

Die dritte Skulptur bezieht sich auf den Bau des Zürcher Architekturbüros E2A aus dem Jahr 2022. Ein Blick in das Gebäudeinnere gibt Hinweise auf die Situation gegenwärtiger Bildung. Unter dem Dach befindet sich eine grosszügige Lernlandschaft (Abb. 3), wo Schüler*innen nicht mehr in Klassenverbänden synchron lernen (Abb. 4), sondern in asynchroner Weise gemäss ihrem individuellen Tempo arbeiten. Das Paradigma des Individualismus, das sich in diesem postindustriellen Modell abzeichnet, ist unter anderem eine Reaktion auf die Anerkennung der verstärkten Heterogenität der Schülerschaft. Die Vielfältigkeit der postmigrantischen Gesellschaft konfrontiert die Volksschule zunehmend mit dem Umstand, dass die Voraussetzungen sehr unterschiedlich sind. Zugleich ist im neoliberalen Konkurrenzkampf die Einzigartigkeit zu einem Wettbewerbsvorteil geworden.[9]

Die Paradoxie zwischen Freiheit und Disziplinierung verläuft hier zwischen der performativen Singularität des Individuums und dem nicht mehr allzu belastbaren Kollektivsingular *Wir*.[10] Die Volksschule sieht sich vor die schwierige Aufgabe gestellt, der Singularität jedes Individuums gerecht zu werden und diese zugleich auf einen gemeinschaftlichen Nenner zu bringen. Der Körper des Subjekts ist hier ein Ort sichtbarer Partikularitäten, wie Geschlecht, Ethnie oder Träger religiöser Attribute und schliesslich deren intersektionaler Verbindungen.

8 Siehe dazu Karl Jaspers, *Die geistige Situation der Zeit*. Leipzig/Berlin 1932.

9 Siehe dazu Luc Boltanski / Ève Chiapello, *Der neue Geist des Kapitalismus*. Konstanz 2003.

10 Zu dieser Paradoxie siehe auch Andreas Reckwitz, *Die Gesellschaft der Singularitäten. Zum Strukturwandel der Moderne*. Berlin 2018.

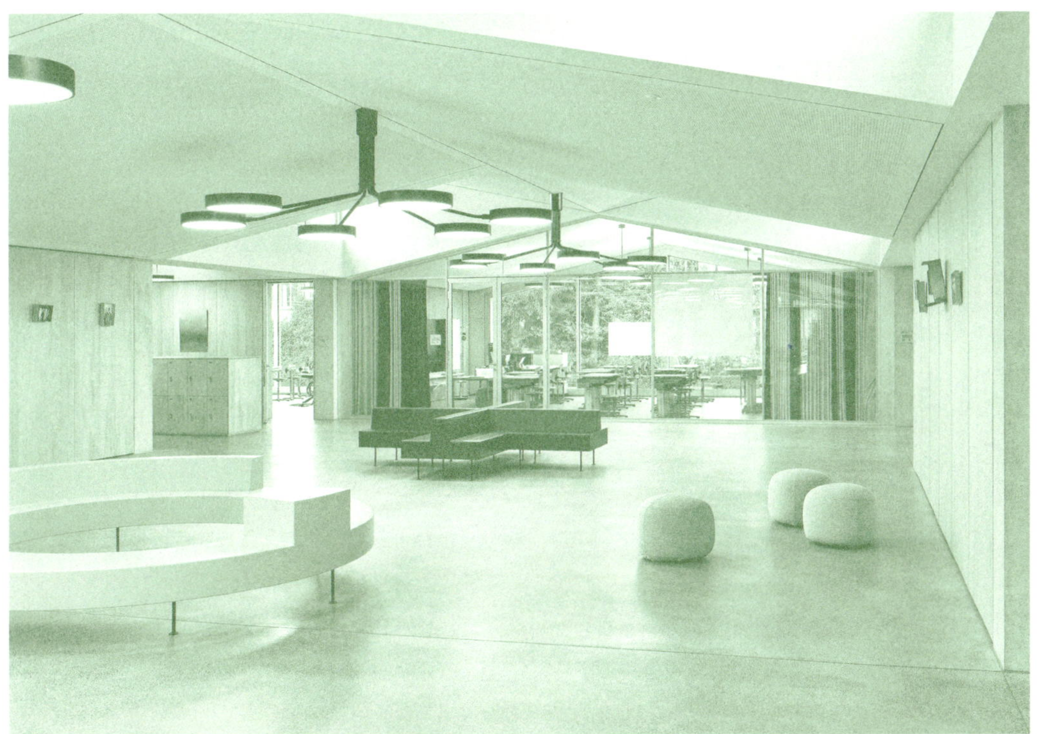

Abb. 3 Schulanlage Hofacker, Neubau, Lernlandschaft im 1. OG, E2A Architekten, 2022

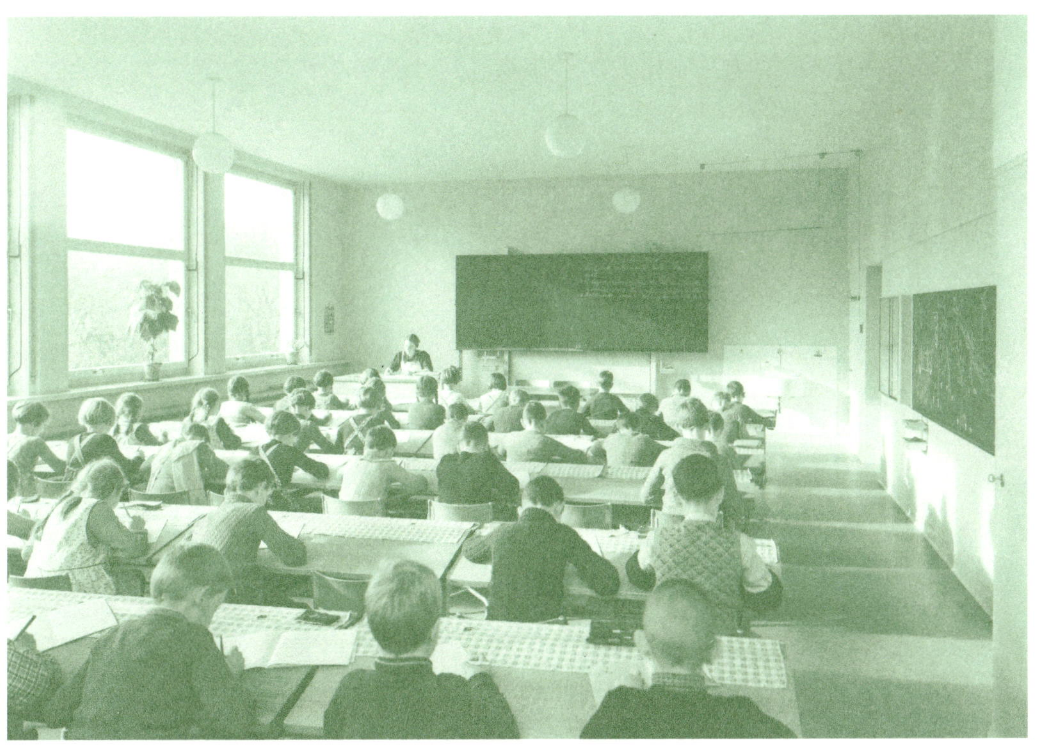

Abb. 4 Schulanlage Hofacker, Herter-Bau, Klassenzimmer, 1938

Die von *School Models* ermöglichte Selbstüberschreitung trägt auf subtile Weise zur Bewältigung dieser Aufgabe bei, denn der ermöglichte Überflug entkommt auch der gesellschaftlichen Überdeterminierung, die vor allem den Körper des Subjekts überfrachtet. Der durch *School Models* befreite Blick schüttelt den sozialen Körper imaginativ ab, freilich ohne die körperliche Erfahrung aufzugeben, denn die *School Models* sollen auch angefasst und erklommen werden. Ruhend auf den Terrazzo-Spielklötzen, stehen sie den Schüler*innen zur Disposition und lassen sich von ihnen vereinnahmen. Die Vereinnahmung durch den sehenden und tastenden Körper[11] verändert die funktionale Richtung der Skulpturen: Zunächst hergestellt als Modelle *von* einer Schule werden sie zu Modellen *für* eine Schule,[12] deren Sinn und Potenzial noch nicht feststehen. In dieser Richtungsänderung ins Offene markieren die *School Models* den Scheitelpunkt der Paradoxie von Disziplinierung und Befreiung, an deren Fluchtpunkt das moderne Subjekt steht.

11 Dies erinnert an Albertis Emblem des geflügelten Auges, das dank seiner ausgestreckten tastenden Tentakel die Welt auch zu spüren vermag. Markus Rath hat dem Charakter von Albertis Emblem als «Tastauge» hervorgehoben, vgl. Markus Rath, «Albertis Tastauge. Neue Betrachtung eines Emblems visueller Theorie», in: *kunsttexte.de – Journal für Kunst- und Bildgeschichte*, Nr. 1, 2009, S. 1–7.

12 Für eine differenzierte Analyse des Modellbegriffs siehe Bernd Mahr, «Ein Modell des Modellseins. Ein Beitrag zur Aufklärung des Modellbegriffs», in: Ulrich Dirks/Eberhard Knobloch (Hg.), *Modelle*. Frankfurt a. M. 2008, S. 187–218.

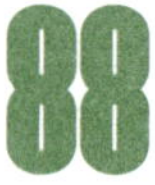

Transcending the Self: Florian Graf's *School Models* and the Paradoxes of Education

Dominique
Laleg

Dominique Laleg is Senior Lecturer in the Institute of Art History at the University of Zurich. His research focuses on the theory and history of modern art, the nexus between aesthetics and politics, and the relationship between art, architecture, and democracy. He teaches at the University of Basel, the University of Vienna, and the University of Applied Sciences and Arts Northwestern Switzerland.

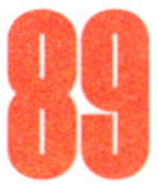

“Before anything else, therefore,
one must have understood
that the point is a sign,
so to speak, that in no way
can be divided into parts.”

Leon Battista Alberti[1]

The above quote from Leon Battista Alberti’s art historical tract of 1436 describes not only a geometric fact but also something of the human condition, because, for Alberti, the central point is a perspectival vanishing point and thus represents the subjective gaze—i.e., the position in space from which the world is perceived. Alberti is referring here to the fact that the human interpretation of the world is perspectival, as the gaze can only ever take in the world from an isolated point of view. It is this perspectivity of human perception that is transcended in Florian Graf’s work *School Models*.

In the grounds of Zurich’s Hofacker School, Graf has carefully installed three Muschelkalk limestone models of the surrounding architectural ensemble. Placed on oversized blocks of colored terrazzo, the work inverts the perspectival relationship between the human and the built environment. While the multistory buildings are viewed from ground level, slowly changing as the viewer moves around the schoolyard, the same buildings are simultaneously looked at from above as models. In no more than a few steps, one’s gaze has flown over the entire ensemble. The limits of human perception are outwitted, the gaze can transcend—if only in the imagination—the isolated point of view.

1 Leon Battista Alberti, *On Painting*, trans. by Rocco Sinisgalli, New Haven, CT: Yale University Press, 1970, p. 23.

Unlike Alberti's perspectival vanishing point, the self-transcendence that this work affords does not take place in a vacuum. It is not based on a geometric fact but on a specific architectural ensemble. The specificity is typological on the one hand: the models are of school buildings. On the other, it is also historical: the ensemble consists of three buildings from three different centuries. It is this specificity that lends the perspectival transcendence of *School Models* its true meaning and potency. The school building typology suggests that it is an institution caught in the very paradox that characterizes the modern human: the paradoxical relationship between *freedom*—the core concern of liberal-democratic society—and the discipline needed to maintain it. Freedom is contingent upon empowerment, which in turn can only be achieved through discipline. The work *School Models* operates with the paradox of the *Volksschule* and the human subject it produces, which Graf's work places at the vanishing point.[2]

In the first building that is referenced in *School Models*, the historical configuration of this paradox is that of nineteenth-century bourgeois modernity (fig. 1). Erected in 1898, the building indicates that the aim of the still youthful institution of the *Volksschule* was to achieve its educational goals by teaching classics. The introduction of compulsory schooling in 1874 envisioned that every member of society should have their intellect shaped in this way, at least to some degree. The transcendence of subjective limits here is spiritual in nature, the aim of education being "to provide *within* ourselves a free existence."[3] The paradox between freedom and discipline thus appears here as one that exists between the

2 The *Volksschule* covers the compulsory years of kindergarten, primary school, and middle school.

3 Johann Heinrich Pestalozzi, *How Gertrude Teaches Her Children* (1801), Norderstedt: Hansebooks, 2021 (emphasis in quotation: D.L.).

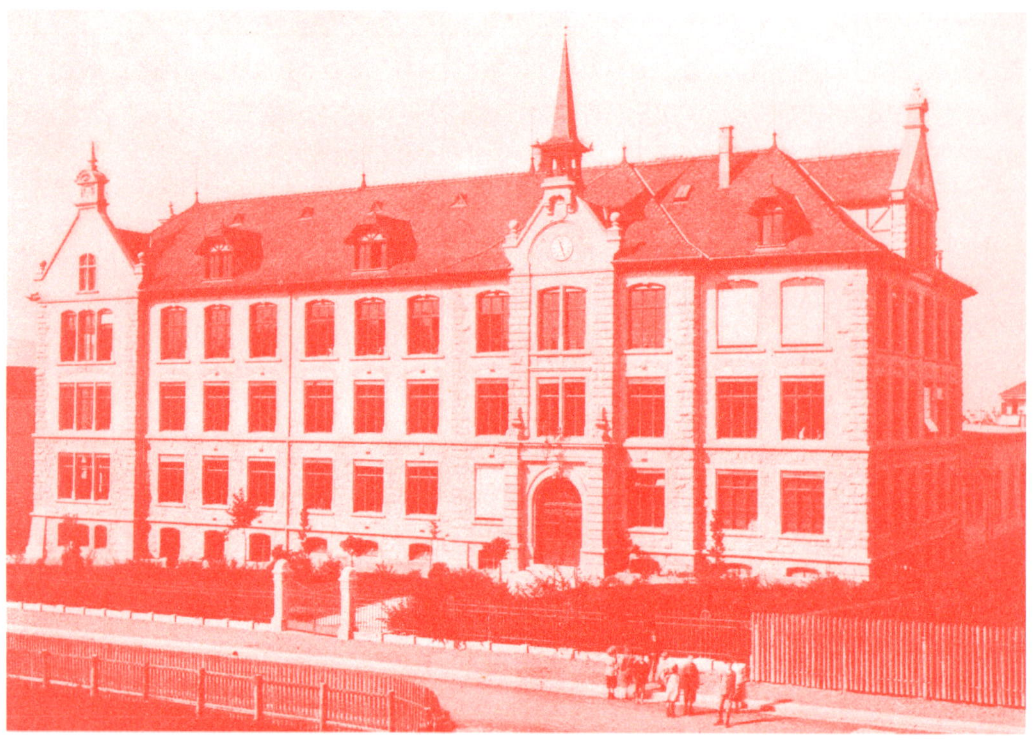

fig. 1 Hofacker school complex, first building, Friedrich Wehrli, 1898

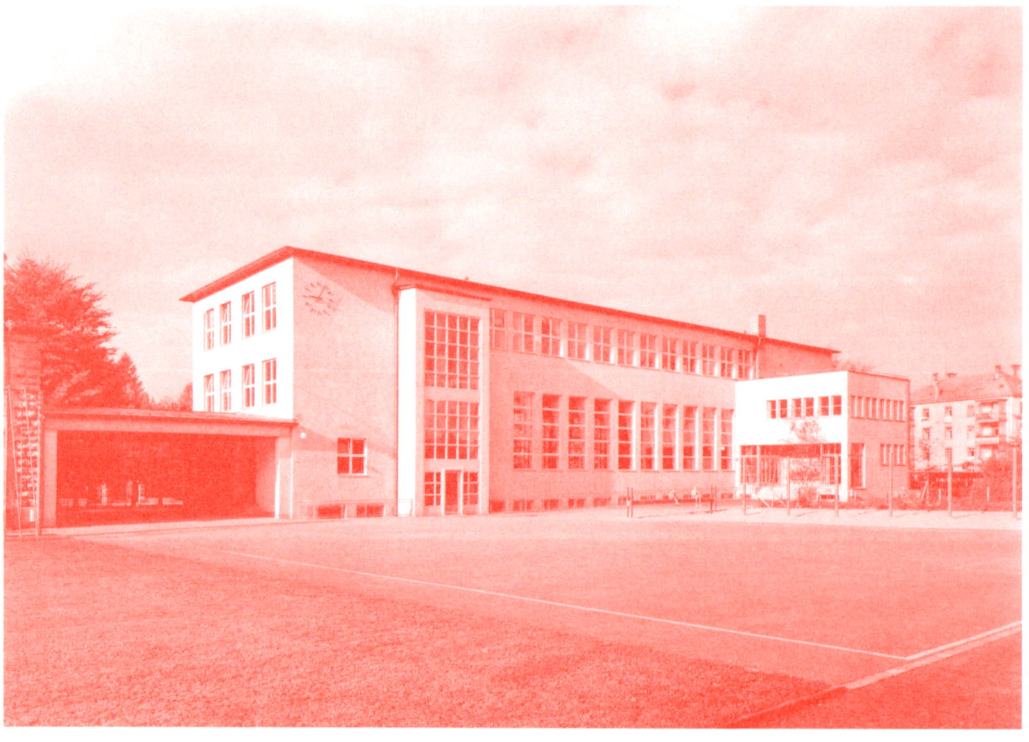

fig. 2 Hofacker school complex, second building, Hermann Herter, 1938

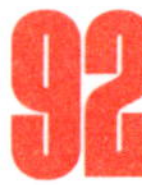

subject's exterior and interior worlds.[4] The spiritual flight of the neo-humanist subject is essentially a self-transcendence of the body and its "pathological" tendencies, which make bourgeois discipline necessary.[5] "The spirit moulds the body for itself,"[6] as Schiller writes in *Wallenstein*.

The second building that Graf refers to in his work is the neighboring building, completed in 1938 (fig. 2), whose pragmatic functionalism and modern industrial references have almost completely effaced all memories of classicism. Such effacement was symptomatic of the modernism of the interwar period, which abandoned neo-humanist educational ideals. These were replaced by a technologically obsessed love of progress, with a focus on bringing man and nature under the control of rationality.[7] In this context, the school became a place for the reproduction of the skills necessary for capitalist production, and would later lead Louis Althusser to describe it as a place that ensures "subjection to the ruling ideology."[8] The paradox between freedom and discipline here is between technological progress and its flip side, the alienation of the modern subject.[9]

4 This tension is powerfully prefigured in the idealistic systems philosophy of Immanuel Kant and Georg W. F. Hegel and was applied to pedagogical effect in the nineteenth century in the writings of Friedrich Schiller and Johann Heinrich Pestalozzi.

5 Immanuel Kant, *Critique of Pure Reason* (1790), Cambridge: Cambridge University Press, 1998.

6 Friedrich Schiller, *Wallenstein: A Dramatic Poem* (1800), Edinburgh: Cadell and Co., 1827, p. 139.

7 The crisis this provoked features in the writings of Max Horkheimer, Karl Jaspers, Martin Heidegger, and Edmund Husserl. See, for example, Max Horkheimer, "Notes on Science and Our Crisis" (1932), in *Critical Theory: Selected Essays*, trans. by Matthew J. O'Connell and others, New York: Continuum, 1972; Karl Jaspers, *Man in the Modern Age* (1931), trans. by Eden and Cedar Paul, Abingdon, UK: Routledge, 2010.

8 Louis Althusser, "Ideology and Ideological State Apparatuses" (1969), in *Lenin and Philosophy and Other Essays*, trans. by Ben Brewster, New York: Monthly Review Press, 1971.

9 See Jaspers, *Man in the Modern Age*.

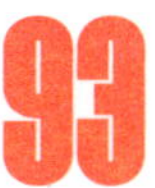

The third sculpture refers to the building designed by the Zurich architecture office E2A from 2022 A glance into the building's interior provides insights into the state of contemporary education. Under the roof is a spacious learning landscape (fig. 3), where students no longer learn synchronously in class groups (fig. 4) but work at their own pace. The individualistic paradigm that emerges in this postindustrial paradigm is at least in part a response to the acknowledgement of the increased heterogeneity of the student body. More and more, schools are having to confront the fact that the diversity of post-migrant society means very different requirements for each student. At the same time, in the neoliberal rat race, individuality is seen as the way to gain a competitive edge.[10]

The paradox between freedom and discipline here runs between the performative singularity of the individual and the dwindling resilience of the singular collective *We*.[11] The *Volksschule* is faced with the difficult task of doing justice to the singularity of each individual and at the same time reducing it to a common denominator. The body of the subject is here a place of visible particularities, such as gender, ethnicity, or religious signifiers and their intersectionalities.

10 See Luc Boltanski and Ève Chiapello, *The New Spirit of Capitalism*, trans. by Gregory Elliott, London: Verso, 2018.
11 On this paradox, see Andreas Reckwitz, *The Society of Singularities*, trans. by Valentine A. Pakis, Cambridge: Polity, 2020.

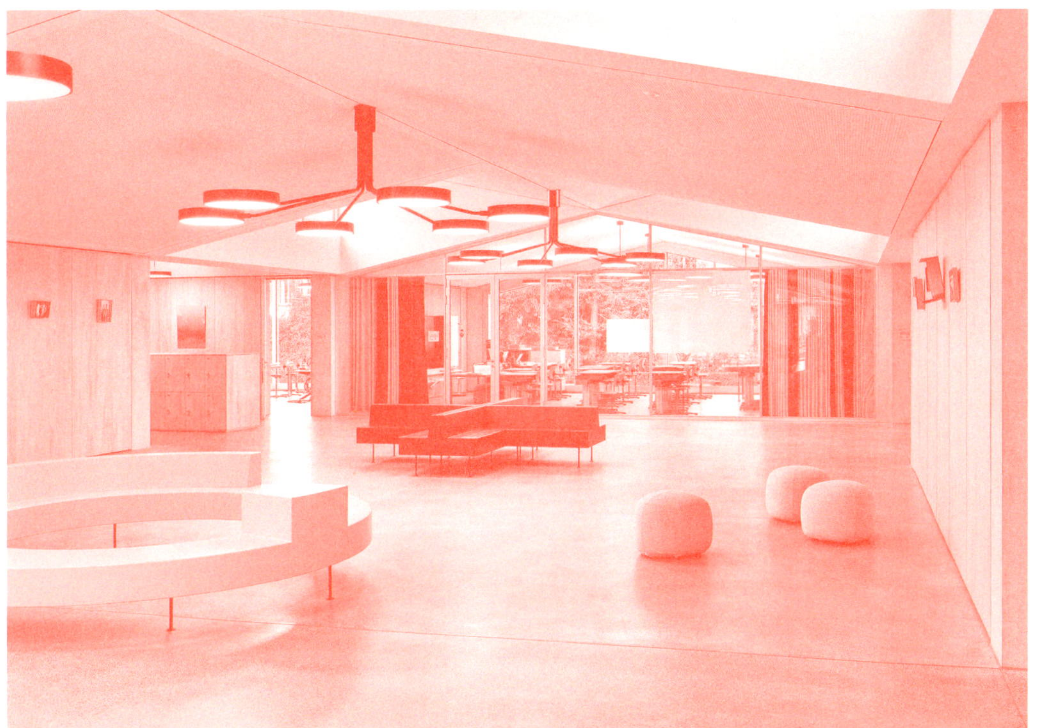

fig. 3 Hofacker school complex, new building, learning landscape on the 1st floor, E2A Architects, 2022

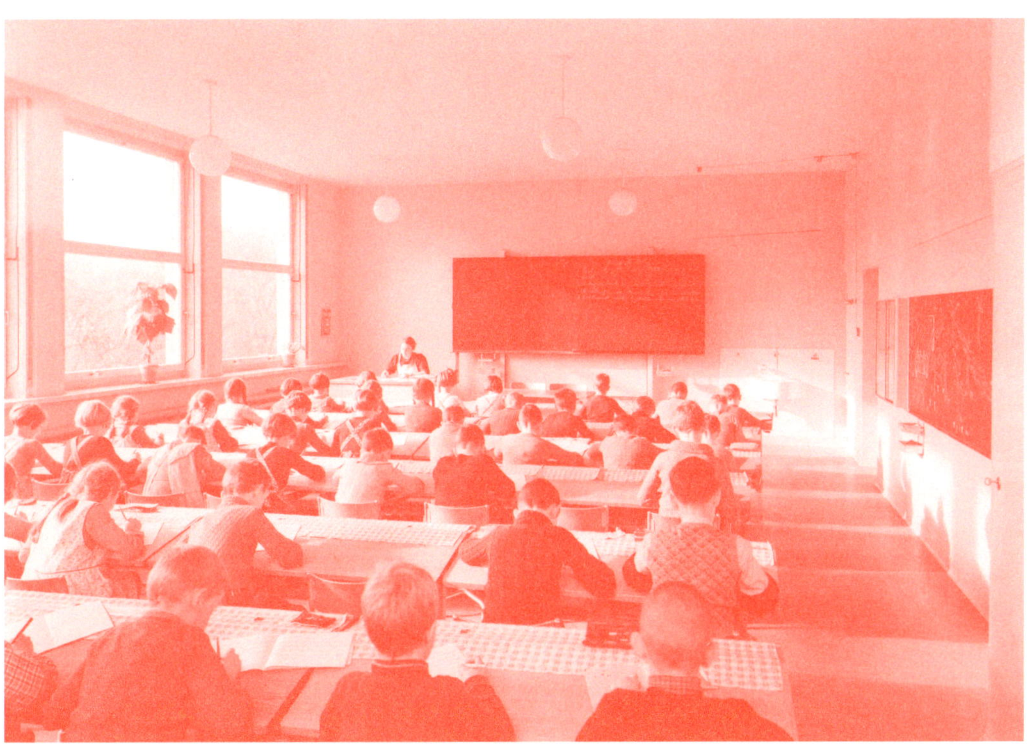

fig. 4 Hofacker school complex, Herter building, classroom, 1938

The self-transcendence afforded by *School Models* itself subtly contributes to the accomplishment of this task, because the bird's-eye view that it provides also evades the social over-determination that is a particular burden on the body of the subject. The liberated gaze that *School Models* facilitates shakes up the social body on the level of the imagination, without, of course, neglecting the physical experience, because the *School Models* are there to be touched and clambered on. Resting on their giant terrazzo toy building blocks, they are readily appropriated by the schoolchildren. This appropriation by sensing bodies changes the functional direction of the sculptures:[12] initially produced as models *of* a school, they become models *for* a school whose meaning and potential have yet to be determined.[13] In this shift of direction toward openness, *School Models* marks the peak of the paradox of discipline and liberation, at the vanishing point of which the modern subject stands.

12 This is reminiscent of Alberti's emblem of the winged eye, which is also able to feel the world with its outstretched tentacles. Markus Rath has characterized Alberti's emblem as a "tactile eye." See Markus Rath, "Albertis Tastauge: Neue Betrachtung eines Emblems visueller Theorie," *kunsttexte.de: Journal für Kunst- und Bildgeschichte*, 1 (2009), pp. 1–7.

13 For a nuanced analysis of the model concept, see Bernd Mahr, "Ein Modell des Modellseins: Ein Beitrag zur Aufklärung des Modellbegriffs," in *Modelle*, ed. by Ulrich Dirks and Eberhard Knobloch, Frankfurt am Main: Peter Lang, 2008, pp. 187–218.

über die veränderten Grenzverläufe auf dem Laufenden sein.

(Aus dem Roman:)

ZEITZEUGE ~~+~~ und STEINZEUG

(aus der Serie:)

KANNIBALEN KÖNNEN NERVEN

FG

165

Kultur

- Grabbeigabe
- Urnen
- Souvenirs: Eiffelturm, Colosseum etc.
- Swiss Miniature
- Modelleisenbahn/Lego (Spielzeug)
- Puppenhaus
- Marionettentheater
- Wissenschaft
- Architektur

Typus

- Alice i.W. / Gulliver
- Lebkuchen
- japan. Laterne

Modello + Disegno (Zeichnung + Modell) als Zwischenschritt

Monument / im Moment

Matt Mullican, M. Pernice
Stephen Craig, Thomas Schütte
Kirkeby, Wim Delvoye
Charles Simonds
Langlands & Bell, Thomas Demand
J. Hedjuk, van Lieshout
Carlos Garaicoa, Absalon, Dan Graham
E. Wurm, Hans op de Beeck
Rita McBride
Hans Haacke
Mike Kelley
R. Mucha

Kunst

Reconstruction

REPRESENTATION

Stellvertreter

Face – Fassade
offen / geschlossen
abweisend, abgeschieden,
gealtert (Gebäude selbst mit menschl. Charakteristika)
Metapher, Analogie

Modell

IMAGINATION

VORSTELLEN

Vorbild (funktion)
(ermutigende Kraft)*

Entwurf, Experiment, Plan, Idee, Erfinden, Test

Massstäblichkeit

Verhältnismässigkeit
Spielplatz

Erinnerung

OBSERVATION

NACHDENKEN

Overview-Effect
(seeing earth from space or like New Year / when sb dies → looking back, consciousness, self-awareness
Übersicht + Einsicht)

Betrachten, Vereinfachung / Abstraktion
Mimesis, Anschauungsobjekt
Nachbildung, Erklären

1. noch nicht → aber sein könnte
2. nicht mehr → REKONSTRUKTION
3. (Souvenir) noch da → Vedute als Objekt

ZH

Was bleibt länger? Original oder Modell? Denk mal!
→ Sarkophag

200 cm

10 2 20

98/99

* Horst Bredekamp: "Modelle der Kunst u. der Evolution"

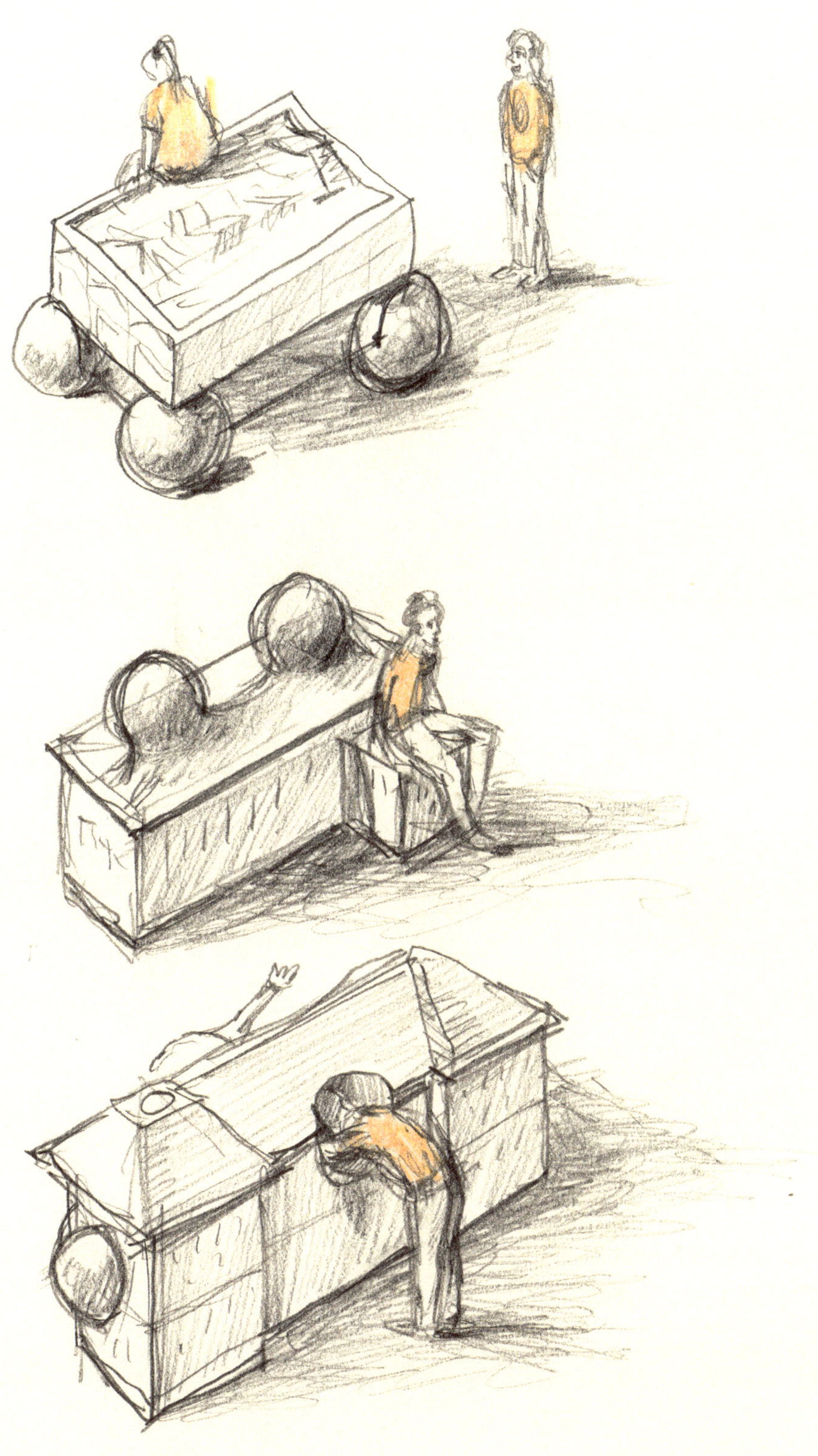
21 2 20 FG

166

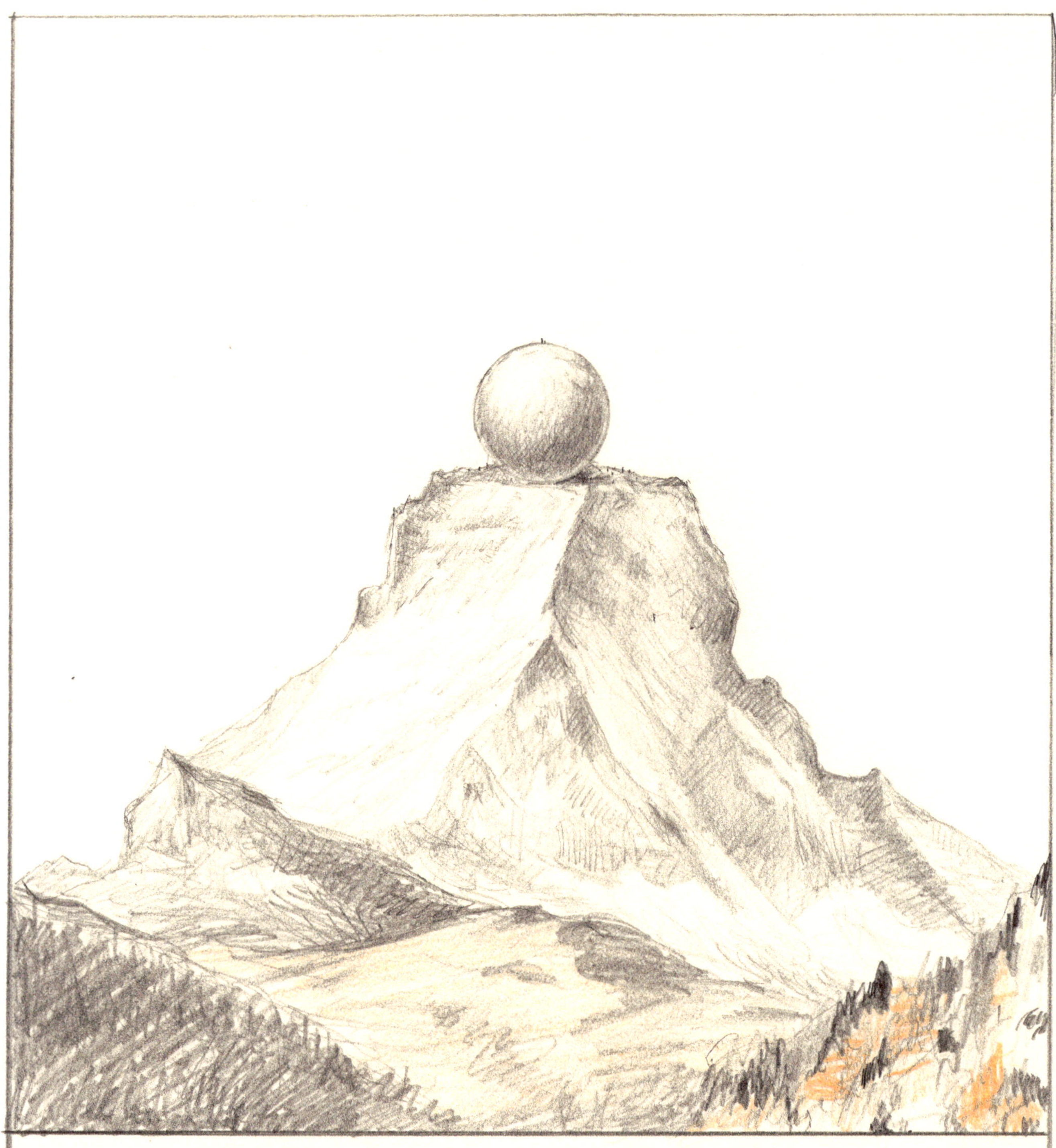

I just started chiseling

1 4 20 FG

79

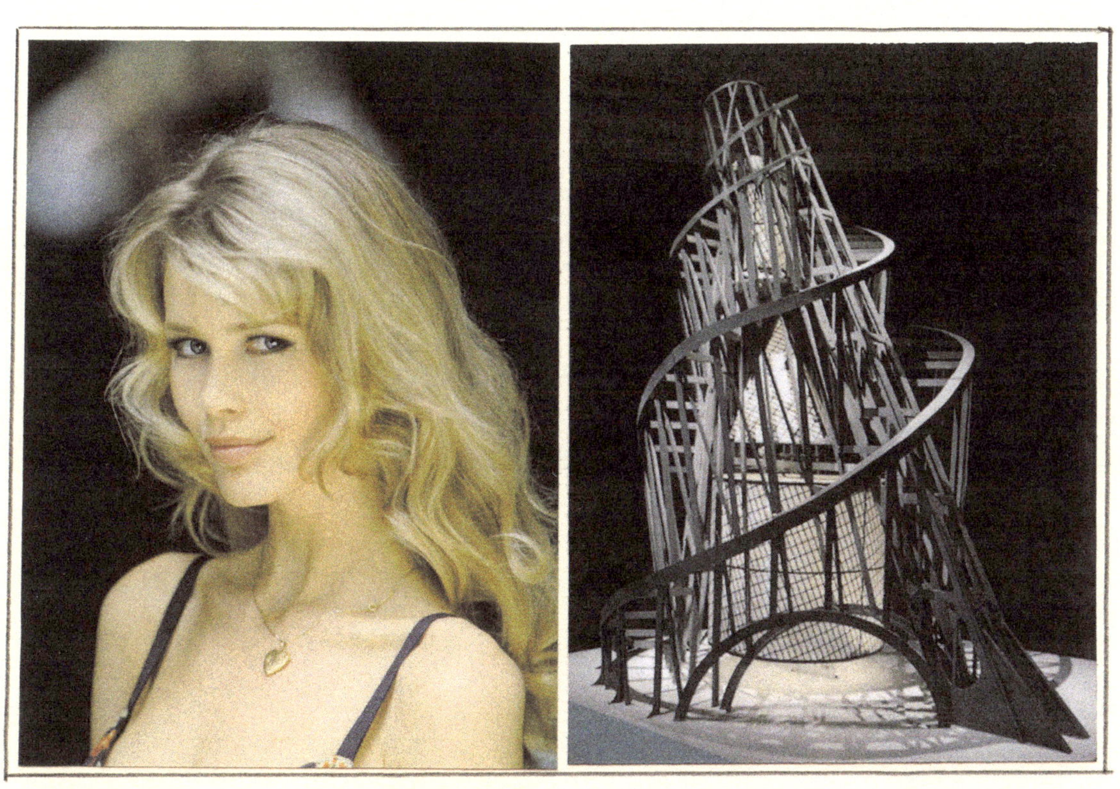

TWO MODELS XI

18. 8. 2020 II FG

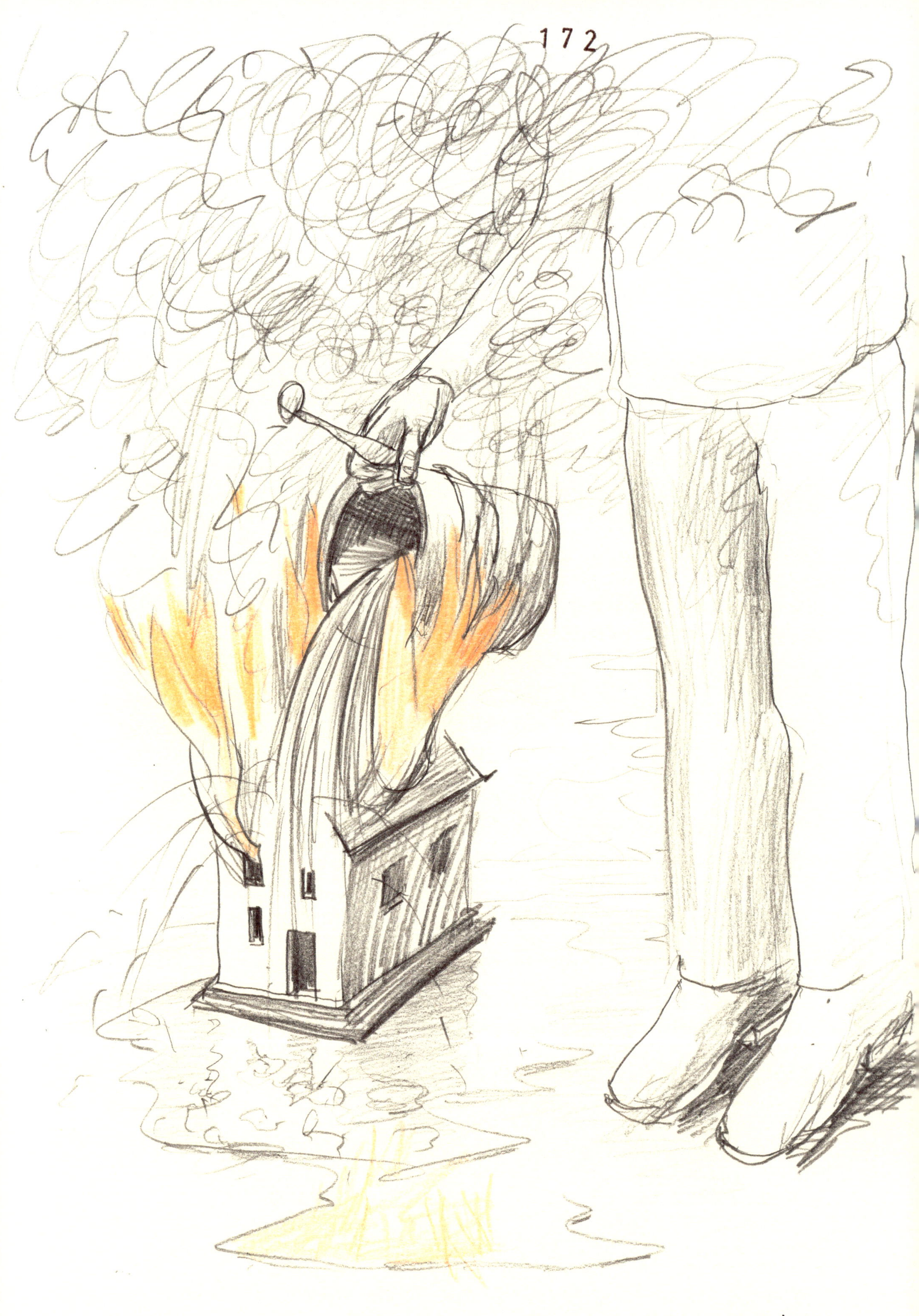

102/103

Der destruktive Charakter ist heiter und freundlich, will Platz schaffen + räumen (→ W. Benjamin)
ICH BIN DER HEILIGE FLORIAN

5 2 21 FG

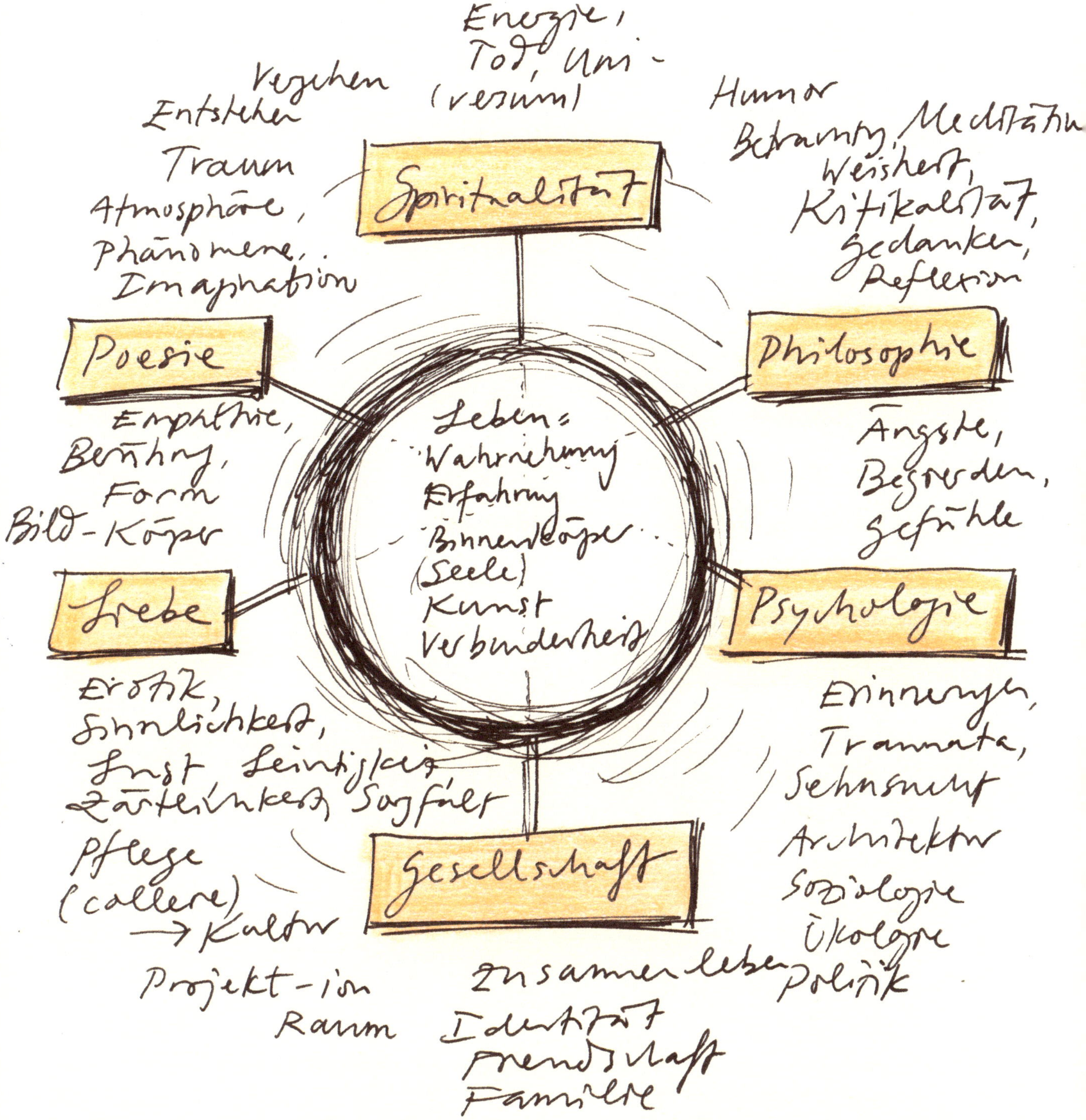

Energie, Tod, Universum

Vergehen
Entstehen
Traum
Atmosphäre,
Phänomene,
Imagination

Humor
Betrachtung, Meditation
Weisheit,
Kritikalität,
Gedanken,
Reflexion

Spiritualität

Poesie

Philosophie

Empathie,
Berührung,
Form
Bild-Körper

Leben:
Wahrnehmung
Erfahrung
Binnenkörper
(Seele)
Kunst
Verbundenheit

Ängste,
Begierden,
Gefühle

Liebe

Psychologie

Erotik,
Sinnlichkeit,
Lust, Leiblichkeit
Zärtlichkeit, Sorgfalt
Pflege
(collere)
→ Kultur
Projekt-ion
Raum

Erinnerungen,
Traumata,
Sehnsucht
Architektur
Soziologie
Ökologie
Politik

Gesellschaft

Zusammenleben
Identität
Freundschaft
Familie

6 wichtige Aspekte meiner Kunst

6 5 21

172

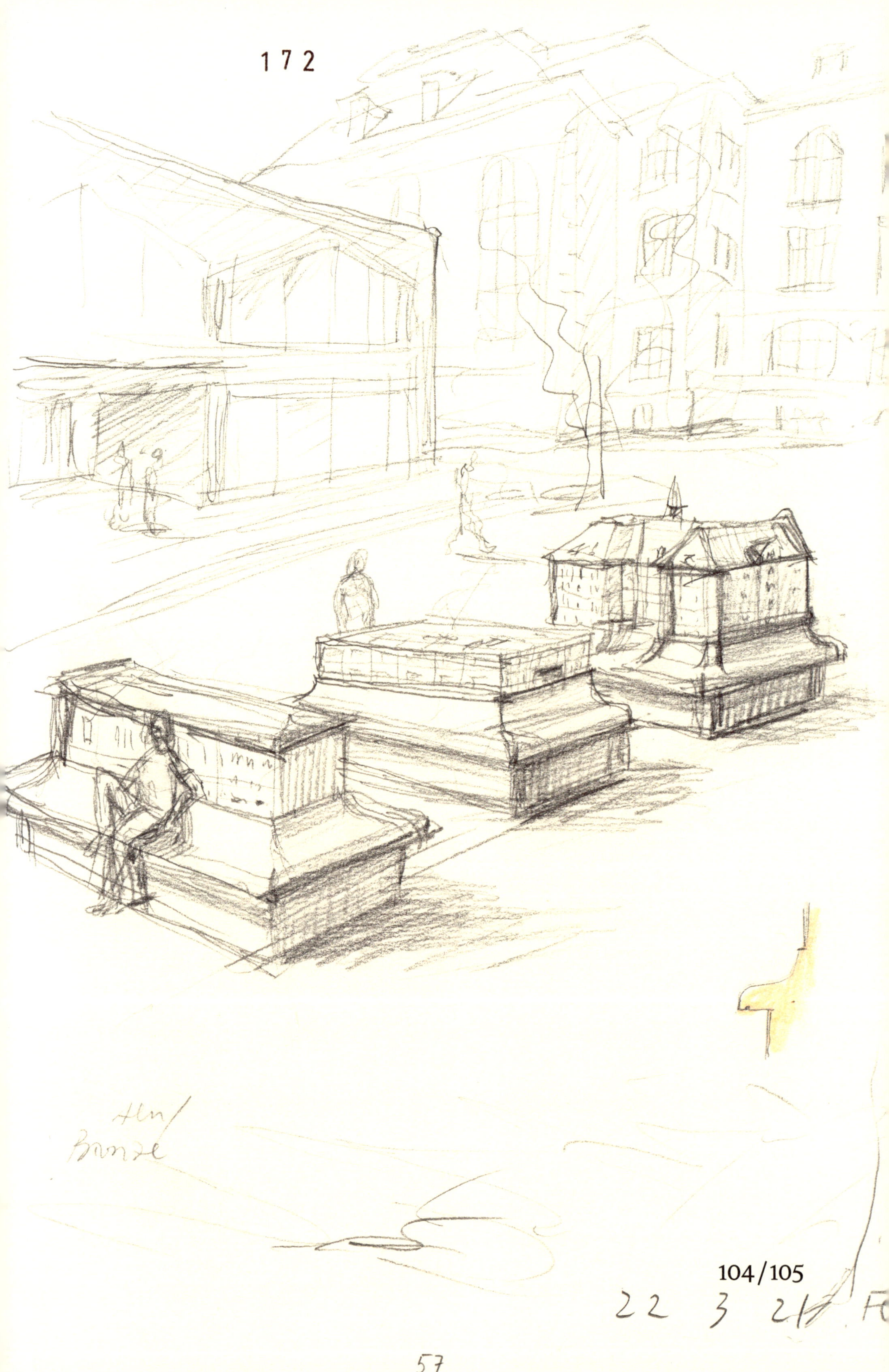

104/105

26 · 5. 22

out
Model
SPACE
SPACE
PERCEPTION
NARRATION
IMAGE
Body
Sculpture
Building
Volume
(Container)
ENCOUNTER
DIALOGUE
SPACE
SPACE
Installation
in

Image
Body
Text
(Perception + Encounter + Dialogue + Narration = (Communication)
political
(society)
sensual
(body, touch)
perception
social
(community,
love, friends)
individual
Image
Space
psychological
(feelings, soul
dreams)
historical
(memory, culture
tradition)
collective
philosophical
(thoughts, wisdom
cognition)
economical
(values)
Ethik
ecological
(nature
Lebensraum
interconnected
8 Layers

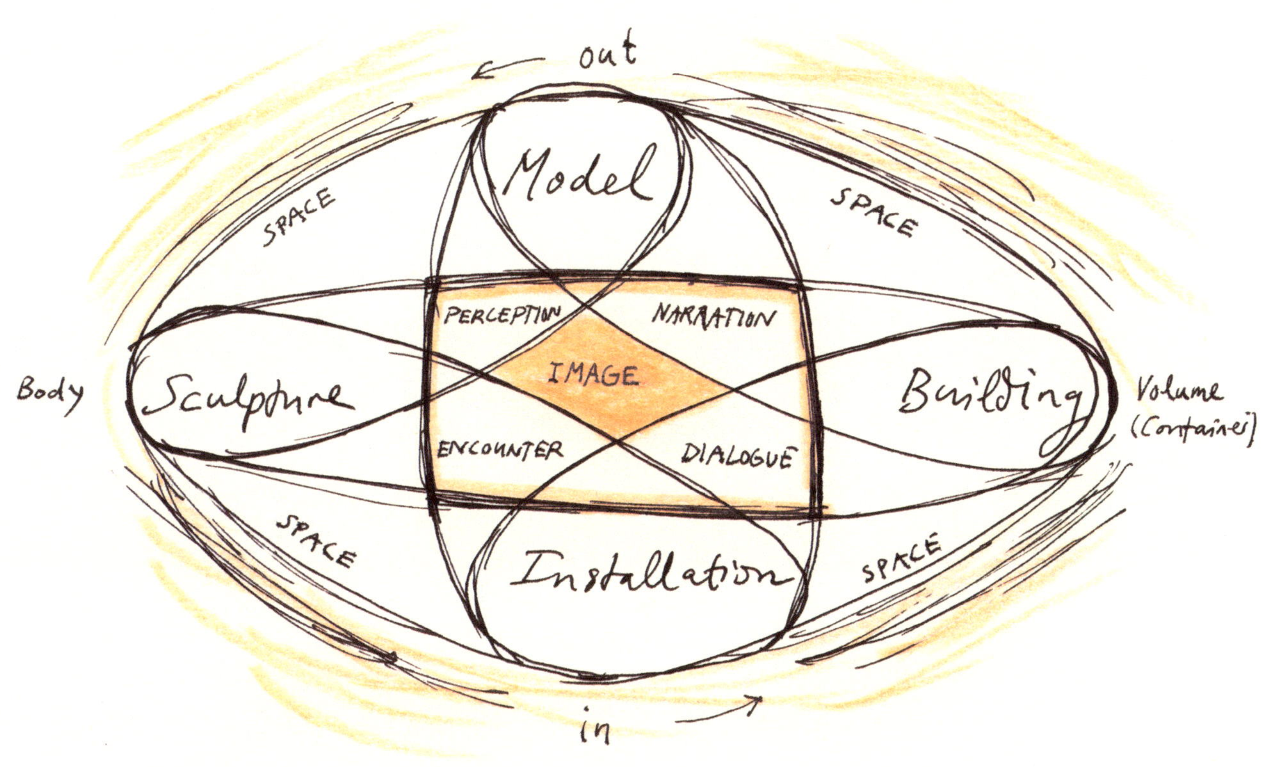

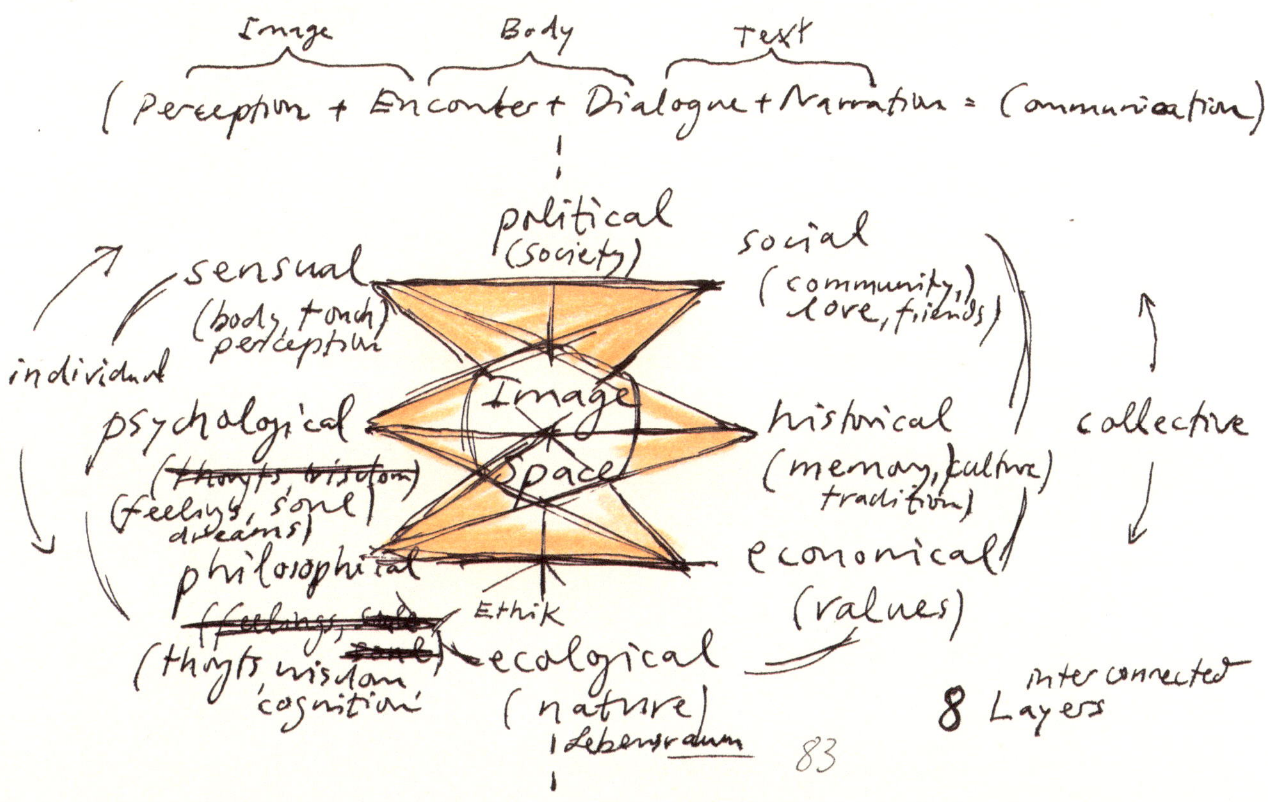

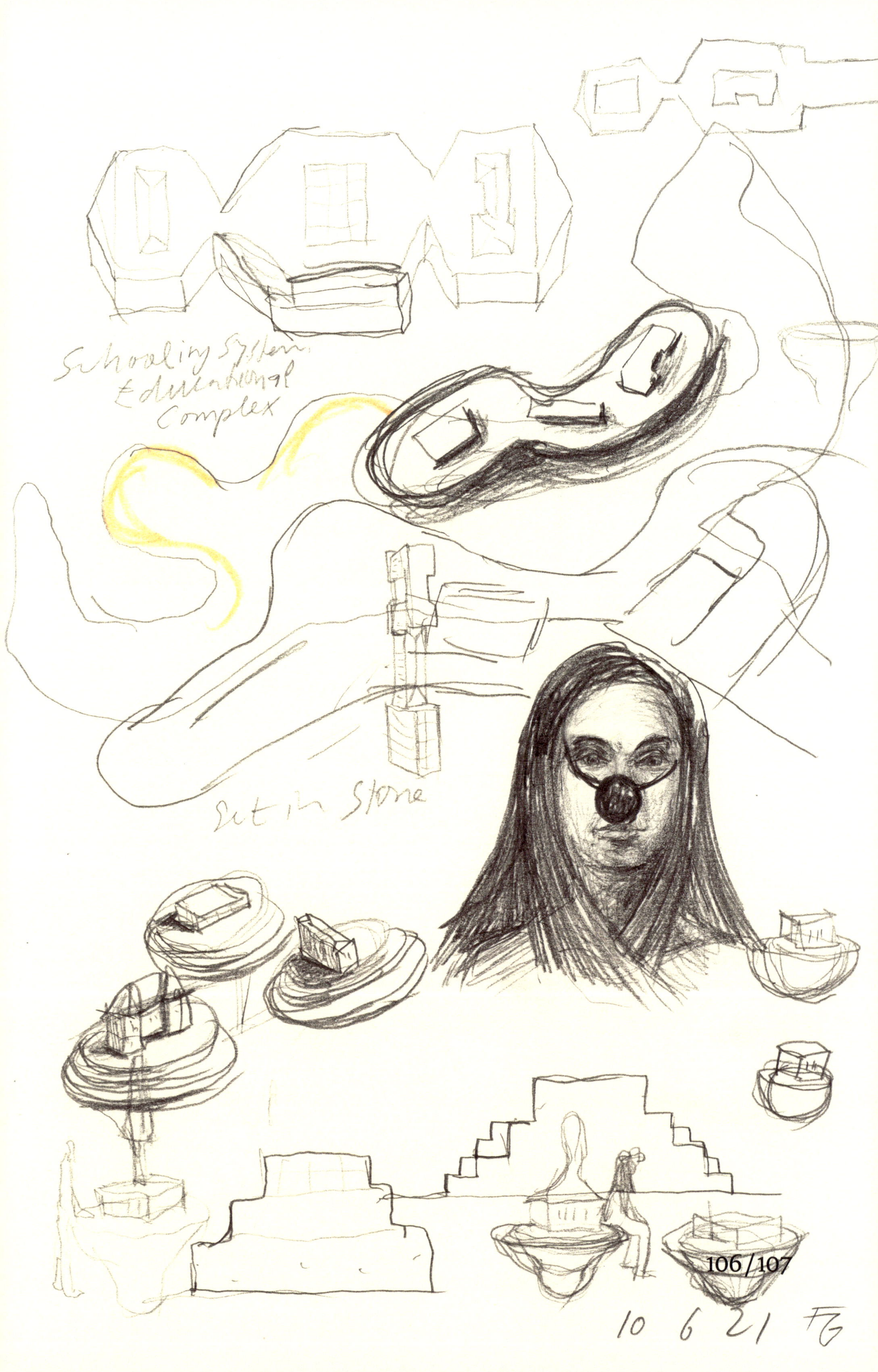
Schooling System
Educational
Complex
Set in Stone
10 6 21 FG

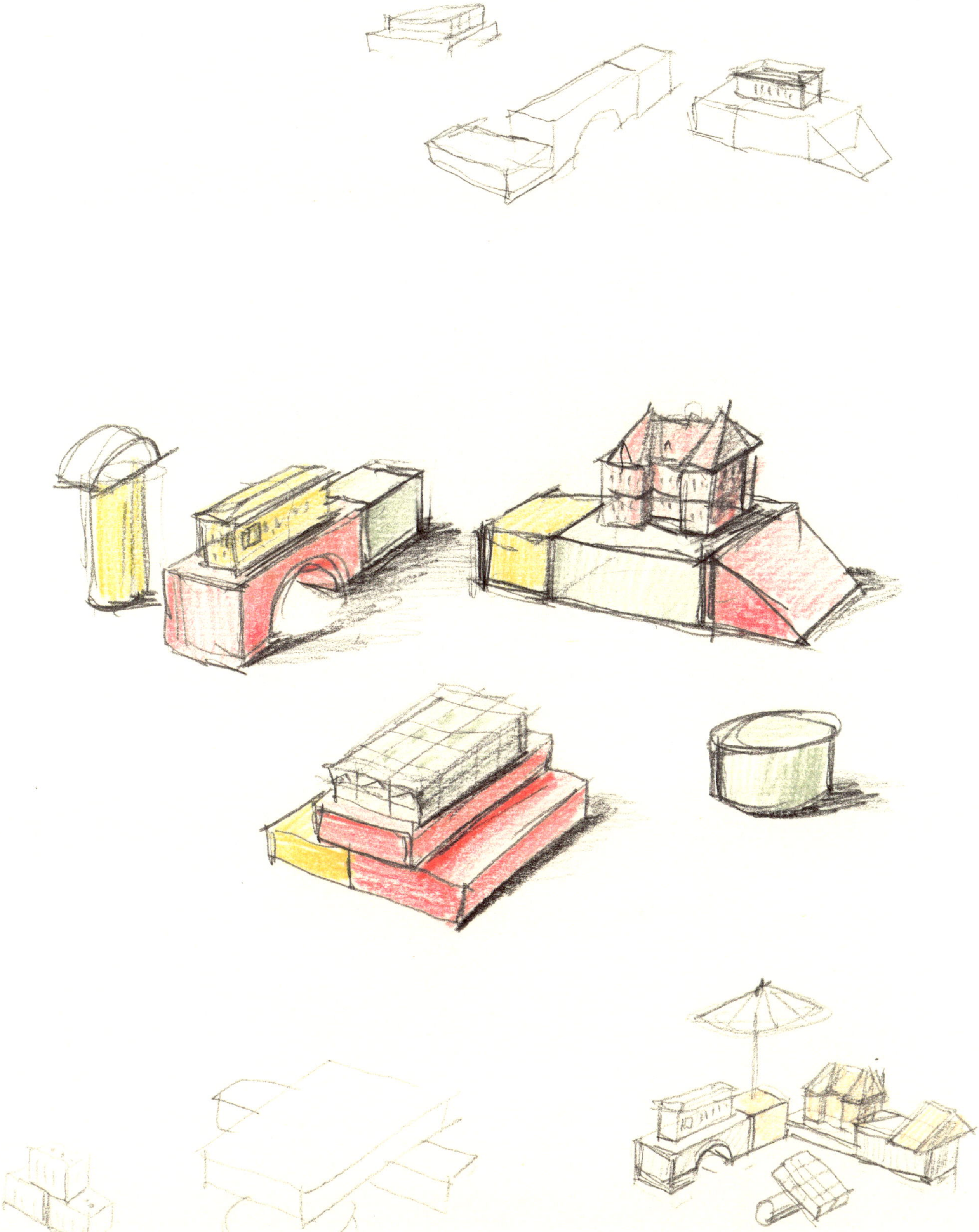

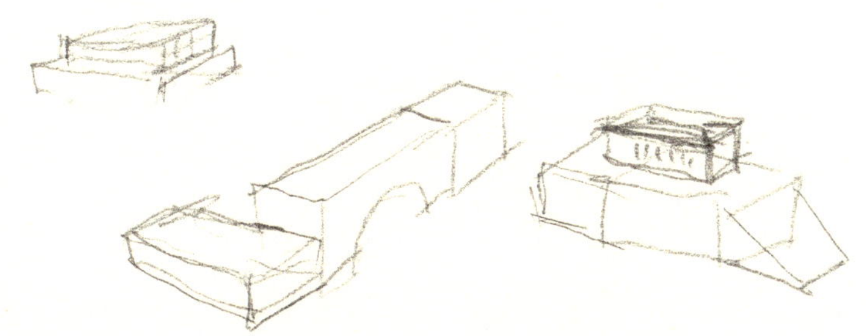

7 7 21

FG

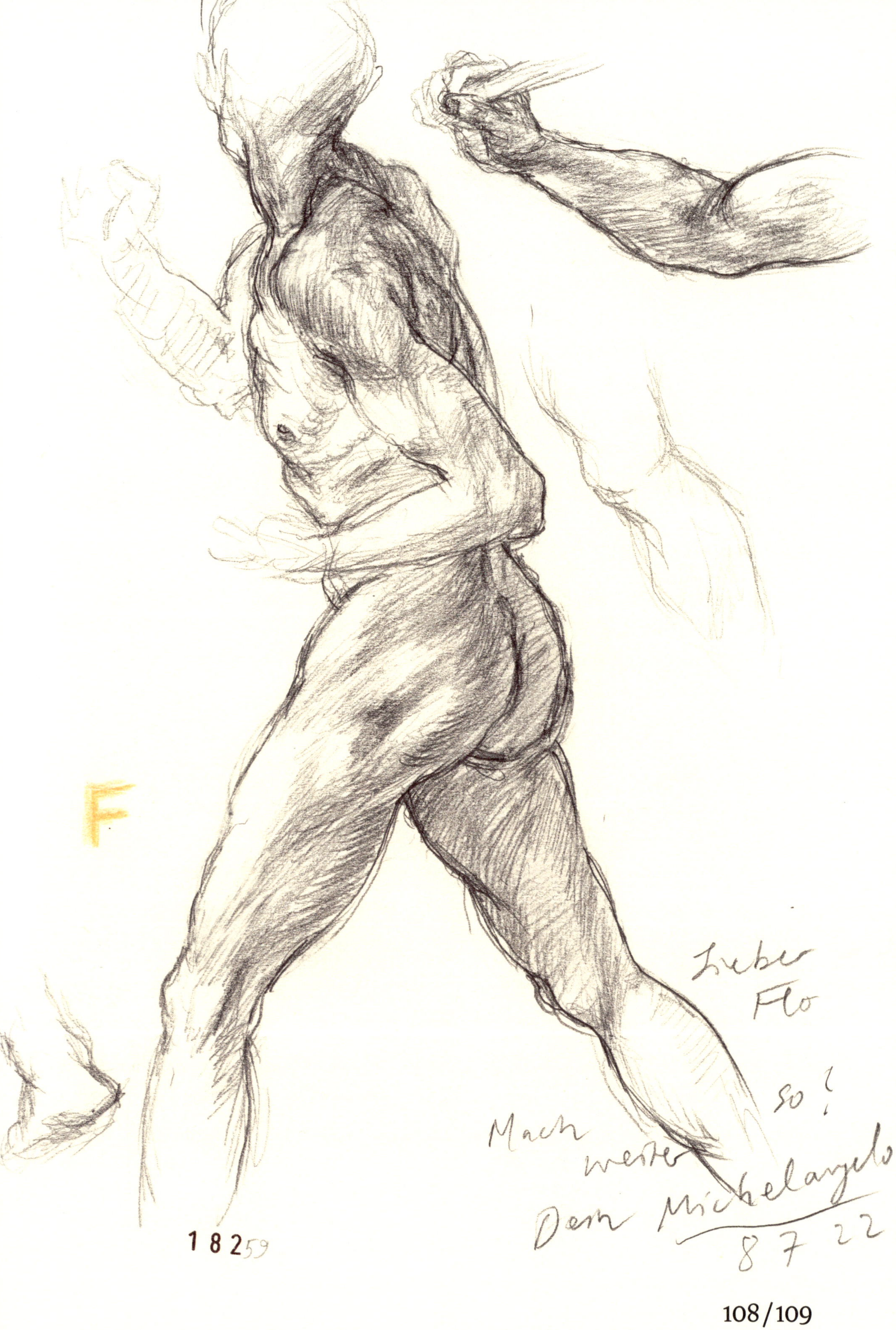
Lieber Flo
Mach weiter so!
Dein Michelangelo
8 7 22

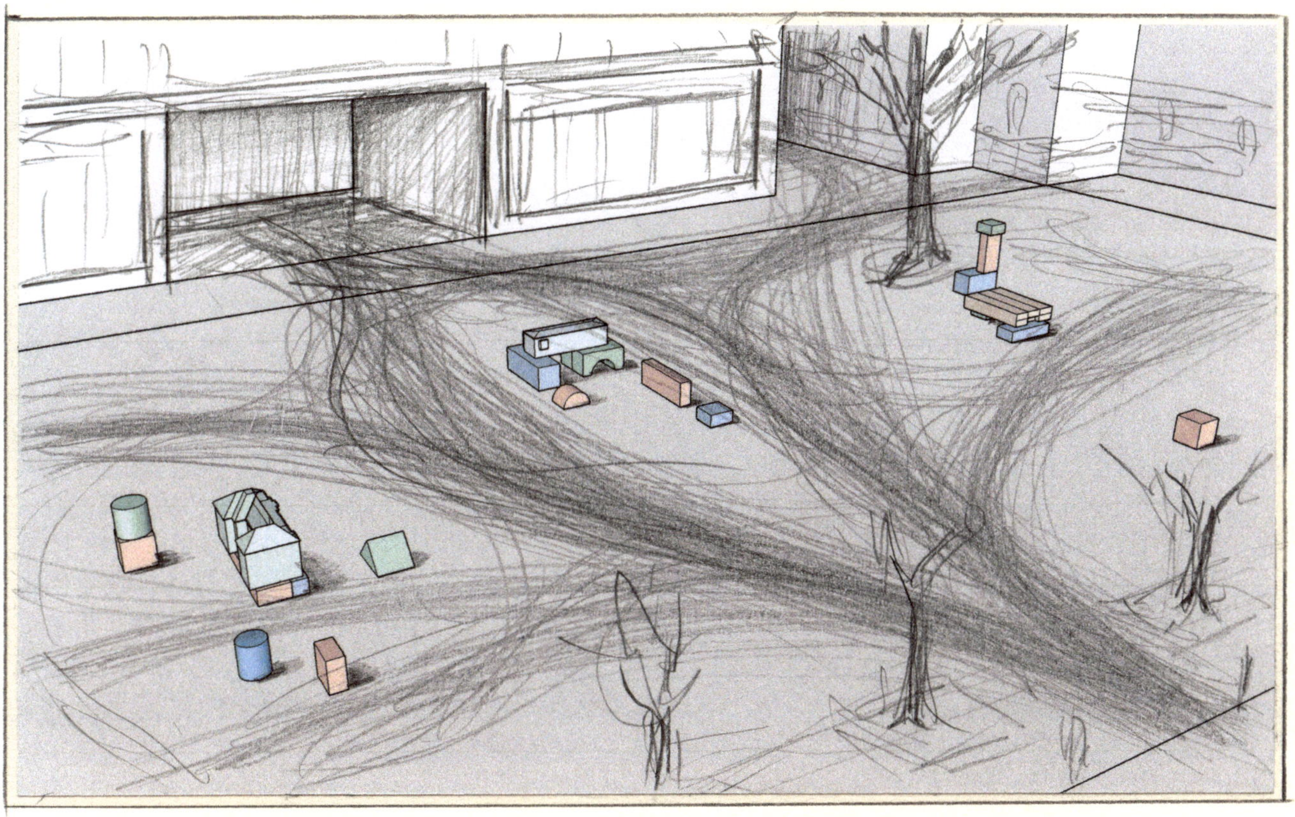

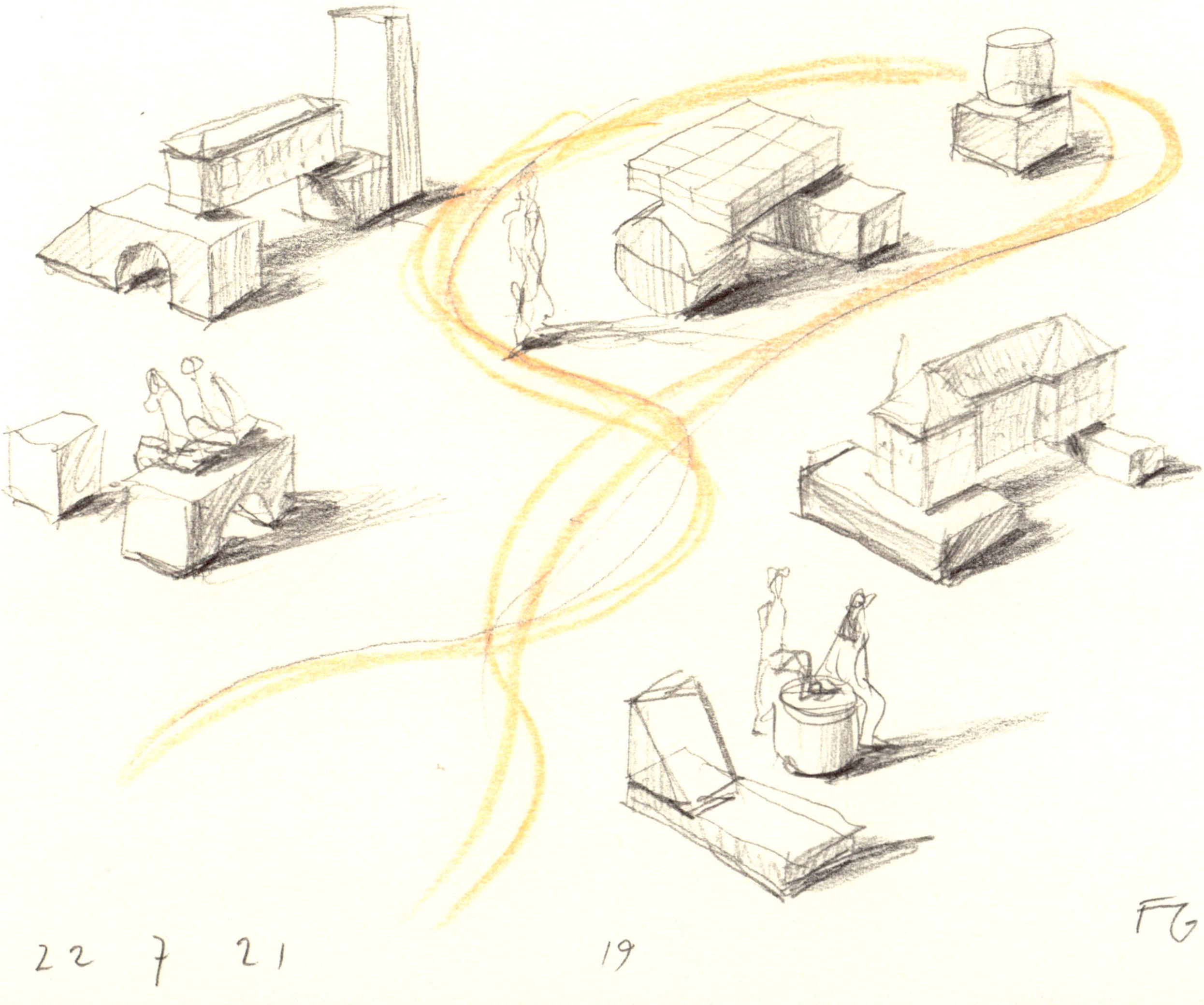

22 7 21 19 FG

183

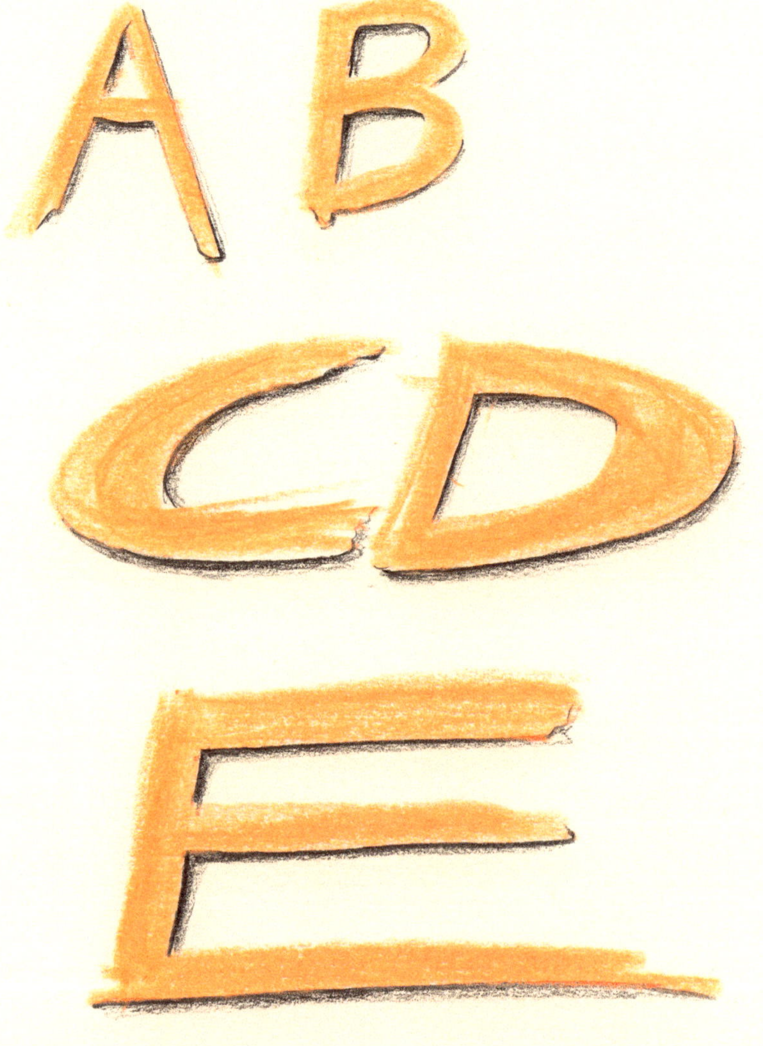

FG

Love
Mystery
(Inter)connectivity
Devotion
Meditation
(Self) Transcendence
Ecstasy
Care
Dialogue (free)
Exchange (social)
Society, (Politics)
Ethics
Zusammenleben
Spiritual Space
Meeting Point
Art
emotional
cognitive
Learning Place
Play Ground
(Self) Reflection
Observation
Understanding
Meaning
System
Experiment
Model Making
Freedom
Rules
Party
Science
Technology
Vita meditativa
(Reflection)
retreat
Vita activa
(Action)
Collaborate

9 10 22

FG

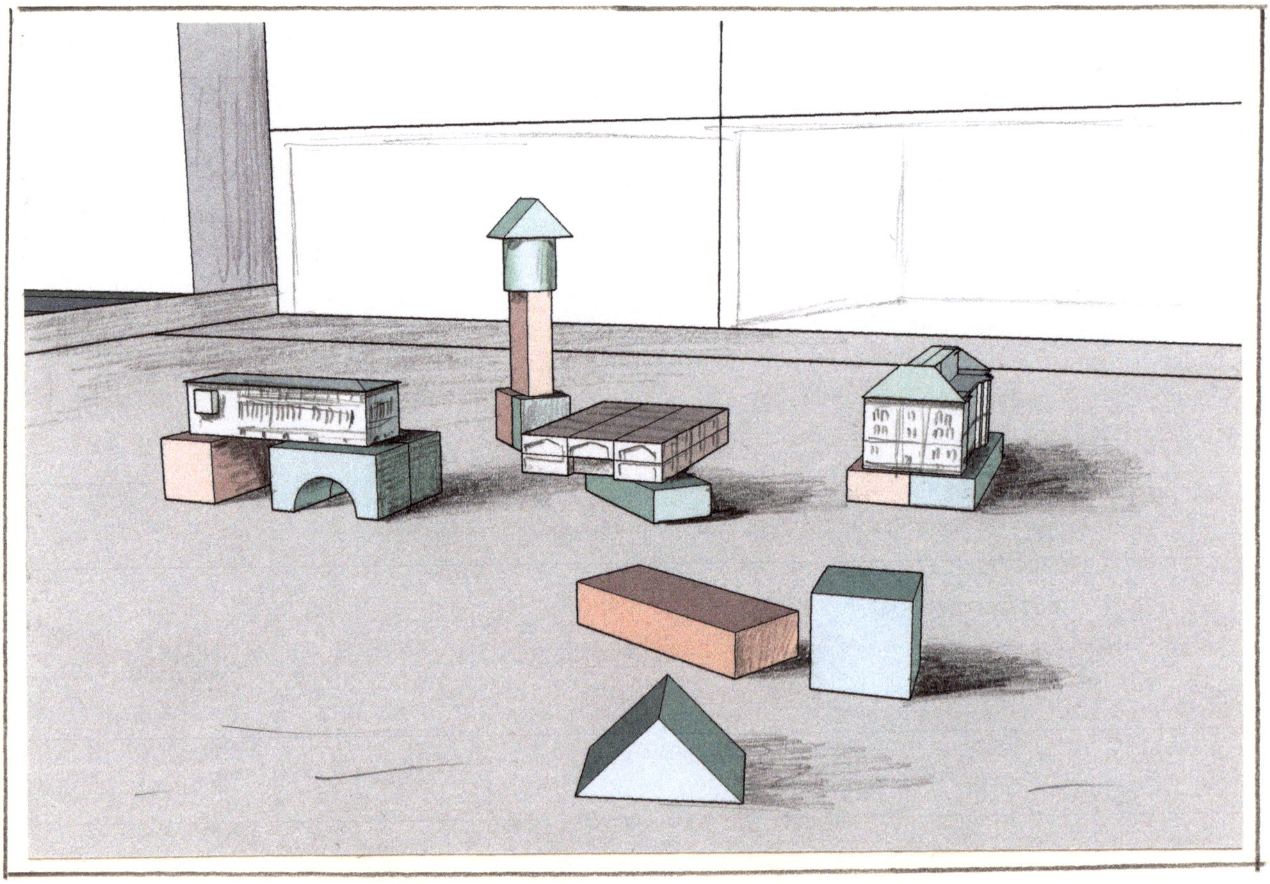

1x ⌀ 30, 60 cm

1x 150 × 60 × 60 cm

2x 120 × 60 × 60

2x 60 × 60 × 60 cm

2x 150 × 60 × 30

2x 240 × 60 × 30 cm

2x 85 × 60 × 42,5 cm

2x 60 × 60 × 30 cm

1x 120 × 60 × 30 cm

77

Fondation?

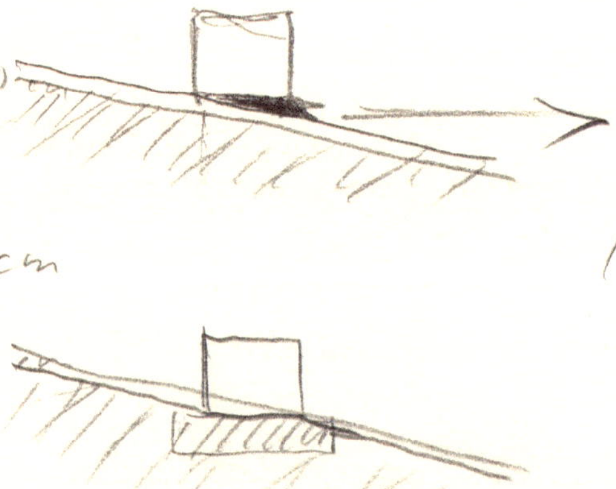

Schatten fuge! (wie hinge- streut gestellt nicht in Grund verankert)

FG

Florian Graf
School Models, 2023
Muschelkalkstein, Terrazzo
Skulpturenensemble:
860 × 780 × 280 cm (total Dimension)

Die Arbeit *School Models* von Florian Graf ist im Rahmen des Neubaus und der Sanierungen der Gebäude der Schulanlage Hofacker in Zürich-Hirslanden entstanden. Die Fachstelle Kunst und Bau, Amt für Hochbauten, Stadt Zürich hatte sieben Künstler*innen eingeladen, ein künstlerisches Projekt für die Schulanlage zu entwickeln. Aus den eingereichten Vorschlägen ging das Projekt von Florian Graf als Sieger hervor.

In der Arbeit bezieht sich Graf direkt auf die besondere architektonische Zusammenstellung des Schulareals, das sich aus drei Gebäuden aus ganz unterschiedlichen Epochen zusammensetzt: aus den zwei denkmalgeschützten Bauten von Friedrich Wehrli (1898) und Hermann Herter (1938) und dem von E2A Architekten 2022 erstellten Neubau. Der Künstler lässt von jedem Schulhaus ein Steinmodell im Verhältnis 1:20 herstellen. Statt die verkleinerten Schulhäuser auf Sockeln zu platzieren, setzt Florian Graf die Modelle auf überdimensionierte Spielklötze mitten auf den Pausenplatz. Die Bausteine aus eingefärbtem Terrazzo und die Schulhäuser aus Muschelkalk können von den Schüler*innen als Sitzgelegenheit benutzt werden. Sie können also ihr Schulhaus beklettern, sich draufsetzen oder auch mal von oben herab auf die Schule schauen. Die Gebäude werden so (an-)fassbar. Florian Grafs Skulpturenensemble ist ein augenzwinkerndes Spiel mit Grössenverhältnissen und mit unserer Wahrnehmung: Es regt dazu an, die Betrachter*innen-Positionen zu wechseln, andere Blickwinkel einzunehmen und sich zwischen Modell und Wirklichkeit zu bewegen.

Als wichtiger Bestandteil des Projektes wurden die *School Models* in einem Schulfest und einem Performance-Programm um und an den neuen Skulpturen eingeweiht. Das Performance-Programm wurde in Zusammenarbeit mit Elise Lammer und dem Cabaret Voltaire, Zürich entwickelt.

Ausführungsplanung und Realisation *School Models*:

- Daniel Friedmann, Projektleiter,
  Amt für Hochbauten, Stadt Zürich
- Franziska Holenstein,
  Schmitt Natursteinwerk AG, Herisau
- Paul Junker,
  Ganz Landschaftsarchitekt*innen GmbH, Zürich
- Christiane Rekade, Projektleiterin,
  Fachstelle Kunst und Bau,
  Amt für Hochbauten, Stadt Zürich
- Urs Schmitt, Schmitt Natursteinwerk AG, Herisau
- Tobias Weise,
  E2A Piet Eckert & Wim Eckert Architekten, Zürich

Schulfest und Performance-Programm:

- Astrid Hänggi und Christoph Widmer,
  Schulleitung Schule Hirslanden Sek
- Marianne Saller, Lehrperson Schule Hirslanden Sek
- Péter Völgyi, Koch Mensa Schulhaus Hofacker
- alle Schüler*innen, Lehrpersonen und Personal
  der Schule Hirslanden Sek
- Raffaela Boss, Charlotte Horn, Künstlerinnen, Basel
- Monster Chetwynd, Künstlerin, Zürich
- Nina Emge, Nils Amadeus Lange, Künstler*innen, Zürich
- Salome Hohl, Direktorin Cabaret Voltaire, Zürich
- Elise Lammer, Kuratorin, Lausanne
- Julie Monot, Künstlerin, Lausanne
- Christiane Rekade, Projektleiterin,
  Fachstelle Kunst und Bau,
  Amt für Hochbauten, Stadt Zürich
- Yorgos Sapountzis, Künstler, Berlin
- Monica Unser, Cabaret Voltaire, Zürich

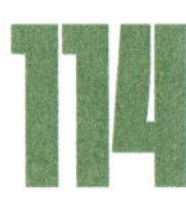

Florian Graf
School Models, 2023
Muschelkalk limestone, terrazzo
Sculptural ensemble:
860 × 780 × 280 cm (overall size)

The work *School Models* by Florian Graf was created as part of the new construction and renovation of the Hofacker school complex in the Zurich-Hirslanden district. The Fachstelle Kunst und Bau, Amt für Hochbauten, Stadt Zürich (Art and Architecture Unit, Building Surveyor's Office, City of Zurich) invited seven artists to develop an artistic project for the school complex. Florian Graf's project emerged as the winner from the proposals submitted.

In the work, Graf makes direct reference to the unique architectural composition of the school complex, which features three buildings from very different eras: the two listed buildings by Friedrich Wehrli (1898) and Hermann Herter (1938) and the new build by E2A Architekten (2022). The artist had a 1:20 stone model made of each building. Instead of placing these models on plinths, Graf placed them on oversized toy building blocks made of colored terrazzo in the middle of the square. The building blocks and the Muschelkalk limestone models of the school buildings can be used by the pupils however they wish. They can clamber over them, sit on them, or even look down on the school from above. This lends the buildings a tangible reality. Graf's sculptural ensemble is a tongue-in-cheek play with proportions and perception: it encourages viewers to move around, adopt different perspectives, and shift between model and reality.

The *School Models* were inaugurated as part of a school festival, which included a performance program based on and around the new sculptures–a key aspect of Graf's project. The performance program was developed in collaboration with Elise Lammer and Cabaret Voltaire, Zurich.

Design and realization of *School Models*:

- Daniel Friedmann, project manager, Amt für Hochbauten, City of Zurich
- Franziska Holenstein, Schmitt Natursteinwerk AG, Herisau
- Paul Junker, Ganz Landschaftsarchitekt*innen GmbH, Zurich
- Christiane Rekade, project manager, Fachstelle Kunst und Bau, Amt für Hochbauten, City of Zurich
- Urs Schmitt, Schmitt Natursteinwerk AG, Herisau
- Tobias Weise, E2A Piet Eckert & Wim Eckert Architekten, Zurich

School festival and performance program:

- Astrid Hänggi and Christoph Widmer, head teachers at Schule Hirslanden Sek
- Marianne Saller, teacher at Schule Hirslanden Sek
- Péter Völgyi, cook, Schulhaus Hofacker canteen
- The students, teachers, and staff at Schule Hirslanden Sek
- Raffaela Boss, Charlotte Horn, artists, Basel
- Monster Chetwynd, artist, Zurich
- Nina Emge, Nils Amadeus Lange, artists, Zurich
- Salome Hohl, director Cabaret Voltaire, Zurich
- Elise Lammer, curator, Lausanne
- Julie Monot, artist, Lausanne
- Christiane Rekade, project manager, Fachstelle Kunst und Bau, Amt für Hochbauten, City of Zurich
- Yorgos Sapountzis, artist, Berlin
- Monica Unser, Cabaret Voltaire, Zurich

Florian Graf

Florian Graf studierte Architektur an der ETH in Zürich und bildende Kunst am Edinburgh College of Art. Er war Postgraduierten-Stipendiat an der Royal Drawing School in London und Fulbright Fellow an der School of the Art Institute of Chicago. Als Student war er Mitbegründer des ETH House of Science in Afghanistan. Er arbeitete mit Robert Wilson in New York, lebte während einer IAAB-Residency in Berlin, in Rom als Stipendiat im Istituto Svizzero und, nach einiger Zeit in Athen, als Stipendiat an der Cité Internationale des Arts in Paris. Seither ist Florian Graf durch Ausstellungen in Museen und Galerien und durch Kunstprojekte im öffentlichen Raum international präsent. Er erhielt mehrere Auszeichnungen, darunter den Swiss Art Award, das DAAD-Stipendium, das Stipendium der Sommerakademie im Zentrum Paul Klee und den Prix Visarte. Sein Werk wurde weit verbreitet publiziert und befindet sich in namhaften Sammlungen.

Florian Graf

Florian Graf studied architecture at the ETH in Zurich and fine art at the Edinburgh College of Art. He was a postgraduate scholar at the Royal Drawing School in London and a Fulbright Fellow at the School of the Art Institute of Chicago. As a student, he was a co-founder of the ETH House of Science in Afghanistan and subsequently worked with Robert Wilson in New York. He has lived in Berlin during an IAAB-residency, in Rome as a member of the Istituto Svizzero and, after some time in Athens, as a scholar at the Cité Internationale des Arts in Paris. Since then, he has had an international presence through exhibitions in museums and galleries and art projects in public space. His work has received several prizes, including the Swiss Art Award, a DAAD scholarship, a fellowship from the Sommerakademie Paul Klee, and the Prix Visarte. His work has been widely published and can be found in a number of prominent collections.

Dank

Mein Dank für dieses Projekt gilt Urs Schmitt und Franziska Holenstein von Schmitt Natursteinwerk AG für die professionelle und anregende Zusammenarbeit. Vielen Dank auch an Christiane Rekade. Ihre kuratorische Projektbetreuung war eine grosse Bereicherung. Vielen Dank an Astrid Hänggi und Christoph Widmer von der Schule Hirslanden Sek. Sie haben mit ihrer Offenheit und mit viel Einsatz das Fest ermöglicht und unterstützt. Herzlichen Dank auch an Elise Lammer und Salome Hohl für ihre kuratorische Mitarbeit am Fest und tausend Dank den beteiligten Künstler*innen für ihre wunderbaren Performance-Beiträge. Zuletzt möchte ich noch herzlich den Autor*innen Yasmin Afschar, Teresa Fankhänel und Dominique Laleg und den Grafiker*innen Martin Stoecklin und Melina Wilson danken, mit denen ich gemeinsam dieses Buch gestalten durfte.

Mein Dank gilt ausserdem den Menschen, die mich in den letzten Jahren unterstützt und begleitet haben, meiner Familie, meinen Freund*innen und all den Künstler*innen und Kolleg*innen, mit denen ich in inspirierendem Austausch sein darf. Auf der gegenüberliegende Seite möchte ich diejenigen erwähnen, ohne die schlussendlich auch dieses Projekt nicht möglich gewesen wäre. →

Acknowledgements

My thanks for this project go to Urs Schmitt and Franziska Holenstein of Schmitt Natursteinwerk AG for their professional engagement and the inspiring process of collaboration. I would also like to thank Christiane Rekade. Her curation and management of the project were a great asset. Many thanks too to Astrid Hänggi and Christoph Widmer from the Hirslanden Secondary School, who made the festival possible and whose openness and dedication were an invaluable support; to Elise Lammer and Salome Hohl for their curatorial work at the festival; and to the participating artists for their wonderful performances.

Finally, I would like to thank the authors Yasmin Afschar, Teresa Fankhänel, and Dominique Laleg and the graphic designers Martin Stoecklin, and Melina Wilson, my fellow creators of this book, as well as the people who have supported me over the last few years, my family, my friends, and all the artists and colleagues who have provided me with inspiration in our discussions of the work. On the opposite page, I would like to give a mention to all the many contributors who helped bring the project to fruition. →

Basma Abu-Naim, Katharina Ammann, Mark Angélil, Charles Asprey, Ursula Badrutt, Simon Baier, Tenzing Barshee, Daniel Baumann, Isabel Belherdis, Andrey Bartenev, Lisa Beck, Philippe Beck, Andreas Beyer, Mladen Bizumic, Rinny Biberstein, Alexandra Blättler, Ayako Bornhäusser, Michael Bornhäusser, Hugh Brady, Kathleen Bühler, Jacqueline Burckhardt, Ralph Bürgin, Dieter Brunner, Heidi Brunnschweiler, Robert Böcklin, Benedikt Boucsein, Renata Burckhardt, Gion A. Caminada, Giovanni Carmine, Gian Luigi Cavalli della Torre di Porto Corsini, Zhenya Chaika, Efi Chalikopoulou, Stefan Charles, Jessica Cochran, Melanie Dankbar, Raphael Dietschy, Clementine Deliss, Nele Dechmann, Pierre de Meuron, Nikola Dietrich, Christoph Doswald, Gabriel Eckenstein, Marianne Eigenheer, Sebastian Engelhorn, Jacqueline Falk, Elena Filipovic, Christian Flamm, Fabrizio Fracassi, Thomas Geiger, Joël Gessler, Hedy Graber, Aglaia Graf, Agnete Graf, Daria Graf, Peter-Lukas Graf, Damian Grieder, Patrice Gruner, Adrian Hagenbach, Nora Halpern, Zuni Halpern, Vilhelm Hammershøi, Beatrice Hatebur, Jakob A. Hauser, Irène Hediger, Tamara Henderson, Dunja Herzog, Jacques Herzog, Helen Hirsch, Stefanie Hirsch, Benjamin Hirte, Sven Hoffmann, Jan Hostettler, Nicola Hüll, Lea Hummel, Axel Humpert, Melli Ink, Moritz Josch, Anastasia Kandoba, Tony Karman, Bettina Kaufmann, Sabine Kaufmann, Aida Kidane, Kevin Klapka, Christoph Klauke, Nils Kohler, Diemut Köstlin, Clemens Köstlin, Markus Krajewski, Schirin Kretschmann, Stefanie Kreuzer, Hans Landolt, Michaela Langenstein, Max Leiß, Samuel Leuenberger, Nathalie Loch, Kairi Look, Luca Lo Pinto, Andrea Lötscher, Silvia Lüdi-Sokalski, Felicity Lunn, Melissa MacRobert, Anna Matevosyan, Philippe Meerwein, Dorothee Messmer, Massimo Milano, Frank-Thorsten Moll, Giorgio Morandi, Chrissie Muhr, Dominik Müller, Tobias Mueller, Michael Newman, Caroline Nicod, Sascha Nikitin, Laura Niklaus, Eva Oertle, Gregory Olympio, Olga Osadtschy, Camillo Paravicini, Flurina Paravicini, Giacomo Paravicini, Gianni Paravicini, David Pia, Bianca Pedrina, Manfred Pernice, Paula Pöpl, Markus Raetz, Nadine Reinert, Max Renkel, Isabella Ritter, Werner Rohner, Denis Roueche, Viviane Ruof, Tom Ryhiner, Karin Sander, Claudia Schachenmann, Christoph Schifferli, Lea Schleiffenbaum, Hagar Schmidhalter, Sebastian Schmitt, Johannes Schneider, Benno Schubiger, Florian Schweighauser, Moritz Schweighauser, Sandra Sheckter, Kiki Seiler-Michalitsi, Daniela Settelen-Trees, Christine Siegfried, Jeremy Siegfried, Joël Siegfried, Felix Siegrist, Miroslav Šik, Francisco Sierra, Dominique Simonnot, Katrin Sperry, Emil Steinberger, Niccel Steinberger, Dominique Stich-Jehle, Andrea Stieger, Noah Stolz, Agustina Strüngmann, Pierre-Jean Sugier, Daniel Sutovsky, Simmy Swinder Voellmy, Jan Teunen, Daniel Blaise Thorens, Reto Thüring, Iris Touliatou, Ralph Ubl, Philip Ursprung, Esmé Valk, Oriol Vilanova, Philipp Voellmy, Valerie von der Malsburg, Seraina Von Laer, Benedikt von Peter, Jolanda Wackernagel, Renate Wagner, Yves Waldmann, Leopold Weinberg, Carole Wiesmann, Robert Wilson, Nikolai Winter, Pedro Wirz, Brigitte Wyss-Sponagel, Chiona Xanthopoulou-Schwarz, Thomas Zacharias, Nina Zimmer, Annina Zimmermann, Vania Zschokke, Marco Zünd

Bildnachweis/Photo credits

Charlotte Aeb	S./p. 14
Stefan Altenburger Photography Zürich	S./pp. 121–130, Umschlag/Cover
Katja Bode	S./p. 10
Florian Graf	S./pp. 16–29, S./p. 31, S./p. 38, S./p. 46, S./pp. 97–112
Romain Mader	S./pp. 49–80
Christiane Rekade	S./p. 30, S./p. 32
Martin Stoecklin	S./pp. 1–2, S./p. 4, S./p. 40, S./p. 48, S./pp. 131–132
Annik Wetter	S./p. 8
Seraina Wirz	S./p. 87 oben/top, S./p. 95 oben/top
Wolf-Bender's Erben/heirs, Baugeschichtliches Archiv, ETHZ	S./p. 87 unten/bottom, S./p. 95 unten/bottom
	S./p. 84 oben/top, S./p. 92 oben/top
unbekannt/unknown, Baugeschichtliches Archiv, ETHZ	S./p. 84 unten/bottom, S./p. 92 unten/bottom

Impressum/Colophon

Diese Publikation erscheint anlässlich der Fertigstellung des Kunst-und-Bau-Werkes *School Models*, 2023 von Florian Graf für die Schule Hofacker in Zürich./This book is published to mark the completion of Florian Graf's art and architecture project *School Models*, 2023, for the Hofacker School in Zurich.

Konzept/Concept: Florian Graf und/and Yasmin Afschar
Lektorat und Korrektorat: Dorit Aurich
Translations, copy editing, and proofreading: Tradukas GbR
Visuelles Konzept und Gestaltung/Visual concept and design: Stoecklin & Wilson, Zürich, a-language.net
Lithografie/Image processing: Marjeta Morinc
Schriften/Typefaces: Mosaic, Maxitype; Herbik, Counterforms
Druck und Bindung/Printing and binding: DZA Druckerei zu Altenburg

Verlag Scheidegger & Spiess
Niederdorfstrasse 54
8001 Zürich
Schweiz/Switzerland
www.scheidegger-spiess.ch

ISBN 978-3-03942-250-0

Der Verlag Scheidegger & Spiess wird vom Bundesamt für Kultur mit einem Strukturbeitrag für die Jahre 2021–2025 unterstützt./Scheidegger & Spiess is being supported by the Federal Office of Culture with a general subsidy for the years 2021–2025.

unterstützt von/supported by:

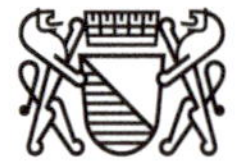

Stadt Zürich

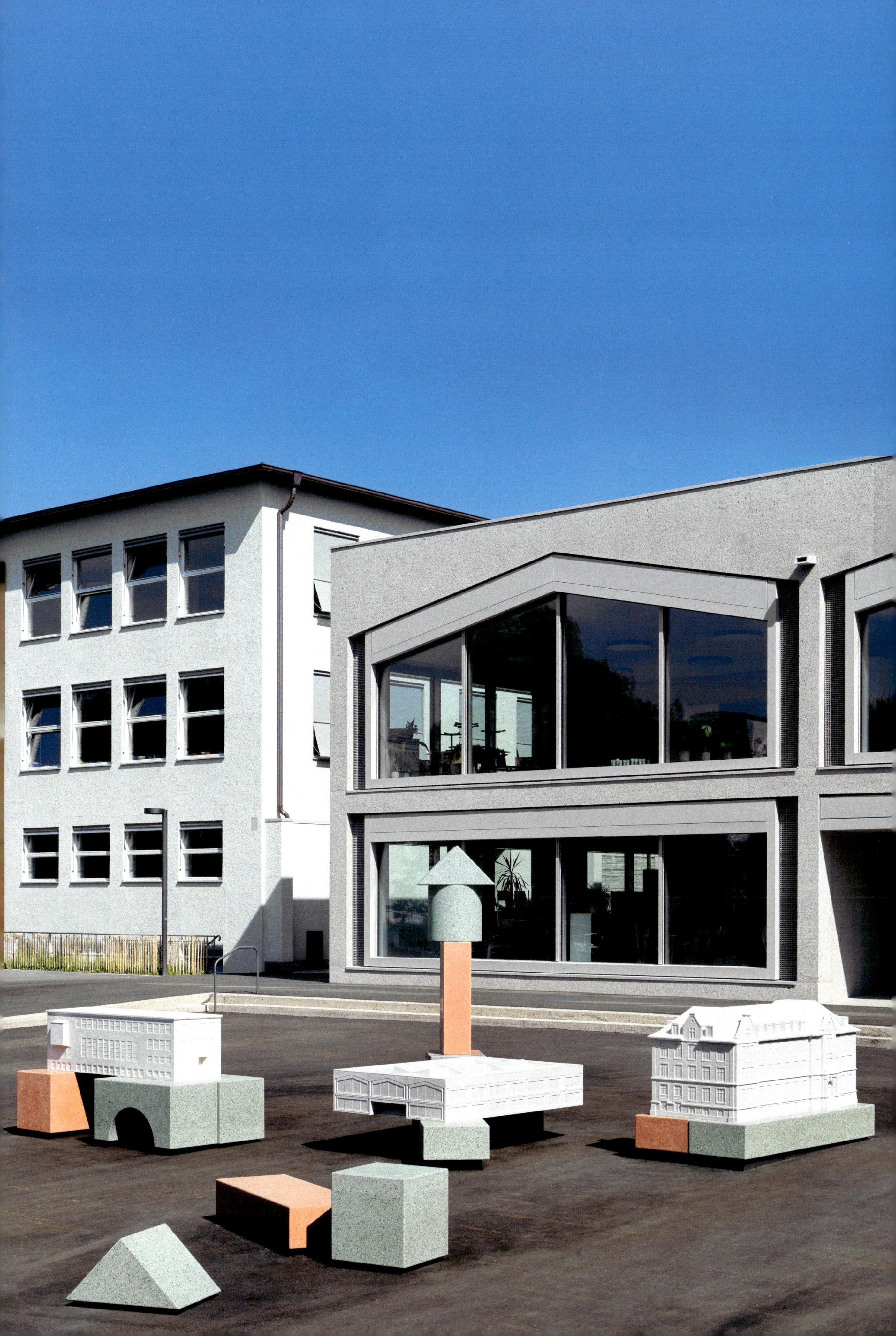

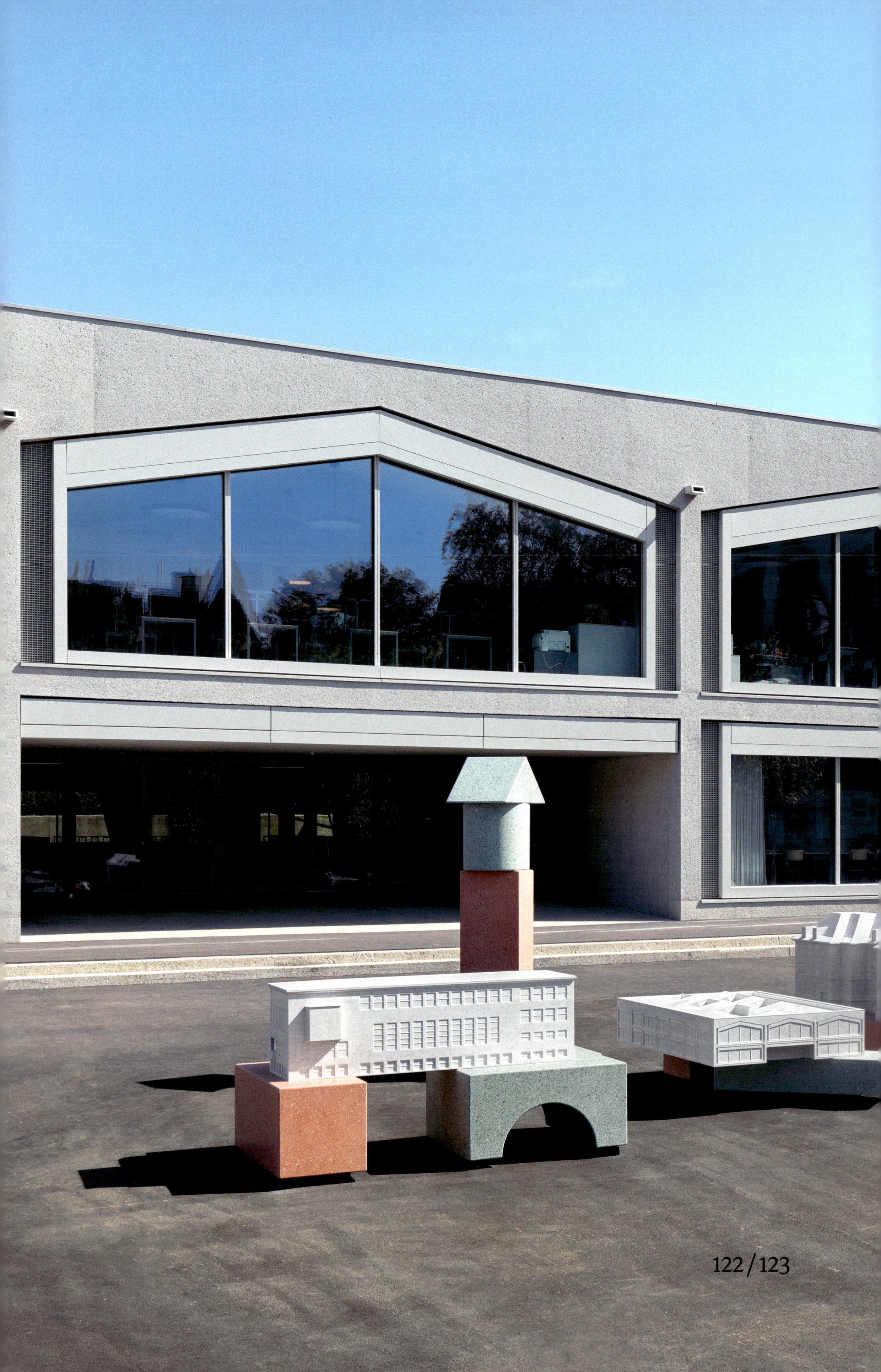

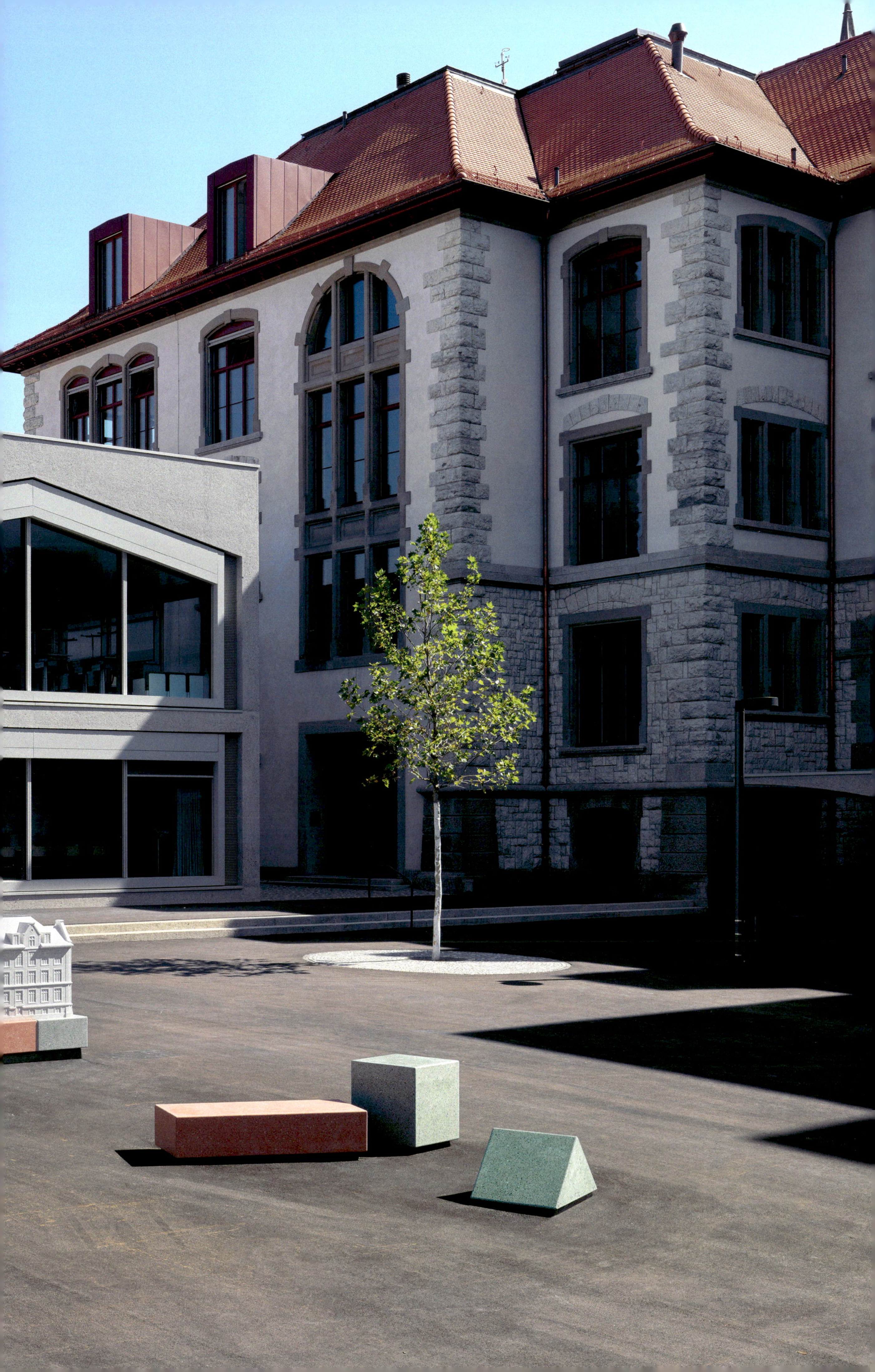

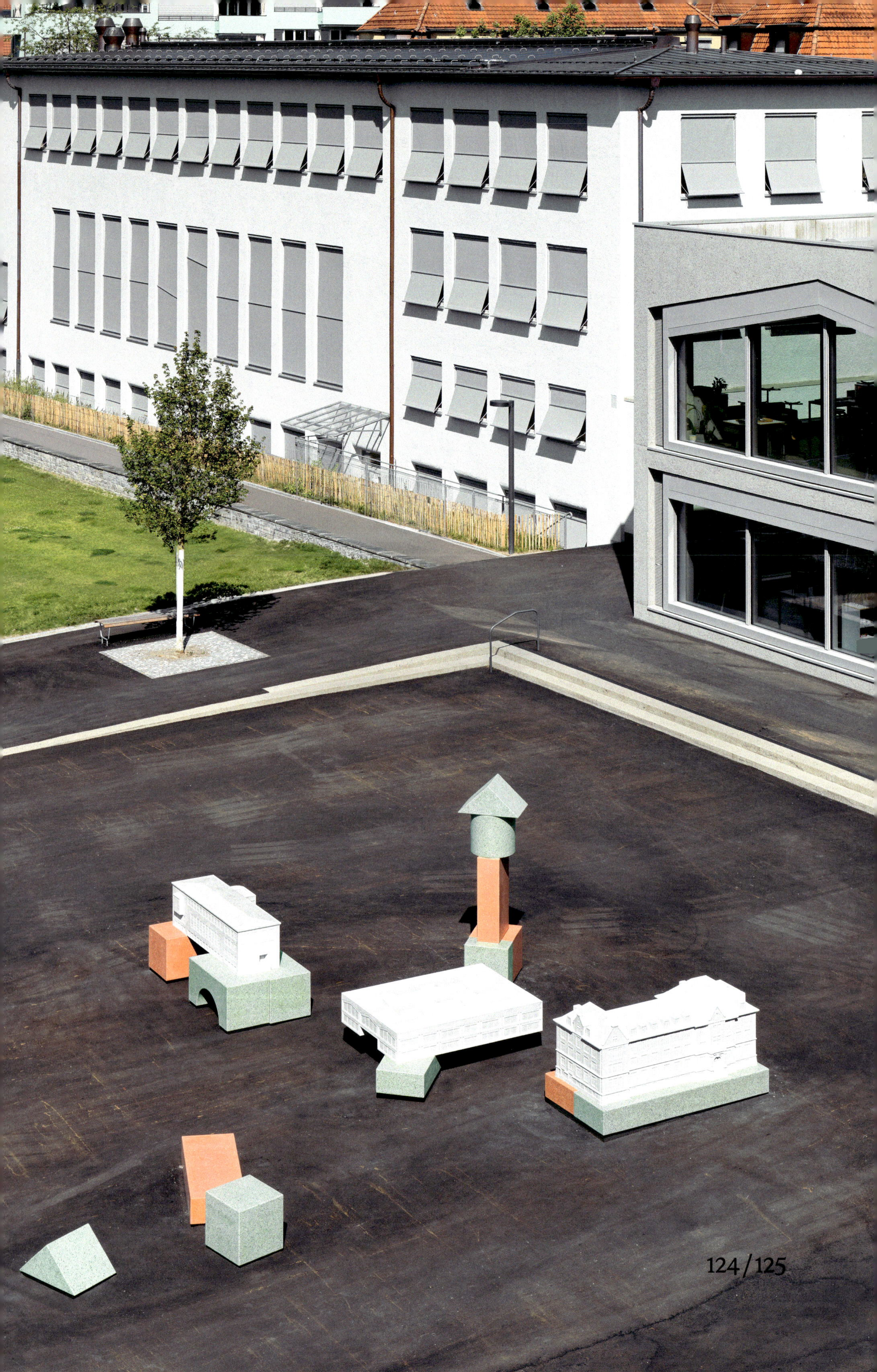

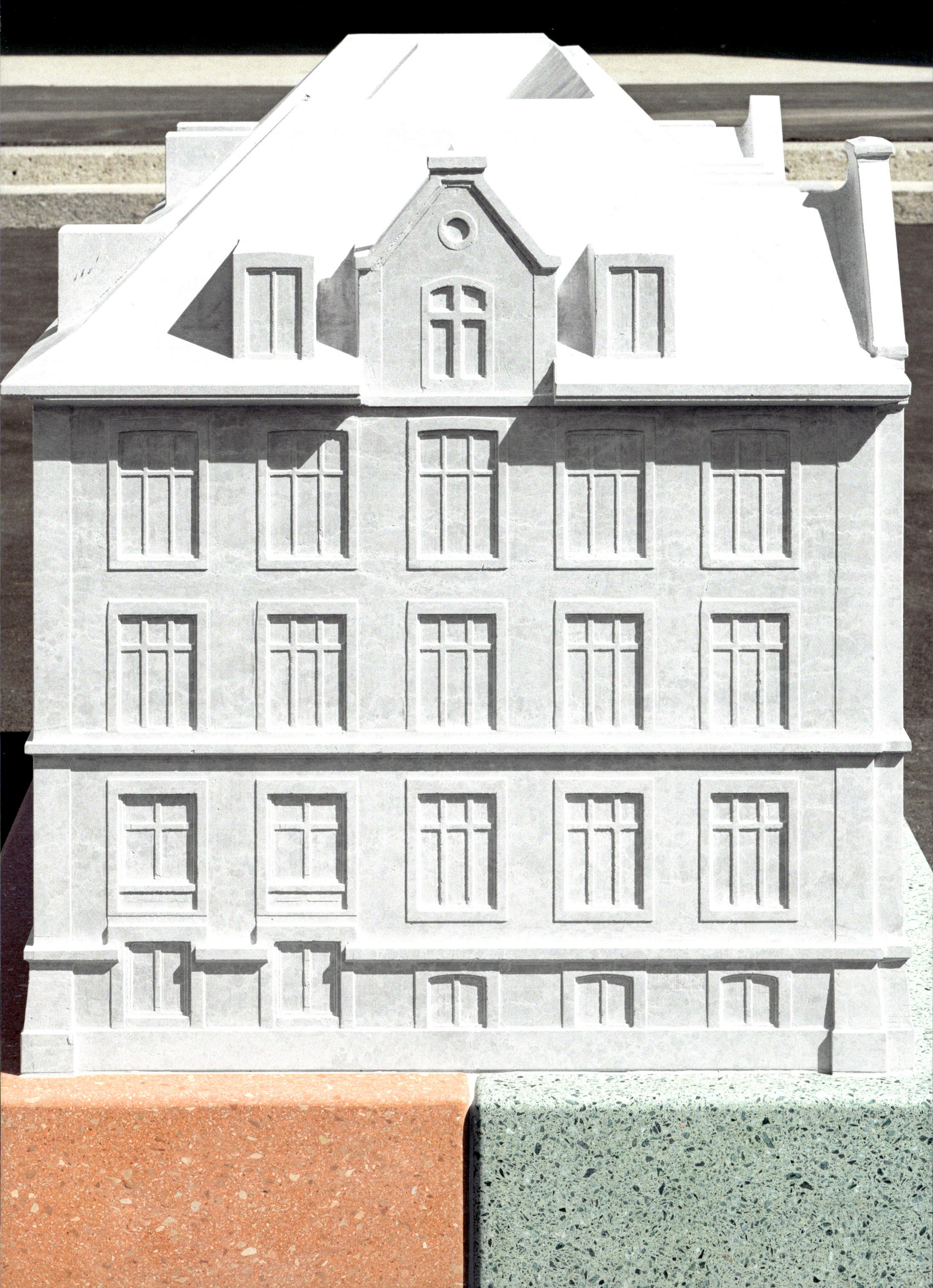

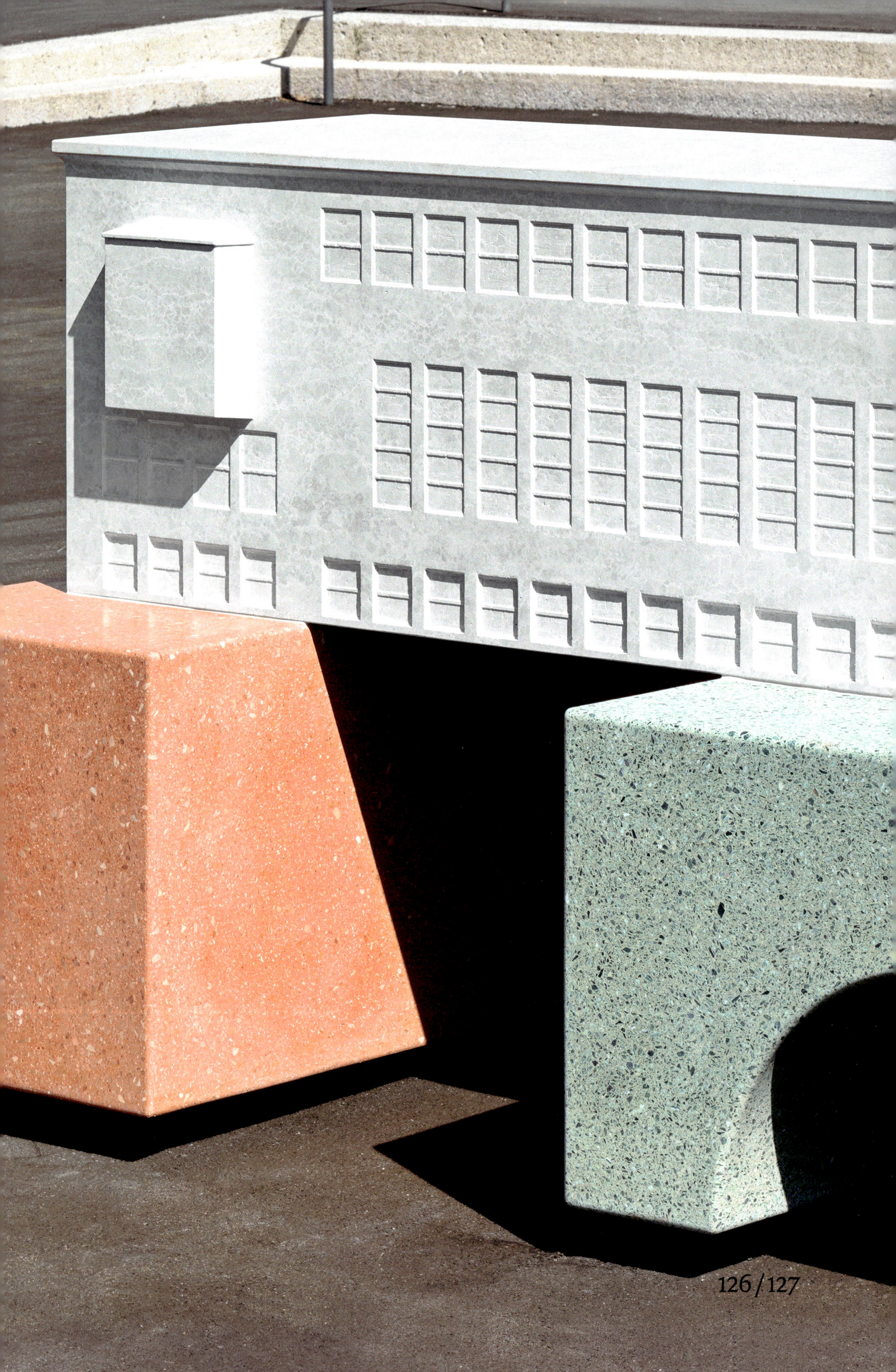

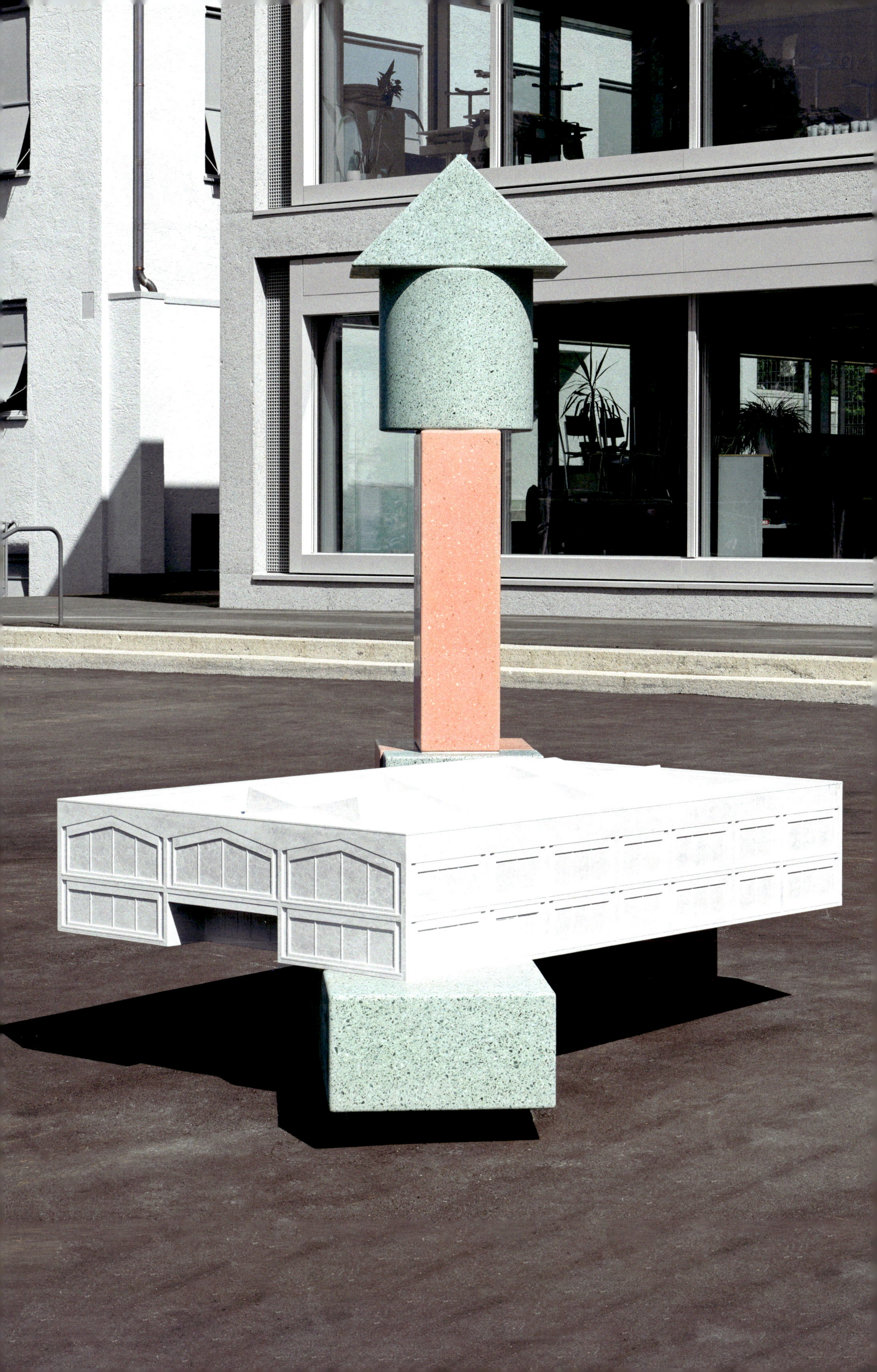

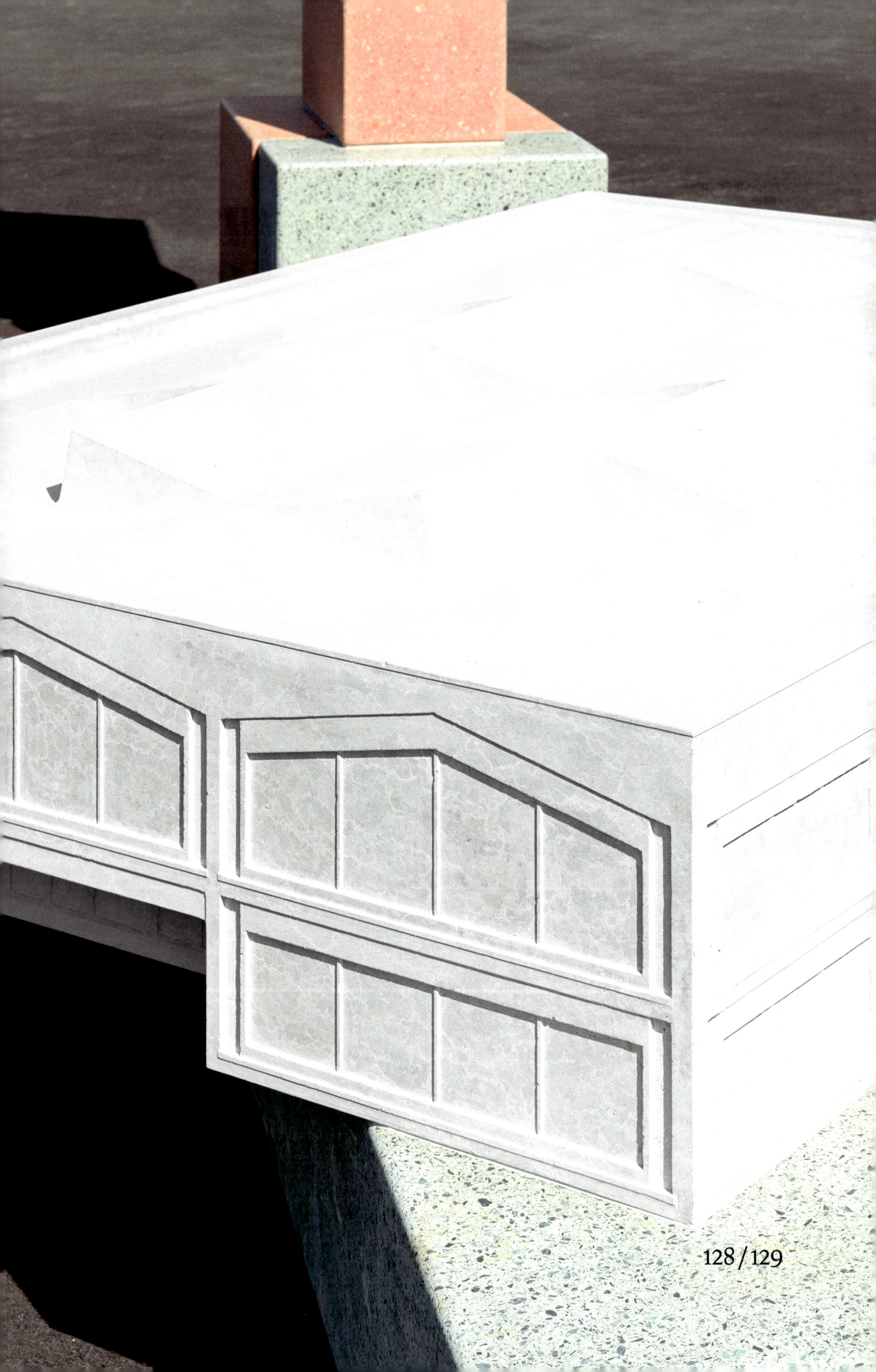

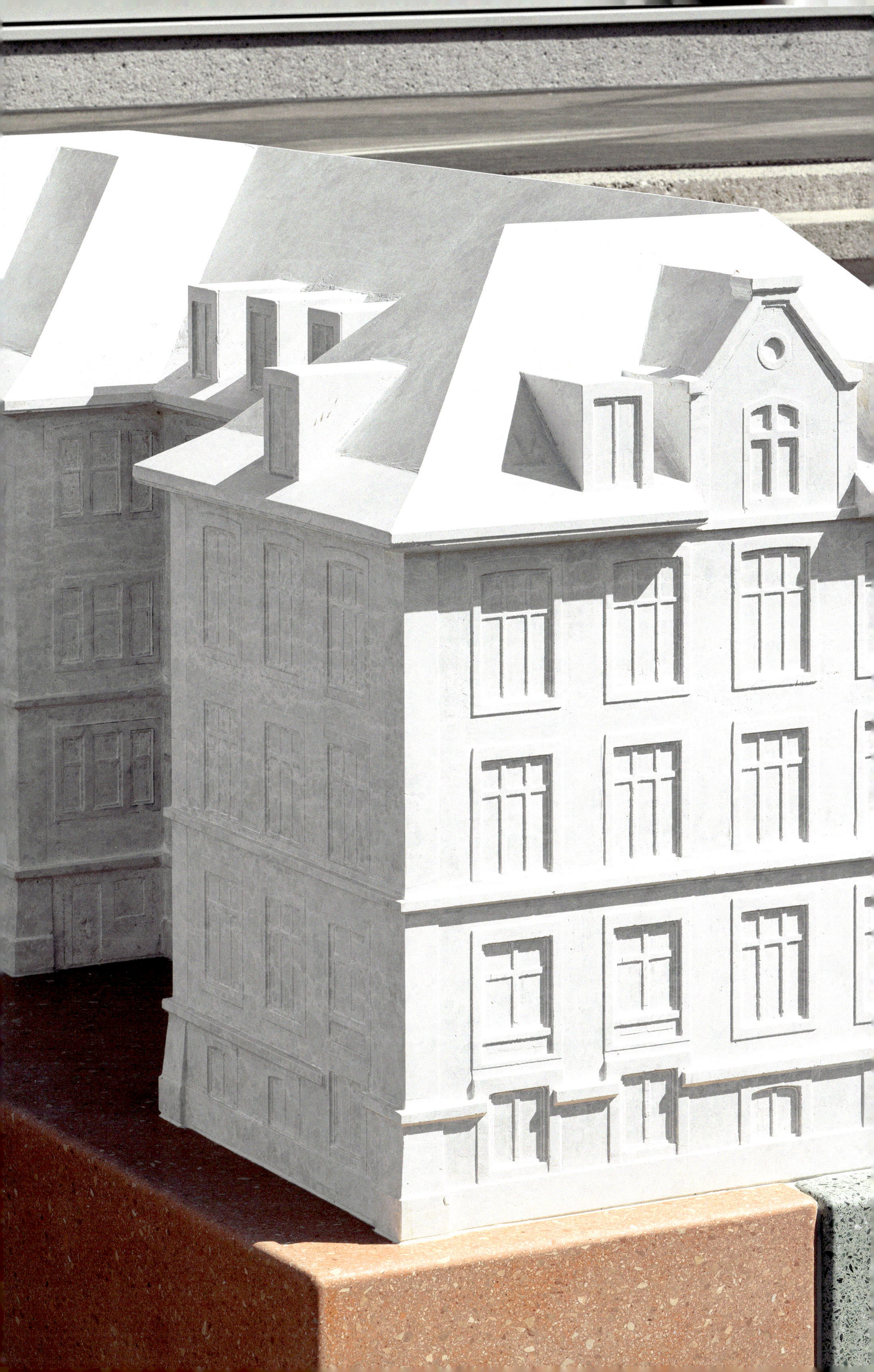

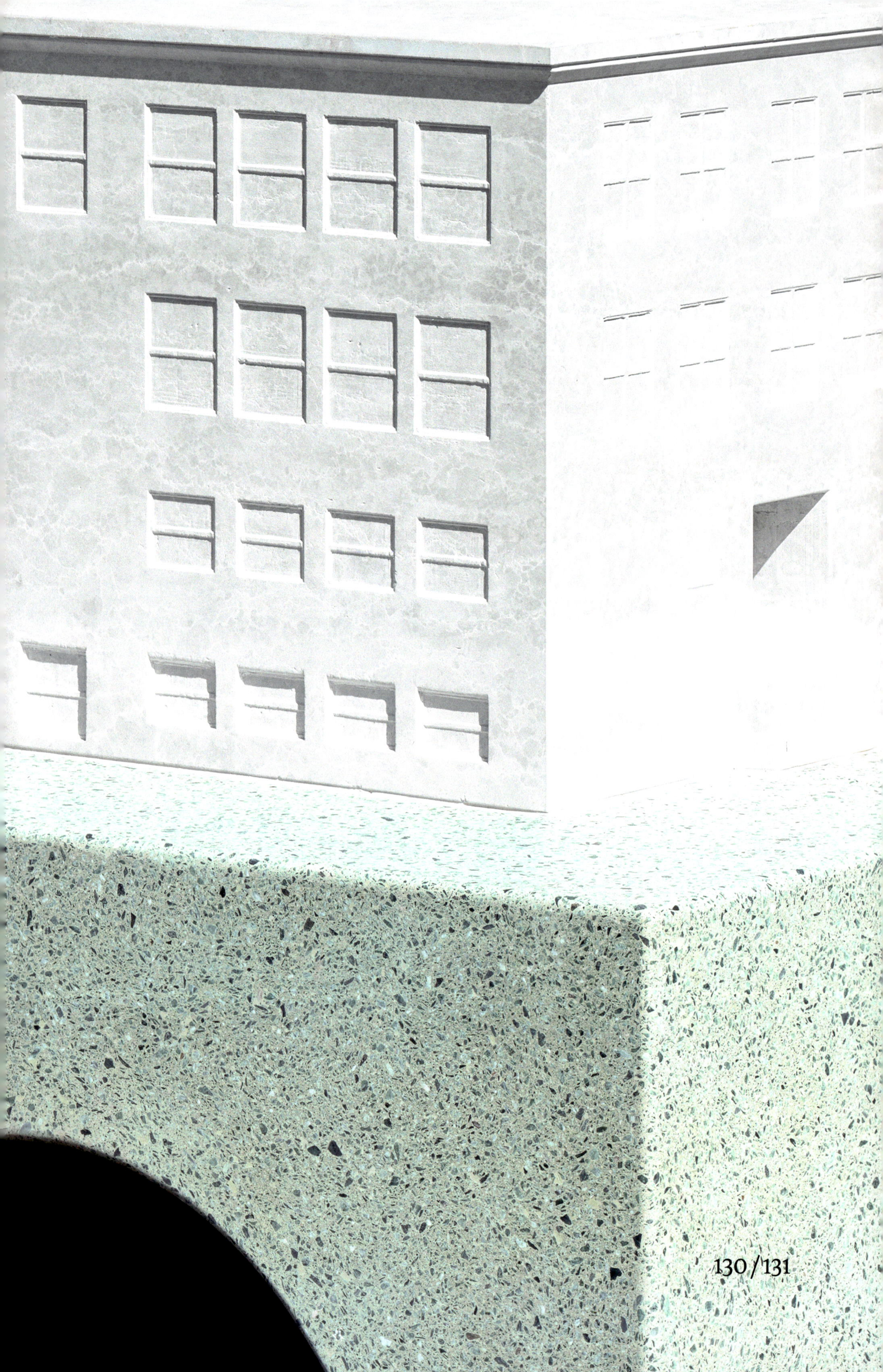

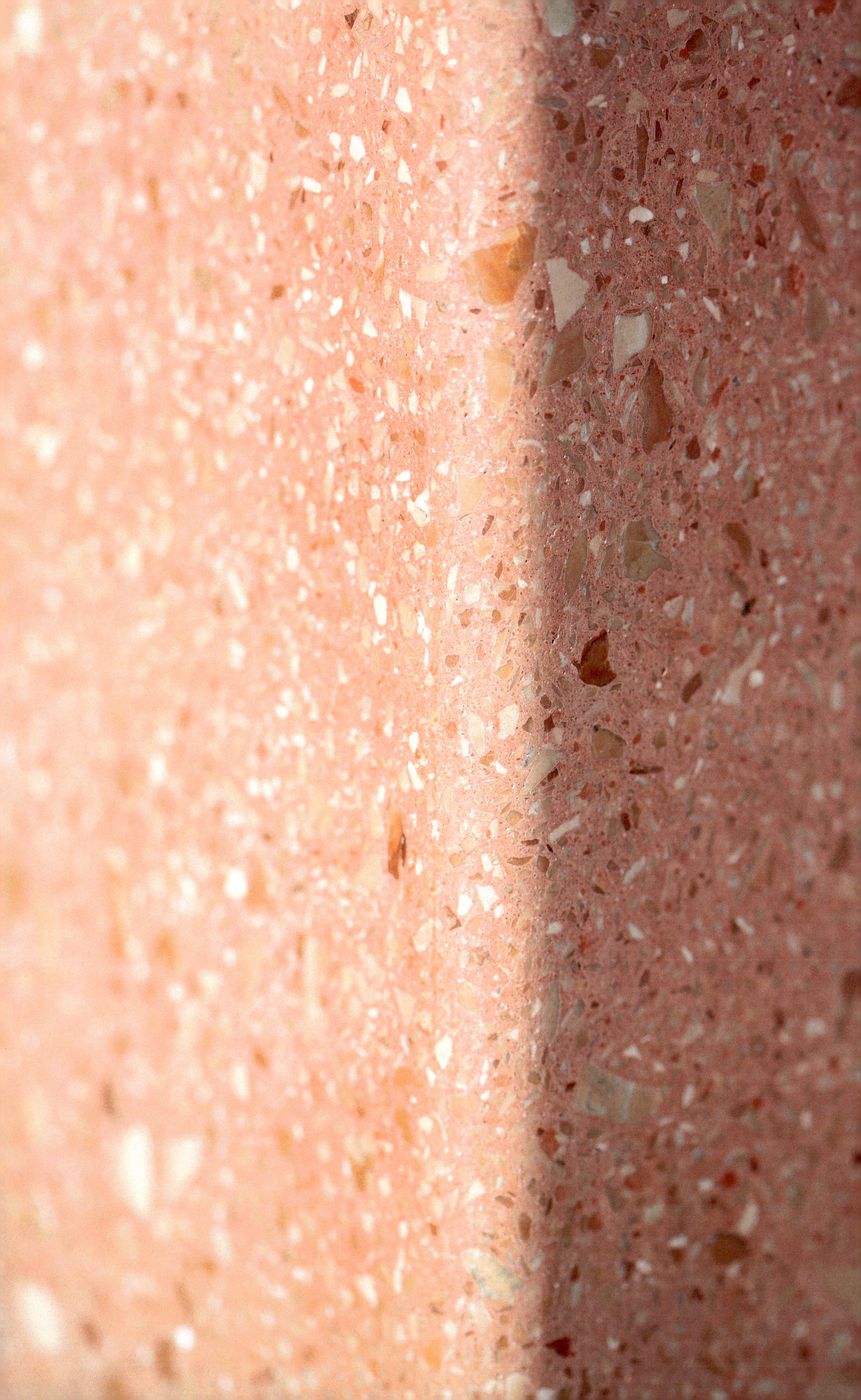

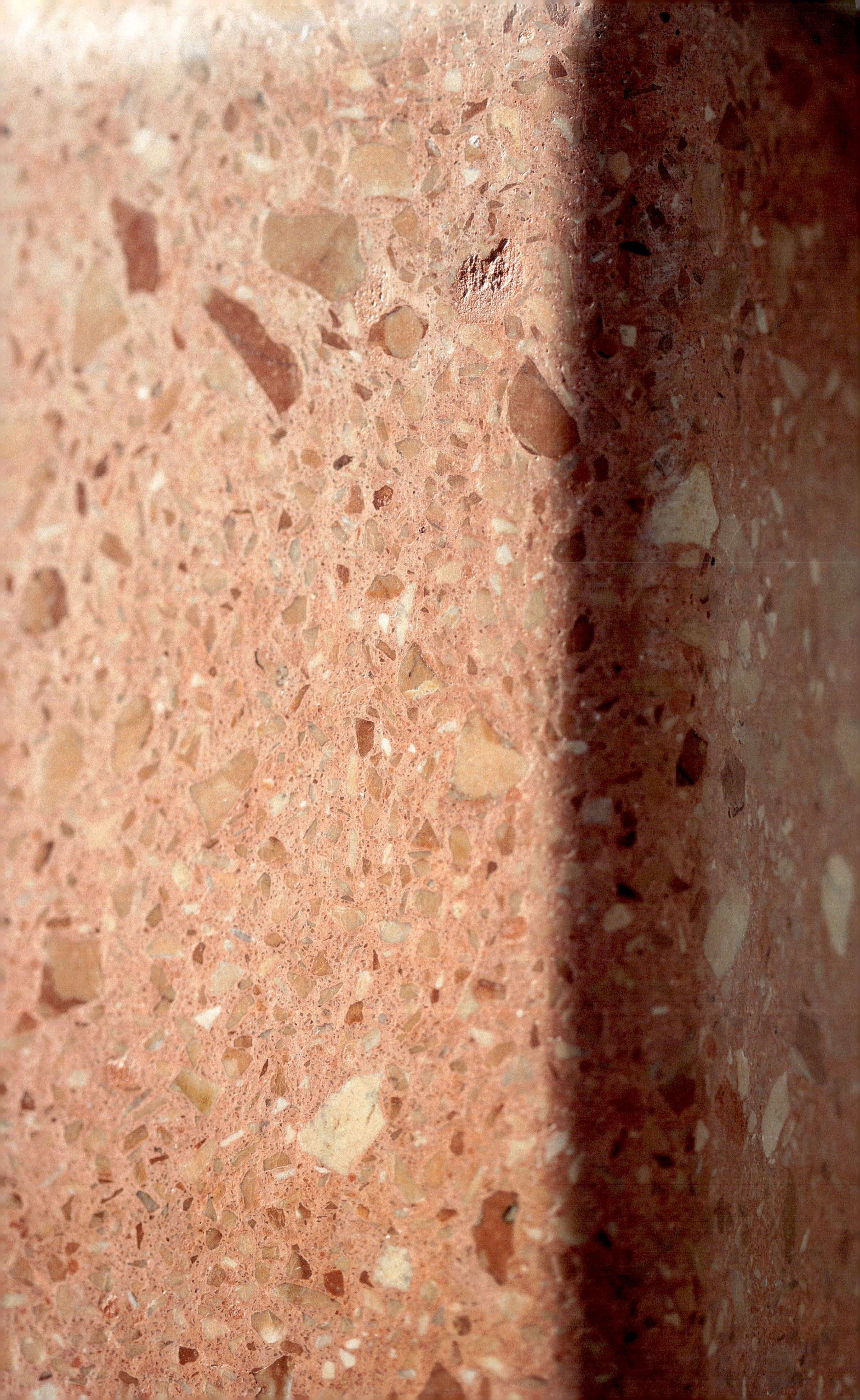

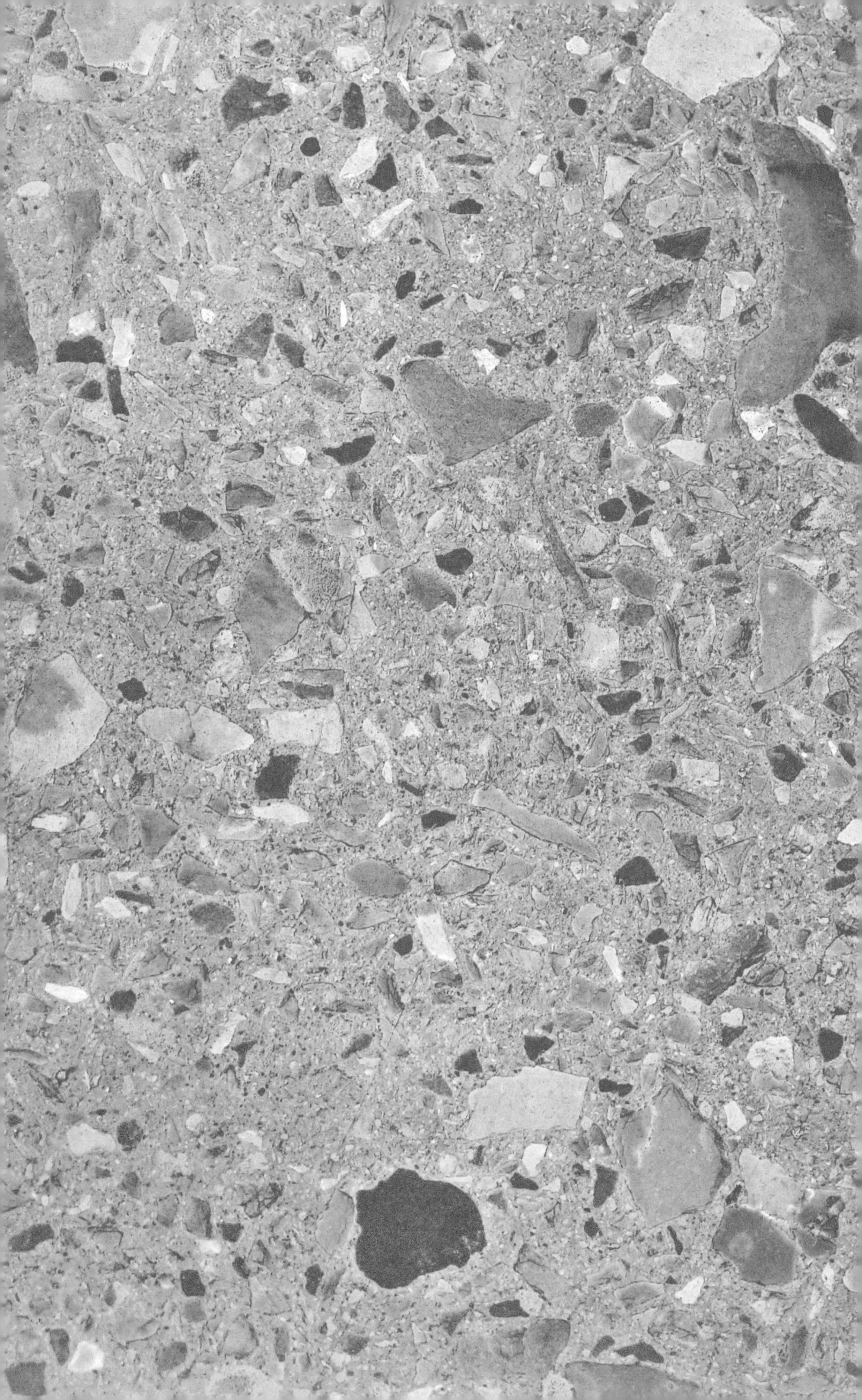

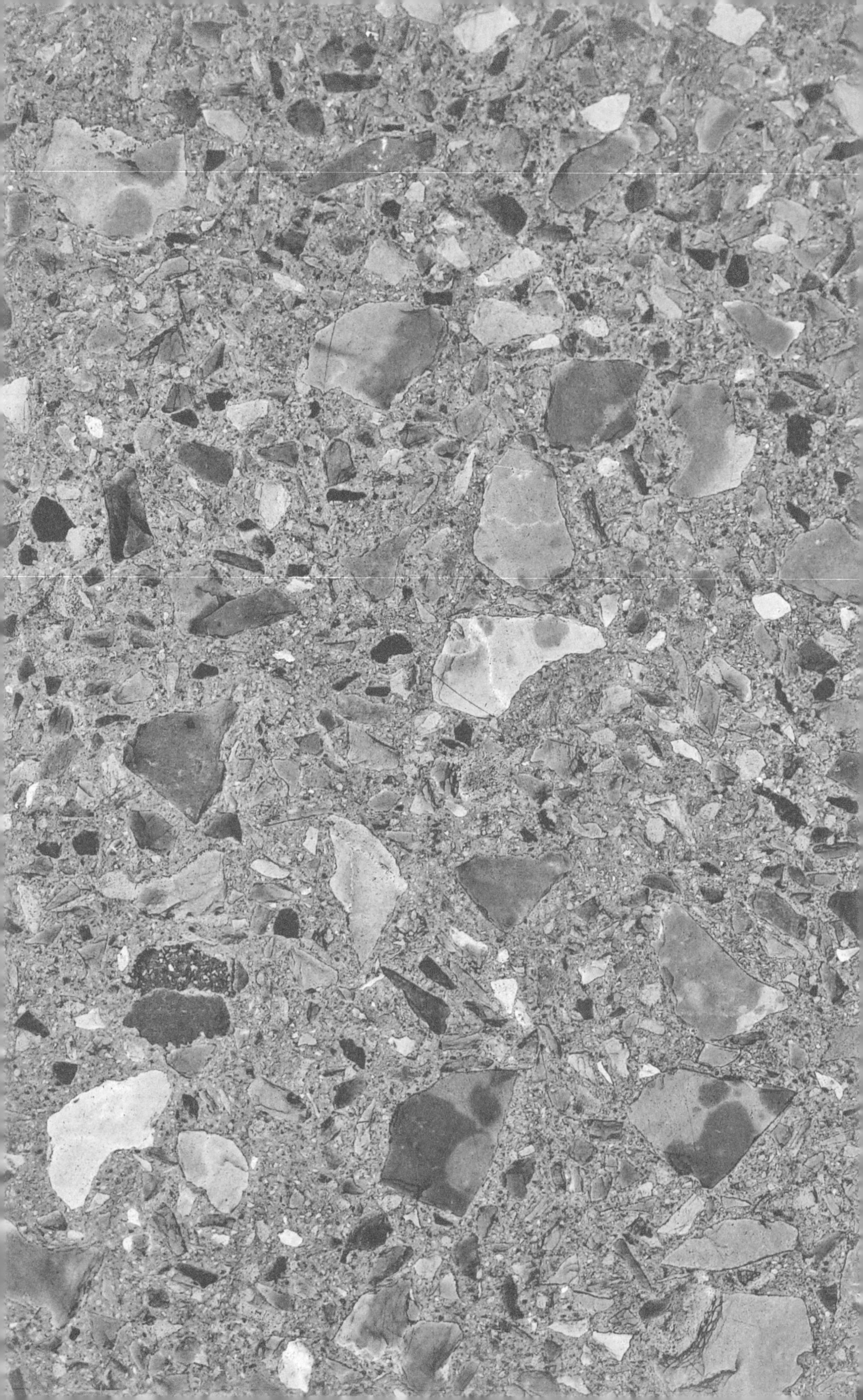